12/21/08

To My Wonderful Colleggue and friend

Ann Gunkel

Jagarathth

Arab Modernities

POSTCOLONIAL STUDIES

Maria C. Zamora
General Editor

Vol. 1

PETER LANG
New York • Washington, D.C./Baltimore • Bern
Frankfurt am Main • Berlin • Brussels • Vienna • Oxford

Jaafar Aksikas

Arab Modernities

Islamism, Nationalism, and Liberalism in the Post-Colonial Arab World

PETER LANG
New York • Washington, D.C./Baltimore • Bern
Frankfurt am Main • Berlin • Brussels • Vienna • Oxford

Library of Congress Cataloging-in-Publication Data
Aksikas, Jaafar.
Arab modernities: islamism, nationalism, and liberalism
in the post-colonial Arab world / Jaafar Aksikas.
p. cm. — (Postcolonial studies; v. 1)
Includes bibliographical references and index.
1. Arab countries—Intellectual life. 2. Arab countries—Social conditions.
3. Islamic fundamentalism—Arab countries. 4. Arab nationalism.
5. Liberalism—Arab countries. 6. Postcolonialism—Arab countries. I. Title.
DS36.88.A418   909'.0974927083—dc22   2008050611
ISBN 978-1-4331-0534-0
ISSN 1942-6100

Bibliographic information published by **Die Deutsche Bibliothek**.
Die Deutsche Bibliothek lists this publication in the "Deutsche
Nationalbibliografie"; detailed bibliographic data is available
on the Internet at http://dnb.ddb.de/.

The paper in this book meets the guidelines for permanence and durability
of the Committee on Production Guidelines for Book Longevity
of the Council of Library Resources.

© 2009 Peter Lang Publishing, Inc., New York
29 Broadway, 18th floor, New York, NY 10006
www.peterlang.com

All rights reserved.
Reprint or reproduction, even partially, in all forms such as microfilm,
xerography, microfiche, microcard, and offset strictly prohibited.

Printed in the United States of America

Contents

Acknowledgments vii
Introduction 1
Chapter One. Periodizing Arab Modernities:
  Toward a Political History of the Present 13
Chapter Two. Arab Liberalism: Abdallah
  Laroui and the Politics of the End of History 33
Chapter Three. Tradition, Rationality, and Nationalism:
  Al-Jabri's Critique of the "Arab Mind" 61
Chapter Four. Islamism and Modernity: Abdessalam
  Yassine and Islamizing Modernity 95
Chapter Five. Toward a New Project of Modernity:
  Marxism and the Arab Left 129
Conclusion 151
Select Bibliography 157
Index 173

Acknowledgments

In preparing this book, I have incurred great debts to numerous people: family, friends, colleagues, teachers, and students. I thank them all.

In particular, I would like to thank Jean-Paul Dumont, Paul Smith, Elli Dumont, Dina Copelman, and Roger Lancaster. From beginning to finish, they offered invaluable advice and criticism on both the conceptualization of the project and the written text. They provided a model of generosity, support, and rigor, which sustained me both as an individual and a scholar.

Special thanks also go to all my colleagues in the Department of Humanities, History, and Social Sciences, Columbia College Chicago, for their constant support and encouragement. In particular, I thank Lisa Brock and Ann Gunkel, who were always interested in discussing what was going on in the intellectual and political arenas. Their patience and kindness, their knowledge and intelligence are truly inspirational.

My life and work as a teacher and scholar have been shaped by two committed teachers and intellectuals: Jean-Paul Dumont and Paul Smith. Although I have moved in different directions, to different places, I still and will always look up to them.

I must also recognize the guidance and help afforded by the editorial team at Peter Lang, and especially Caitlin Lavell, Jackie Pavlovic, and Valerie Best, to mention just a few.

Last but not least, I would like to thank my wife Madiha and my son Ayman. But for their love, generosity, and support, this book would not have been possible.

For the flaws that remain, however, I am NOT responsible!

Introduction

[People] make their own history, but they do not make it just as they please; they do not make it under circumstances chosen by themselves, but under circumstances directly found, given and transmitted from the past. The tradition of all the dead generations weighs like a nightmare on the brain of the living. And just when they seem engaged in revolutionizing themselves and things, in creating something that has never yet existed, precisely in such periods of revolutionary crisis they anxiously conjure up the spirits of the past to their service and borrow from them names, battle-cries and costumes in order to present the new scene of world history in this time-honoured disguise and this borrowed language.

—Karl Marx (1852)

The present book is fundamentally a critical interrogation of some of the ideologies of so-called modernity and modernization in the post-colonial Arab world, with a specific focus on three political movements and ideologies: liberalism, nationalism, and Islamism. However, this intervention is also best understood as an attempt to grapple with what appears to be one of the central paradoxes in post-colonial Arab societies (and Middle Eastern societies more generally): the rise of Islamism and fundamentalist Islamist movements at a time when global neo-liberalism has declared "the end of history." Among other things, it is an attempt to "name" contemporary Islamism and Arab nationalism and liberalism—to delineate the social, cultural, economic, and political conditions under which they first emerged, evolved, and ultimately failed, and thereby to construct a political history of and shed light on Arab-Islamic societies at present.

For reasons, both theoretical and strategic, it seems only logical to start with an interrogation of the discourses of modernity and modernization. The problematic of modernity and modernization has been a central preoccupation of intellectual debates and political discourses and practices for more than three hundred years. The modernist ideology originated in the industrialized North and has even a longer history there than in the so-called underdeveloped South, where it is no less central. Ironically, in the last few decades, the debate over modernity and modernization, and in specific historical circumstances (namely colonialism and the structural dependency produced by it), has been even more heated in the "underdeveloped" South than in the more advanced North, its place of origin. The industrialized North has become "post-industrial"; it has left the era of modernity to fully embrace "postmodernity." But even in the North, while modernity has been redefined, challenged, and even rejected as the dominant logic, it has never been eliminated altogether. Far from it, the modernist ideology seems to be regaining some of its long lost vigor and vitality. Frederic Jameson, whose work is precisely a critique of (post)modernity, devotes one of his most recent interventions, *A Singular Modernity*, to the "return of the repressed" ideology of modernity in the North. Here, Jameson grapples with what seems, in his assessment, to be a recent universal attempt to revive modernity as a social ideal in traditional and political philosophy, as well as in political economy and even aesthetics (1-3). While acknowledging the possibility of a post-modern break, which could be associated with a more or less "completed" form of industrial and technological capitalist modernization (an advanced stage of capitalism), especially in the North, it is also important to recognize the continued presence of modernity—in one form or another—in our ideas and practices all over the world today. The ideology of modernity, which is tied to a situation of "incomplete" modernization, has equally been the focus of public discourses and practices, especially in the underdeveloped South.

What exactly is modernity? How dare one ask what many would consider a rather naïve question? Should not the modern be self-evident? I will challenge this understanding by trying to question what is supposedly self-evident and ask precisely: What is modernity? The notion of modernity carries with it an inherent contradiction. At a literal level, the word "modern" simply means present-day or contemporary and can be dated back as far as the fifth century AD (Jameson 17), when it was used to refer primarily to a distinction between the present and the past, between the now and then, between life now and life when Jesus Christ was still alive. This pre-modern use of the word modern is turned to the past, to that unique historical moment when Jesus Christ (in the context of the dominantly Christian world) was alive. As an ideal,

INTRODUCTION 3

the past provides an example of wisdom, beauty, and glory that needs to be revered and regained at the same time.

As a theoretical category, however, modernity cannot be defined in relation to its literal meaning alone. Such conception is very limited, and of very little use, for otherwise, any historical period would be modern in its own day. In social and cultural analysis, modernity is usually said to refer to the special features of the industrial capitalist society that have been developing in the West since the late sixteenth and early seventeenth centuries, thus steadily weakening and gradually replacing the more traditional systems of thought and modes of experience and practice. It has always been associated with such key social processes as rationalization, secularization, urbanization, and industrialization and with such ideals as freedom, happiness, democracy, and progress. These characterizations, however, only complicate the concept even further and raise more questions about the relationships of the processes to the ideals and also of both of these to the material world.

In late capitalist society, while modernist ideology exists as a discursive formation and while it is central to major intellectual debates and public discourses and practices all over the world, modernity's material referent does not in fact match the rhetoric, or the formal narratives modernity relates about itself. The bourgeois ideals of modernity—such as individual freedom, science, progress, and democracy—cannot and will never fulfill themselves in a society whose very structural existence is dependent on a fundamental form of social injustice, namely the division of labor and class antagonism. Thus, capitalist modernity carries with it an inherent contradiction, a contradiction between its ideal discursive promises and the inherently exclusionary tendencies of the capitalist mode of production. Even the essential quantitative changes of social practices and systems cannot be explained by reference to the emergence of these ideals alone. For example, the limited acceptance and incorporation of poor working class men and women into the political system was not the product of formal discursive modernity alone, but was primarily the result of hard and at times violent struggles.

According to most conventional accounts, the notion of modernity had its discursive origins and was given its decisive formulation during the European Enlightenment of the late seventeenth and early eighteenth centuries, mainly through the work of Voltaire, Montesquieu, Hume, and Diderot, although it was anticipated much earlier in the work of Machiavelli, Bacon, and Descartes, and did not come to fruition until the nineteenth century and even later. However, modernity is not the product of Enlightenment philosophy alone; it is not merely a cultural vision or a set of visions, but is also a historical situation, a set of processes, and as such, it cannot be relegated to the realm of ideas or philosophy alone. It is the product of a conjunction of socio-economic developments (the ascendancy of capitalism and the industrial revolution), political events (the French revolution, the class struggle, the early interventions of the workers' movements), as well as theoretical elements (the Enlightenment philosophy) in the early development of the capitalist system. Modernity refers to the historical situation and the experience associated with, yet different from, modernization processes and the modernist visions (both ideologies and counter-ideologies). Here, modernization refers to a set of social processes; it refers, among other things, to scientific discoveries, industrial revolutions and upheavals, political revolutions, the growth of nation-states, demographic transformations, and urban expansions—all of which were unleashed by the advent of a crisis-driven, yet ever-expanding capitalist world market. In a sense, all these are objective processes of socio-economic change, which for lack of a better phrase, can be called processes of socio-economic modernization. Modernist ideologies and counter-ideologies refer to the various cultural visions, values, theories, ideologies, and ideology critiques that emerged as a response to these very objective processes of socio-economic modernization, in an attempt to either celebrate, understand, and justify them on the one hand, or to question, critique, and change them—in a word, to either come to terms with the world thus created or to transform it, or both. The question that unites the modernization socio-economic processes and the modernist cultural visions relates to what it means to live (to be both subject and object) in a modern world, in a world driven by certain processes of socio-economic modernization and characterized by an attempt to theorize and transform them (and in the process be transformed by them, as well).

Thus, as a set of cultural visions, modernity has two aspects to it, one celebratory and the other critical. On the one hand, celebratory modernity consists of an ensemble of triumphant conceptions and images of self, of a consciousness of the "new," of a mere ideology, whose pretensions, dreams, illusions, and projects seek to affirm and reproduce the dominant capitalist relations of production and with them the existing social relations. Critical modernity, however, is different; it is a genuine, yet incomplete, critical reflection on these very conceptions, images, and projects in an attempt to explore, to reveal their hidden contradictions and confusions and also to go beyond them. It should be emphasized, however, that while the distinction between celebratory modernity and critical modernity is necessary, both are aspects, in fact parts, of the modern world. Without the former, we cannot speak of the latter. No theory or history of modernity can be written without the history of modernist ideology.

Starting from the middle of the nineteenth century, and as a consequence of the colonial encounter between Arabs and the West and of the challenges posed by the reality of colonialism, Arabs developed a certain kind of consciousness of the necessity of modernization and national *nahda* [renaissance]. As time went on, ideologies of national modernization and renaissance became more and more powerful and more anti-colonial in nature. Throughout the colonial and post-colonial history of the Arab world, these ideologies have assumed different forms: liberalism, state capitalism, and Islamism. But regardless of the differences, all these ideologies shared common concerns, which centered on the following issues: anti-imperialism and the search for political independence; the search for unity of all Arabs and/or Muslims; modernity and social development; and cultural authenticity.

This intervention is a critique of some of the dominant discourses of modernity, modernization, and globalization in the postcolonial Arab world and the Middle East more generally. More specifically, it provides a critical analysis of the work of major Moroccan intellectuals-activists, namely Abdallah Laroui, Mohammed Abed al-Jabri, and Abdessalam Yassine, thus bringing together what have hitherto been considered competing and even incompatible ideologies in the Arab world: liberalism, state capitalism/nationalism, and Islamism. Although these ideologies and ideologues—products of a specific historical conjuncture—have enjoyed some currency in debates on modernity and globalization throughout the Arab world, they provide an ahistorical understanding of the processes of social change—cultural, economic, and political—in this part of the world. My major concern is to provide a critical account of the work of Laroui, Al-Jabri, and Yassine, and, through them, of liberal, nationalist, and Islamist ideologies of modernity in an attempt to problematize the very assumptions that animate these theories, to locate them in their proper historical context, to reveal their hidden contradictions, and also to point to some alternative paths to a non-capitalist modernity.

Conventional analyses have generally attributed the rise and subsequent decline of liberalism and nationalism, as well as the current rise of Islamism to purely cultural, religious, or ideological factors: the nature of Arab culture; the nature of Islam; the irrationality of the Arab mind, and so on and so forth. This book argues against such facile analyses. My critique is grounded in a distinctly cultural studies materialist reflexivity, locating as it does the basis of all phenomena—economic, political, ideological, and cultural—in the capitalist mode of production, and arguing that ideology critique and analysis is necessarily complex. It requires that we relate ideologies and ideas themselves to ongoing social struggles, as these are embedded in their political, cultural, and economic context. It is one of the central tenets of my analysis here, and my work in general, that ideas and ideologies cannot be understood outside the historical situation from which they emerge and develop, that we should approach all phenomena—ideological, economic, cultural, and political—in the context of their social totality, that is, by pursuing their hidden interactions and interconnections in real life. The kind of methodological assumption informing my work is much closer to what Frederic Jameson and Paul Smith (as well as other cultural studies practitioners) call a "logic of totality", or, to use the words of Smith the "attempt to show the interrelations amongst the several realms of social life—the economic, cultural, and political"(*Millennial Dreams* 2). In other words, the full significance of an event or phenomenon—be it economic, cultural, ideological, or political—cannot be properly assessed outside a dialectical understanding of the structure of totality, outside the concrete unity of all interacting spheres of social life.

By extension, Arab ideologies and discourses of modernity and modernization, including their present critique here, cannot be understood outside the particular historical situation within which they have developed and to which they have responded. The second chapter will depict the broader ways in which these ideologies have been shaped by and have helped to shape their social, economic, political, and cultural environment. Here, we examine the Arab-Islamic trajectory to modernity and propose a historical periodizing hypothesis, according to which modern Arab Islamic history is divided into four phases, four dominant ideological and political movements: Colonial liberalism; Post-colonial liberalism;

Nationalist state capitalism or Nasserism; and Contemporary Islamism. Arab liberalism, nationalism, and Islamism are part of a much broader Arab general problematic, that of modernity and national *nahda* [renaissance] at all levels of society—economic, cultural, and political.

Abdallah Laroui, Mohammed Abed al-Jabri, and Abdessalam Yassine, whose active lives date back to the middle of the last century, provide critiques of the contradictions of contemporary Moroccan society and Arab Islamic societies in general. But they are more than the critics of the Arab world's, and, in the case of Yassine, the Islamic world's, cultural and social crisis; they are its symptoms and victims as well. I have chosen these three thinkers not because their ideas are particularly original, but precisely because their work is symptomatic of different ideological perspectives and demonstrates the existence of a social crisis in the Arab world at the current historical conjuncture, which they affect and by which they are affected. These three intellectuals were the "legitimate children" of a very specific social formation—and as such they have played an important role in Moroccan and Arab contemporary history. Living and writing at around the same time, these three men attack the same social forces, but from seemingly different perspectives: liberal, nationalist, and Islamist.

The second chapter provides a critical analysis of the work of Abdallah Laroui, one of the major contemporary cultural critics, historians, and politicians writing in the Arab world today. Here, I explore the following question: what concept of modernity does Laroui's work produce? To read Laroui means immediately to be confronted by the basic tension between his early and later visions of modernity. For the former, where Marx is still at play, modernity can be implemented only by an elite group of dedicated intellectuals through a "dialectical" look at their past. The "dialectical method" not only describes and analyzes the contradictions and dualities of reality and other ideologies, but it also indicates the means by which capitalist liberalism, which, according to Laroui, is the highest stage of social development, can be achieved. For the latter, where Laroui breaks with Marx, modernity is identified with liberalism and liberal capitalism. Laroui's transformation from a neo-Marxist into a liberal was concomitant with the rise and subsequent fall of Arab state capitalism, and it would be impossible to fully appreciate Laroui's work without due consideration of the historical situation in which it developed. Laroui's abandonment of Marx and the incoherence of his work reflect not only the failure, but also the ideological vacuity of Arab state capitalism.

The third chapter looks at the work of Mohammed Abed al-Jabri, one of the most prominent living Arab cultural critics and philosophers, at various stages of his intellectual career. Al-Jabri has written extensively on Arab-Islamic philosophy and tradition, and most of his work speaks to what became a prevalent concern with *turath* [Islamic tradition] in the wake of the failure of Arab state capitalism and the Arab unity project from the 1970s onward. As a result of the defeat of Nasserism in the 1967 Arab-Israeli war, it became common-place to relate defeat to the neglect of Islamic tradition and religion. Islamism— the ideology that Islam should guide social, political, cultural, and personal life—was becoming more and more powerful throughout the Arab world, especially after the 1979 Iranian Revolution. The work of Al-Jabri is both a reflection of and on the failure of Arab state capitalism and the Arab unity project and the rise of Islamism and Islamist ideologies. It is a nostalgic reflection on the failure of Arab state capitalism and nationalism, as well as a reaction to contemporary Islamism.

The fourth chapter is a critical analysis of the work of Abdessalam Yassine, one of the most powerful ideologues and activists of contemporary Islamism in the Arab world. Abdessalam Yassine is the "spiritual" *murshid* [guide] and political leader of *Al-Adl wa Al-Ihssan* [Justice and Spirituality], which is the largest Islamist opposition movement in Morocco and North Africa. Here, I address the following interrelated questions: How does Yassine perceive modernity and modernization? What vision of modernity and modern society does his work produce? And what kind of alternative, if any, does his work present?

As mentioned earlier, Islamist movements emerged in the wake of the failure of modern Arab liberalism and nationalist state capitalism to achieve true social development and true modernity. The thought/practice of Yassine, like that of other Islamists, is not only a mere reaction against the uneven development and unequal modernization of Arab societies, but is also the product of that very development and modernization.

How does one explain the decline of Arab liberalist and state capitalist ideologies? Why could they not achieve true development and true modernity? To be sure, neither liberalism nor nationalism did represent the interests of society as a whole; they represented the interests of only one social class or another, without due consideration for the subaltern classes of society. But do Islamists provide an alternative that represents the interests of all social classes? Are they able to provide such an alternative without destroying some of their basic foundations and ideas about life and society?

There is a tendency in much of contemporary postcolonial studies to disregard Marxism, jettisoning it as an essentialist narrative unable to provide a comprehensive analysis of colonial history and ideology, or even worse, complicit with the project of imperialism. What many postcolonial studies scholars fail to realize is the significant contribution Marxism can make (and has made) to the global South. The project of this book is to work against such facile disregard and to argue for the importance of the work of Marx and Marxism for understanding the complicity of capitalism and colonialism and for the development of any serious emancipatory project of true modernity in the post-colonial South.

One fundamental criticism of orientalist, liberal, nationalist, and Islamist ideologies is that they tend to overlook—partly or completely—the historical nature of social and cultural phenomena, thereby serving to naturalize and eternalize them. Laroui's celebration of liberalism and liberal capitalism as the highest stage of social and human development, Al-Jabri's emphasis on the role of medieval Islamic traditions in underdevelopment, Yassine's claims about the eternal nature of "authentic" Islam, all these reveal the fundamentally ahistorical, undialectical logic informing their thought and practice. What emerges from such ideologies is a worldview that echoes, and thus becomes complicit with, the orientalist view of Arab society and culture as unchanging, fixed, and eternal.

If Morocco and the Arab world are in search of modernity and democracy, is there any alternative to capitalist modernity and formal democracy? In the sixth chapter, I argue that Marx and Marxism provide us with a "theoretical base," with a set of categories that are indispensable for understanding the implication of postcolonial societies in the history of capitalist/Western imperialism and also for developing an emancipatory project of modernity in the global South. More specifically, the work of Marx (and of others in the Marxist tradition) provides critical insights for the development of a foundation for an emancipatory project of modernity in the post-colonial world, and in the Arab world in particular.

Marx's work is a critique of capitalist modernity and modern life under capitalism (in its socio-economic, political, and ideological manifestations), but it is more than mere critique. It provides us with the base on which an alternative vision, an alternative project, another modernity can be developed. This does not mean that the theoretical concepts and categories developed by Marx and others in the Marxist tradition are sufficient or complete; they have to be consistently elaborated, refined, and complemented by other concepts and categories whenever necessary.

What should be the aim of an emancipatory project of modernity? It should provide an alternative to conventional, ahistorical (orientalist, liberal, nationalist, and Islamist) analyses of society, as well as provide a guide for emancipatory political practices. Unlike ahistorical, undialectical methods, Marxian dialectics does not examine social phenomena as static entities but rather looks at them in the processes of their development, movement, existence, and transformation. All social and cultural phenomena are seen as processes. Society and culture are always in movement; they are produced, develop, move, and change.

Marxism's emphasis on the position of all aspects of society within the social totality could lead to a much more profound critique and a much more active sense of revolutionary activity in contemporary Moroccan and Arab society in general than the persistently abstract models derived from the liberal, nationalist, and Islamist theories of Laroui, Yassine, and Al-Jabri. Given the fact that orientalists and auto-orientalists (Arab liberals, nationalists, and Islamists) portray the Arab-Islamic societies as stuck in static, unchanging traditions and cultures, the whole discussion cries out for just what Marxism in general (and contemporary cultural studies) can offer: a view of culture that treats its objects as historically contingent, socially constructed, and politically volatile; an emphasis on historicity and dynamism of traditions.

Equally, the Marxian analysis of the nature and logic of the capitalist mode of production is still relevant and has much to say about capitalism. At different stages of his life, in his attempt to account for and overcome the contradictions of modern capitalism, Marx developed two complementary, interconnected projects of modernity, one of radical democracy and the other of socialist revolution. These two projects, we would argue, provide the Arab left with two critical strategies of political practice, one short-term and the other long-term. At the current historical juncture, it is very unlikely that the establishment of a socialist society, of a collectivist mode of production involving the abolition of private ownership and control of the means of production, will be fulfilled in the foreseeable future. That is why, the Marxist tradition calls on the left to work for another project, that of radicalizing democracy, thereby paving the way for the ultimate dream of all of progressive forces: socialist justice, equality and freedom for all.

· CHAPTER ONE ·

Periodizing Arab Modernities: Toward a Political History of the Present

This book critiques some of the dominant ideologies of modernity and modernization in the post-colonial Arab world, with a specific focus on Morocco and Egypt and on the work of three Moroccan cultural critics and political intellectuals: Abdallah Laroui, Mohammed Abed al-Jabri, and Abdessalam Yassine. For reasons theoretical and strategic, it seems only logical to start with a discussion of the historical context in which this ideological work has emerged and developed.

As I have argued earlier, ideology cannot be understood outside the historical situation from which it emerges and develops. By the same token, Arab ideologies (and ideologues) of modernity and modernization, including their present critique here, cannot be understood outside the particular historical situation within which they have developed and to which they have responded. In many ways, and as will become clearer in the course of this critique, these ideologies, the liberal, nationalist, and Islamist, are part of a much broader Arab general problematic, that of modernity and national *nahda* [renaissance] at all levels of society—economic, cultural, and political. The present chapter will depict the broader ways in which these ideologies have been shaped by and have helped to shape their social, economic, political, and cultural environment.

This chapter examines the Arab-Islamic trajectory to modernity; it proposes a historical periodizing hypothesis. According to this hypothesis, modern Arab societies (and Middle Eastern societies more generally) have passed through four historical phases, four **dominant** cultural-political conjunctures or moments: Colonial liberalism; Post-colonial liberalism; Nationalist state capitalism or Nasserism; and Contemporary Islamism. The notion of historical periodizing is very problematic indeed. As Jameson puts it:

> One of the concerns frequently aroused by periodizing hypotheses is that these tend to obliterate difference and to project an idea of the historical period as massive homogeneity (bounded on either side by inexplicable chronological metamorphoses and punctuation marks) (*Postmodernism* 4).

This is, however, precisely why it is essential to grasp contemporary Islamism as the current cultural-political dominant logic in the contemporary Arab world, just as other ideologies, such as liberalism and nationalism, **were dominant** at previous historical conjunctures. Such conception is much more tenable and allows for the presence and co-existence of very different, yet less dominant or even marginal ideologies, including emergent and residual ideological forms and formations.

The Era of Imperialism and Nationalist Liberalism

In the nineteenth and early twentieth centuries, and as the Ottoman Empire declined, Britain, France, and Italy established Western control over most of the Arab world from western Morocco to Oman, and from Turkey in the north to Yemen and Sudan in the south. Much of the trauma and shock suffered by the people of the Arab world, both in the *Mashreq* [Arab East] and the *Maghreb* [Arab West], during this time can be traced back to the colonial encounter between the native Arabs (as well as people of other ethnicities) and the colonizing Europeans. The colonial encounter between Arabs and Europeans, between the colonized and the colonizer, introduced a series of social, economic, cultural, and political changes and served to highlight and dramatize the unequal and uneven nature of the relationship between the two parties.

One consequence of this was the development among the colonized of a certain kind of consciousness of the exploitative nature of colonialism, as well as consciousness of the superiority of the European colonizers at many levels. Arab societies faced the challenge of the West, of an advanced capitalist, imperialist, and secular society that was scientifically and militarily advanced and more economically developed, a West that even asserted its superiority culturally, claiming that Islamic religion and culture were inherently backward. These dramatic changes led to a period of self-doubt, questioning, confusion, and even a certain "inferiority complex." The fall of the Arab world into colonialism obviously troubled Arab consciousness. Commenting on the fall and conquest of Algeria in 1830, a local singer cries:

> The end of times has come;
> Henceforth no more rest,
> The day of battle has shone,
> Grief to the living, happiness to the dead;
> Times gone by are sorrowfully missed!
> I am grieved, o world, about Algiers!
> The French march on (toward) her
> With troops whose number (only) God knows (Heggoy 20).

Another local song begins:

> O my eyes, cry tears of blood and cry some more
> Happy is the one who rests buried on the sand.
> The news of the world does not reach him.
> At least he rests in peace
> While we, like beasts of burden
> Eat grass that grows in the dung heap (Memmi 28).

Colonialism was a violently shocking and humiliating experience, indeed. And the same feeling of defeat and humiliation is to be found throughout the few popular tales, poems, and songs that have fortunately survived. However, it would be wrong to reduce the colonial encounter to being a mere experience of shock and humiliation. Such understanding is at best partial, one-dimensional. The other side of the colonial experience is also recorded in surviving oral accounts. As a local preacher puts it, "This kingdom is like a muddy pool. Its waters will not clear up as long as the Turks reign over us...We need *the Black man.* My God! Better the unbeliever than such tyranny! *Under the government of the French, no one will go to bed hungry*" (Heggoy 61) [my Italics]. It is very ironic that the French are here initially acclaimed as saviors![1] To be sure, the locals did have a nuanced understanding of colonialism and its implications. This is quite natural given the paradoxical nature and results of the colonial encounter as a whole.

With the passage of time and the further integration of the colonial system into the colonies, anti-colonialism soon became the dominant mood, though not the only mood. In their attempt to frame the events surrounding them, to organize anti-colonial political action, and to secure their various interests, the ruling classes and rural and urban notables, the masses, and the intelligentsia converged on the language of nationalism and national modernization and renaissance. Thus, ideologies of national modernization and renaissance developed, not because of abstract debates, but because of practical, everyday, and ongoing struggles and challenges posed by the realities of colonialism. It was centered on four main issues: anti-imperialism and the search for political independence; the search for unity of all Arabs and/or Muslims; modernity and social development; and cultural authenticity. These issues, however, did not disappear with the end of colonialism, but continue until today.

More specifically, two major events contributed to the development of such early modern renaissance consciousness among Arabs: the invasion of Egypt by the armies of Napoleon in 1798 and the French occupation of Algeria in 1830. In Morocco, in addition to these factors, the defeat of the Moroccan army (which had sided with the Algerians) by the French at Isly in 1844 was concomitant with the development of a future-oriented renaissance consciousness. For the Moroccan ruling elite [*Makhzen*] and the merchant class, the defeat meant the imminent threat to their interests and the loss of their hegemony. This led to a period of self-reconsideration and self-reflection on the part of these dominant classes and the intellectuals among them. Commenting on the defeat, Allal Al-Fassi, the famous Moroccan politician and critic, writes:

> [The defeat of 1844] led Moroccan people and the Moroccan elite to reconsider and reflect on its causes and circumstances. Moroccans immediately realized that old political and military systems were of no use given the progress of modern Europe. Thus, the ruling elite became conscious of the necessity of modern-like innovation and renaissance (85) [My translation].

In the turmoil that followed the Isly defeat, sultan Mohammed Ibn Abdurrahman IV (who ruled between 1859 and 1873) and his son sultan Hassan I (who ruled between 1873 and 1894) after him played the role of "enlightened, reformist" leaders. These so-called nationalist reforms by the ruling elite and the merchant class included the innovation of the sugar cane planting techniques, building of a factory for commercial sugar production, and the introduction of the printing press, as well as other military and educational reforms.

However, the successors of Hassan I would soon abandon these reforms and would soon submit to the eventual French occupation in 1912 (the year Morocco became a French Protectorate). They obtained guarantees from the colonial powers that their privileges would be maintained and their interests protected. In many ways, the ruling class did not have much of a choice because Morocco (as was the case in other parts of the Arab world) had already been integrated into the world market, well before 1912. The socio-economic future of Morocco was planned at the start of the contact of local pre-capitalist social formations and imperialist commercial capitalism in its full expansion throughout the nineteenth century, and political colonization came to confirm a process of structural dependence that had started early in the second half of the 19th century. Starting from the second half of the 19th century, the influence of European imperial capital on the Moroccan social formation was growing larger and larger. At the legal and political levels, it was translated into a series of treaties and agreements which opened the Moroccan market definitively to European capital: the Anglo-Moroccan Agreement of 1856, Spanish-Moroccan Agreement of 1860-61, and the French-Moroccan Treaty of 1863. By the end of the 19th century, there had already been a colonial society of 8000 people; in 1830, this society was almost inexistent (Tebaa 15).

The French defeat of the established ruling class of Egypt in 1789 had played an even more decisive role in the development of anti-imperialist nationalism as a political movement. Immediately after the withdrawal of the French from Egypt in 1801, Mohammed Ali (1769-1849) seized power and launched a series of reforms in an attempt to modernize Egypt. His imposed reforms included the modernization of the agricultural sectors, educational institutions, and the army. As in the case of Morocco, the successors of Mohammed Ali did not continue this nationalist attempt at reform. As Samir Amin puts it:

> The Pacha's [Ali's] successors, from 1848 to 1882 abandoned this autonomous direction, hoping, like Khedive Ismail, to Europeanize and modernize with the help of European capital, by integrating into the world market through cotton growing and by calling on European banking houses to finance this extraverted development (*Arab Nation* 31).

At around the same time, Syria and Iraq underwent a similar experience under the rule of Ibrahim Pasha, the son of Mohammed Ali, and Midhat Pasha respectively. Immediately after the capture of Damascus in 1832, Ibrahim Pasha launched a series of reforms, reorganizing the judicial system, the military system and taxation policies, and founding new schools. In Iraq, between 1869 and 1872, Midhat Pasha introduced similar reforms. He founded new schools and a new press, improved the irrigation system, expanded date production in the south, and established a new water supply system.

In any case, it would be very difficult to talk about what Morocco, Egypt, Syria, or Iraq might have become had these reformist projects been continued. What is sure is that these "nationalist" reforms, these anti-imperialist struggles, in the case of Morocco, Egypt, Syria, Iraq and elsewhere in the Arab world, ended in defeat, and not without reason. They were imposed from above and were very limited indeed. The focus of these reforms was primarily military and bureaucratic, the aim being to create a strong military and central administration. In addition, Morocco, Egypt, Syria, and Iraq did not have a strong local bourgeois class to contend with the other classes. The local merchant class was so weak that it could not contend with the landed and tribal aristocracies, let alone challenge the power of the imperialist bourgeoisie.

The ideology of national renaissance and modernization did not decline in the least with colonialism. Quite the opposite, colonial occupation made this ideology even stronger and more anti-colonial and anti-imperialist in nature. The bearers of this ideology were no longer the ruling classes or the landed aristocracy, who were the second beneficiaries of colonization after their imperialist bourgeois masters. It was artisans and remains of the local merchant class in the city and some tribal leaders in the countryside who embraced this ideology. These social milieus were the first to feel the dangers of colonization not only at the economic and political levels, where their interests were challenged, but also at the cultural levels. Intellectuals in these social layers were beginning to become restive, reflecting on the dangers that colonization presented to tradition, while at the same time worrying about lagging "behind" the Western world materially and wondering what to do about it. Religion from early on provided a convenient starting point from which to begin cultural change and reconstruction. That is why, this anti-imperialist, nationalist, ideological struggle assumed the form of a political movement that was half fundamentalist, half modernist.

In the *Mashreq*, the work of Jamal Eddine Al-Afghani (1838-1897) and Mohammed Abduh (1849–1905), two major religious reformist thinkers, is representative of this movement. It urged Muslims to reform themselves as the first step in rising to meet the challenge from an alien, more powerful culture. It rejected blind adherence *[taqlid]* to Islamic tradition and called for the reformation of religion as the only way to modernize Islam. In the words of Abduh, "What the Islamic political body needs [now] is not mere reforms, but total religious reform...And there is no doubt that what is needed immediately is a new political base in order to fulfill the spiritual needs of all Muslims" (1: 867) [My translation]. The movement was an Islamist movement and called for modernization based on Islamic principles. It was not a homogenous movement, for it included more liberal thinkers, including prominent feminist thinker Qasim Amin (1863–1908), a close friend of Abduh, who wrote two controversial books, *Tahrir Al-Maraa [The Emancipation of Women]*, and, *Al-Maraa Al-Jadida [The New Woman]*.

The movement spread rapidly throughout the Islamic-Arab world. In Morocco, it developed into what one might call a "new nationalist fundamentalism" with such religious leaders and scholars as Chouaib Doukkali (1878–1937) and Mohammed Ben Al-Arbi Al-Alawi (1880–1964). This movement sought to resist Western imperialism, to reconcile Islam and modern rationalism, and to help build a powerful Muslim nation, and even to unite the whole Muslim *umma* [community]. Both Doukkali and Al-Alawi believed that reason and Islam, Islam and modern science, were reconcilable, but that this required the dismantling of the traditional, "unorthodox" social, economic, political, and religious institutions of the Muslim world, which were—in their view—perversions of "true" Islam.

What should be pointed out here, however, is that the existence of colonial powers also played a major role in the development of the liberal nature of the thought and practice of these movements. It is true that these movements were anti-colonialist, but their thought and practice were not only the product of struggle against the colonizers, but also a result of the impact of the latter on Arab society. The colonizers had introduced modern political, economic, and cultural structures, institutions, and practices, all of which have naturally contributed to the development of such liberal-like consciousness among the colonized subjects.

This consciousness was even more liberal and more secular in some parts of the *Mashreq*, especially in Syria, Lebanon, and Egypt. Beginning in the late nineteenth and early twentieth centuries, several Arab Westernized elites, many of whom were educated in Europe and imbued with European ideas, contributed to the development of liberalism in the Arab world. These intellectuals borrowed many elements of their thought from the West and Western intellectual developments. Thinkers such as Salamah Musa in Egypt and Sati Al-Husri in Syria (1880–1968) were part of this liberal, secular Arab nationalist movement. For them, Arab nationalism, not Islamic unity, was the only route out of colonialism and imperialism as well as a route to greater territorial unity as it provided the basis of creating a unified nation that could repel colonial powers and achieve independence. Islamist reformers like Jamal Eddine Al-Afghani and Mohammed Abduh conceived of themselves as primarily Muslims and thought of all Muslims—Arabic-speaking or non-Arabic-speaking—as part of one *umma*, the nation of Islam. More liberal thinkers, such as Al-Husri and Musa, conceived of themselves as primarily Arabs, regardless of their religion, and called for the unity of all Arabs initially as a reaction against the Islamic Ottoman Empire, and later against European imperialism. This is partly understandable given the fact that many of the leading thinkers in this movement were Christians, not Muslims.

This liberal movement was part of a larger process of capitalization and embourgeoisement, a process of the development of a bourgeois, capitalist class that started in the West and was imported into the Arab world. It was an extension of the bourgeois revolution that had already started in the West. Central to this movement, in the context of the Arab world, was the idea of creating a modern, democratic, and bourgeois Arab state, while at the same time preserving Arab cultural identity.

As colonial capitalists established themselves as the new ruling class in the colonies, which themselves became increasingly integrated into the world capitalist system, new economic structures and new social formations began to emerge. On the economic level, the encounter between colonial capitalism, introduced from outside, and the native pre-capitalist modes of production created a peculiar economic structure, which certain economists have described as "dualist."[2] On the social level, imperialism established a new agrarian bourgeoisie. As I have mentioned earlier, there was no local bourgeois class in the historical sense of the word before colonialism, which "implies that in the East the bourgeoisie's development was closely linked to its integration into the imperialist system" (Amin, *Arab Nation* 25). This new bourgeoisie played a major role in supplying certain agricultural products (such as cotton, wheat, and dates in the case of Morocco) to the industrial countries. Later, the activities of the bourgeoisie extended to include some commercial sectors, as well.

But if the development of this new class was engendered by colonial capitalism, it was also delimited and constrained by it. The new local bourgeoisie could not develop naturally and found itself subject to the subordination of the colonial bourgeoisie. Its commercial activities were limited to certain sectors, such as local commerce and part of the import substitution sector, as dictated by the international division of labor. It became increasingly clear to the local bourgeoisie that colonial capital, which had created it, now stood in the way of its natural development. Thus, the local bourgeoisie had no choice but to join the anti-imperialist struggle to secure its class interests and promote its independence.

There were other factors that contributed to this change of venue on the part of the local bourgeoisie. The colonial system had led to an overall crisis, a crisis which was further reinforced by the fact that the institutions and laws introduced by the new "masters" did not serve the interests of the indigenous population. The poor peasants lost their land for ridiculously low prices thanks to procedures that were foreign to them (such as land registration which was very rarely practiced in the ancient social system). Laborers, often employed against their will, were forced to accept outrageously low wages. The new fiscal system forced the peasants to brutally enter into the money economy, thus profoundly and abruptly changing their everyday life practices and social relations. These new social changes which were imposed from outside without any transition led to an almost immediate structural crisis.

As a result, the masses became increasingly marginalized with the proletarianization of small farmers and artisans, the impoverishment of peasants, increasing urbanization, and massive unemployment. The result was not only a crisis at the economic level, but at all levels of the social, cultural and political, an overall crisis which was becoming deeper and deeper as the colonial bourgeoisie was penetrating more parts of the colonies. This brutal and traumatizing penetration could have only led to strong resistance, especially on the part of the marginalized classes.

It was only after the Second World War that most of the Arab world gained its political independence, and in many cases, the independence was, and in many ways still is, more formal than real. In the Arab East, Syria and Lebanon became independent at the end of the war, followed by other countries in the region. Only Palestine never became independent, but was partitioned in 1947 with the establishment of the state of Israel. Most, if not all, post-independence Arab states in the East, especially Egypt, Syria, and Lebanon, embraced some kind of nationalist liberal ideology. They introduced a series of political and economic reforms aimed at reinforcing rather than breaking with imperialism. These reforms, mainly legal and structural, were meant to ensure the continuation of the integration of the economies of the newly independent states into the world market and also to defend private ownership. They were meant to provide the assurances necessary for foreign capital to stay on.

From the very beginning, the national liberal ideology and practice carried with them the seeds of their failure. Instead of eliminating foreign control, they reinforced it. Colonial powers retained most of their privileges and prerogatives. Amin comments:

> The mediocre withdrawal into provincialism of 1920—1947 rested on a social equilibrium based on a class alliance between the dominant imperialism of the area (Britain, and to a lesser extent France) and the latifundist bourgeoisie of the various states. This system could function as long as colonial enchantment of values ensured that some crumbs were left for the petty bourgeoisie (50).

But as was becoming clear, this so-called national liberal system was based on the very same contradictions of the imperialist ideology and practice. However, it took a number of events and new developments for these contradictions to destroy the ruling class. Chief among these were the growth of dissatisfied petty bourgeois and proletariat classes; the increasing unemployment and marginalization of the masses; the emergence of communist and Islamist movements, especially in Egypt. The partition of Palestine in 1947 and Israel's first expansion from 1948 were concomitant. And if the 1948 Arab defeat in the war against the establishment of the state of Israel, and the Palestinian issue in general, served anything, it did reveal the contradictions of the post-independence Arab world; it highlighted for the Arab people not only the incompleteness of independence, but also its rhetorical and formal nature. For the masses, there was essentially no difference between their life during and after colonialism. What is worse, many people felt betrayed by their indigenous ruling classes.

In the Arab west, in the case of Morocco, Tunisia, Algeria, and to a lesser extent, Libya, the struggle for independence was a difficult and long one. Libya did not gain its independence until 1951, followed by Morocco and Tunisia in 1956, followed by Algeria in 1962. Shortly after its independence from France, Morocco started a number of serious social reforms. Between 1958 and 1960, the short-lived socialist-nationalist government, led by Abdullah Ibrahim, started a series of social and political reforms in an attempt to restructure the whole system to make it more national and more autonomous. However, this brief flirtation with "socialism" came to an end when the King Mohammed V dissolved the government in 1960.

The new government, headed by King Hassan II himself, looked at national-liberalism (as a set of mainly legal, institutional, but also political measures introduced to support market-led development models) as a way to solve Morocco's problems and move it forward. "Pragmatic" and "realist" liberalism, it was claimed, would diminish the baggage of the country's colonial legacy and would help it achieve true development. Thus, Morocco started a set of constitutional and self-governmental reforms, which though limited, were to have a great impact on the direction Morocco would take. These reforms arose from a combination of external and domestic challenges to the existing traditional power structures. In the face of growing mass discontent and opposition parties, as well as the pressure of foreign capital, Hassan II initiated a number of political reforms that formed the basis for limited popular participation for the first time in the country's modern history. In 1962, Morocco adopted a new constitution.

Hence, the new constitution essentially transformed postcolonial Morocco into a constitutional monarchy overnight, and national elections were held the following year. This was accompanied by the modernization of educational, legal, and economic systems and institutions. At the legal level, the colonial legal legacy was maintained and modern Western models were embraced as the basis for legal reforms, and Islamic law was restricted to personal status or family law and especially to such matters as marriage, divorce, and inheritance. At the economic level, modern colonial economic systems and institutions were maintained and new ones were established. At the educational level, new schools and universities were created and modern programs were introduced to allow students to acquire modern knowledge and science.

However, it soon became clear that such liberal strategies were more formal than real, given the authoritarian nature and practices of the regime. The brutal suppression of political opponents (especially from the left) and gross abuse of human rights were inconsistent with such stated liberal strategies, which failed to guarantee minimum political democracy and freedom of speech, let alone address the more fundamental social contradictions. In a way, they made things worse: the gap between the rich and poor grew even larger, amidst massive structural unemployment and an economic system in crisis. .

Rise of Arab Nationalist Capitalism

During the course of the 1950s, in the Arab East, and as a result of the new social developments and formations discussed earlier, in addition to the growing hegemonic role of the US and the USSR in the region, there emerged a new intelligentsia, mostly of petty bourgeois origin, who felt excluded from political life. They questioned the inadequate development of their countries and demanded participation in political life.

Among other factors, class tensions, unequal distribution of capital, and continued imperialism, all contributed to the rise of this petty bourgeois class. This class was the mainstay of nationalist movements and statist ideologies all over the Arab world between the 1950s and the 1960s. Its intellectual and political leaders adopted some kind of nationalist ideologies and used socialist ideas as a self-interested justification for a massive revolt in the Arab world, and effectively so. The 1948 Arab defeat in Palestine further deepened the frustration of all Arabs, and there were revolutionary movements everywhere in the region. Between 1948 and 1955, the Arab political scene changed; there were three coups d'état in Syria, a regime change in Lebanon, a revolution in Egypt, a revolution in Algeria and Morocco against the French, the assassination of King Abdullah in Jordan, and many other political changes and events elsewhere in the Arab world. The new regimes were turning increasingly to some form or another of state capitalism.

During the era of Nasserism (1952–1967), Arab countries, following the lead of Egypt, evolved within the framework of a somewhat unique economic model, which could be accurately described as state capitalism, whereby the state takes responsibility for the development of an indigenous capitalism in close relationship with the system of the global economy, and whereby the state supplies the conditions for the emergence of national capital within the narrow framework prescribed by the international division of labor. This is what came to be known as "Arab socialism."

What is "Arab socialism"? Writing in the early 1960s, a Westerner writes:

> Socialism has become the fashionable political costume of the underdeveloped countries. What goes for socialism in Asia and Africa is unrecognizable to Western socialists used to thinking in terms of a specific ideology (Tutsch 98–99).

This clearly applies to Arab "socialism," where the latter was a mere label for all kinds of state intervention and oppression. That is why, it would be more accurate to describe it as state capitalism, rather than socialism. Even the founding fathers of Arab state capitalism claimed their theories had nothing to do with Marxist socialism or with any other type of socialism or communism developed in the West. While such claims are exaggerated and were initially made to highlight the authenticity and originality of Arab state capitalism, they still contain some elements of truth. Arab state capitalism has something to do with Marxism, but it was clearly a distortion of Marxism, rather than an original elaboration or interpretation of it.

The new petty-bourgeois Arab leaders embraced state capitalism as the only route to industrialization and modernity. Economically, and as the experiences of Egypt, Syria, and Iraq show, they initiated a number of reforms, mainly land reform and the nationalization of major industries and banks. They aligned themselves with Stalinist Russia in its conflict with the West. Arab state capitalist systems failed to achieve national economic development, because, among other features, they shared, "a bourgeois vision of the future, deep anti-democracy and anti-communism, a mediocre pragmatic philosophy, overestimation of Soviet military support, and the cynical belief that they could play the American card if circumstances required" (*Postwar Period* Amin 112). They failed to eliminate Western imperialism from the Arab-Islamic world. Arab state capitalism and the Arab petty bourgeoisie failed to accomplish what nationalist liberalism and Arab national bourgeoisie had failed to accomplish more than a century earlier.

Between State and Private Capitalism

The appeal of state capitalism was strong all over the Arab world, so strong that even in a country like Morocco, a country that did not officially adopt socialism as a state policy, certain aspects of land reform and nationalization were gaining ground, especially between 1956 and 1963. There was a serious attempt to restructure the colonial system in a way that would make it national in its structures, directions, and objectives. Progressive elements of the Moroccan petty-bourgeoisie developed a reformist program, the stated aim of which was to acquire sufficient political and economic autonomy for Morocco to become a worthy partner in the world capitalist system from which they could not envisage a divorce. It was within this framework that a series of projects were introduced. These included the following: launching a new customs system replacing the colonial one in 1957, the nationalization of Bank Al-Maghreb in 1958, creating new labor and social security codes, and reforming some aspects of national education.

But in general, Morocco remained faithful to the "liberal capitalism," otherwise called "realist or pragmatic liberalism," of the newly departed colonizers throughout its modern history. The first Moroccan constitution (1962) asserted and protected private property and political pluralism in an attempt to encourage foreign capitalists to stay on. But the political turmoil and instability, the spontaneous occasional revolutions of the masses here and there all over the Arab world in the 1960s and 1970s obliged a number of foreign capitalists investing in Morocco to leave the country, fearful that a political revolution (coup d'état), similar to the ones breaking out throughout the Third World, leading to the nationalization of foreign capital and private property, despite strong assurances from the Moroccan state (as well as the different regulations, both economic and political, taken in this regard).

Decline of Arab State Capitalism

Arab state capitalism carried with it the seeds of its failure and was never able to transcend its petty bourgeois origins. Many contradictions set limits on its functioning, contradictions which were very apparent in the deepening of the social crisis at all levels: on the social level, massive unemployment and increasing proletarianization and increasing misery among the masses. On the political level, new social forces were emerging, especially Islamist movements. The failure of the Arab unity project and the defeat in the 1967 Six-Day war against Israel were only natural results of a system full of contradictions and contrasts, a system that was unable to break with imperialism or eliminate dependency on the world capitalist system. Drawing on Mahmoud Hussein's analysis of state capitalism in Egypt, Amin writes:

> In analyzing the ideology of the 'new class', its forms of government and the stages by which it constituted itself in Egypt, Mahmoud Hussein makes the following point: state capitalism, because it is capitalism, must remain within the capitalist world system. It thus cannot really break with imperialism. Belonging to the world system then perpetuates underdevelopment, ruins any changes for independence or real development. To substitute the Soviet Union for the United States as the commercial partner and source of capital (so-called 'aid') in no way changes this fundamental relation of dependency. The petty bourgeoisie, which brings local dependent state capitalism to the fore, thus becomes the main link of imperialist domination, thereby replacing the old latifundist-comprador bourgeoisie which introduced dependent private capitalism in the previous period (*Arab Nation* 57).

What state capitalism did was simply to substitute the bourgeois agents of imperialist domination without eliminating that domination altogether. It was not enough to move from the sphere of domination by the United States to that of the Soviet Union, to replace one commercial partner with another, for the system to achieve true modernity and true development.

State capitalism was overall an opportunist petty bourgeois movement, which, in its search for political power, overlooked the social question. Its ideology was at best a mishmash, a mixture of Western liberal thought, nationalism, Marxism-Leninism, Arab-Islamic tradition, and, above all, capitalism. The early work of Laroui, discussed below, speaks to this ideology.

Socialism never appealed to the masses, a fact which can be ascribed to the conventional contention that socialism was atheist and, therefore, "immoral." This charge has been effectively exploited by conservatives (the work of Yassine discussed below is a very good example of this development) and liberals alike. In addition, oppressive and repressive measures against communists by state capitalist regimes and movements, especially Ba'thism and Nasserism, have also contributed to the weakening of socialism and communism in the Arab world.

From the very beginning, socialism and communism in the Arab world were tied to nationalism and nationalist movements, and throughout the postcolonial history of the Arab world, they have never been given any serious consideration. As Abu Jaber puts it, "In the Arab world socialism as an ideology remained a wing of the nationalist movement which would develop as soon as independence was won... [Unlike Communist ideology], Ba'th ideology explicitly emphasizes nationalist goals over socialist ones" (101). While Arab state capitalism gave some consideration to the problems of the poor peasantry and the working class, it was inherently petty-bourgeois in nature. It rejected Marxism's call for the abolishment of private property as too utopian, and related to this, it rejected Marx's theory of class struggle as a false interpretation of history. It also rejected the materialist, internationalist foundations of Marxism, as unfit for Arab society, given their atheist nature. Such blind rejection or distortion of Marxism did not allow for any chance for an effective and truly revolutionary alternative to emerge.

Contemporary Islamism

The 1967 Arab defeat in the war between Egypt and other Arab States on the one hand and Israel on the other dealt a serious blow to Nasserism in particular, and to Arab state capitalism in general. The defeat led to a new period of defeat, self-criticism, and self-doubt among all Arabs. There emerged from the lines of the masses new intellectuals, a new group of people who felt they had been betrayed all along. It was the working classes and poor peasants who fought, revolted, died for the sake of independence and social change, but it was the petty bourgeoisie who were the ultimate benefactors of all this, like the bourgeoisie before them. Many intellectuals, especially of working class and peasant origins, desperate and disappointed, started calling for the end of all liberal, nationalist, and socialist ideologies and the return to the Islamic religious tradition, pure and simple. Throughout the Arab world, and as a logical reaction to the failure of the nationalist and revolutionary movements of the 1950s and the 1960s, based, as they were, almost exclusively on Western ideologies such as nationalism, liberalism, and, to a lesser extent, socialism, it became commonplace to relate defeat to the dismissal of tradition and religion.

But what was the alternative proposed by such Islamist ideologies? There was a call for the return to tradition, to Islam not as a religion, but as a political system. Islam was presented as the only way to "salvation" and development. This has become the dominant ideology all over the Arab world, especially in the mid-1970s, and as is well known, the 1979 Iranian Revolution was a significant result and also a major contributing factor to this "awakening."[3] The failure of petty bourgeois state capitalism and its ideological vacuity, along with the collapse of the Soviet Union, ultimately reduced the influence of leftist ideologies. Islamism has emerged as the "only" remaining revolutionary ideology in Arab societies. Rather than being a mere reaction against the modernization of Arab societies, Islamism is also the very product of it. However, Islamism is not without its critics. The work of Al-Jabri, discussed later, could be considered a critique of Islamism and Islamists. But as my subsequent critical analysis of Al-Jabri's work demonstrates, Al-Jabri's concern with Islamic tradition reinforces the importance of Islamism itself.

By the late 1990s, Islamist movements and ideologies had become even more powerful and assumed two major forms. First, the emergence of anti-Western radical revolutionary governments (as in the case of Iran and Sudan) and movements (Algeria and Egypt); and, second, the rise of less radical and more reformist Islamist movements, seeking social and political change from within the existing systems and regimes. Yassine's *Al-Adl wa Al-Ihssan* [*Justice and Spirituality*], discussed later, is one of these movements.

Neo-Liberalism Triumphant

The last 15 years, from 1989 to 2005, have been marked by the following fundamental developments: First, the fall of the Soviet Union; second, the indisputable hegemonic role of the US in the area; third, the decline of leftist ideologies and the triumph of neo-liberalism; fourth, the rise of Islamism and Islamist movements; fifth, the 2001 terrorist attacks on the US; sixth, the defeat of Muslim Afghanistan in 2002; and seventh, the defeat of Iraq twice (in 1991 and in 2003). All these elements, along with the concomitant further entanglement of the Arab world with the world capitalist system, have been interacting to determine the history of the world, and the Arab world in particular, at the current historical conjuncture.

From the late 1980s and the early 1990s onwards, we have witnessed the triumph of neo-liberal capitalism throughout the world. The fall of actually existing socialism in the Soviet Union and Eastern Europe (1989–1991), the unification of Germany (1989), as well as the defeat of Iraq in a US-Led invasion (1991), are significant moments in the scenario I am sketching here.

The weakening and eventual collapse of the Soviet Union, the ex-patron of Arab nationalist regimes, the growing hegemonic role and intervention of the US in the area, as well as the growing penetration of Israel into the Arab world, have dealt serious blows to Arab nationalism and Arab unity.

The 1991 Gulf War dealt a major setback to Arab nationalism. The defeat of Iraq was different from that of three Arab states: Egypt, Syria, and Jordan in 1967. In 1991, only Iraq was defeated, and to the dismay of many, most Arab states joined the US-led coalition, despite public opposition in almost all Arab states, thus putting an end to more than a century-old dream, that of Arab unity. In this context, Michael Hudson writes:

> The Gulf crisis of 1990—91, in the eyes of many analysts, marks the final collapse of the Arab unity project. Apart from occasional raids and border skirmishes, inter-Arab warfare in the post-World War I era has been almost nonexistent. But in August 1990 Iraq launched a massive invasion of Kuwait, and the U.S-led international coalition (including Arab members), which drove the Iraqis out and imposed on them punishing sanctions of long duration, was said by many observers to have marked—once and for all—the end of Arabism. Certainly it was a historic setback for Arab integration, let alone unity (13-4).

More recently, the US attack on Iraq in 2003 and the subsequent occupation of a "sovereign" Arab nation have revealed the very hollowness and futility of Arab nationalism and Arab unity.

Islamist movements have even become much stronger and more popular in the wake of the failure of modern Arab neo-liberalism and global liberal capitalism in general. Many factors have contributed to the intensity of the growth of this "Islamist revolt." These included, among others, social marginalization, class divisions, economic deprivation, and state oppression. The failure of capitalist ideologies, liberal and statist, and American "new" imperialism, all have contributed to the rise of Islamist movements all over the Arab world. The overwhelming majority of people in the Arab world (and elsewhere) have found themselves subject to a system that, despite all its claims, only deepened their suffering, both at the material, psychological, and spiritual levels.

As a reaction to such unpropitious circumstances, which neither statist nor private capitalism has been able to end, the oppressed classes—lost, disorganized, and uneducated—found a refuge in the one thing they had: religion and tradition. At the core of the recent Islamic revolt, there are two interrelated struggles, one anti-imperialist and the other class-based. On the one hand, there is a struggle against American "new" imperialism (and even colonialism). On the other hand, there is a struggle between two major classes, between the oppressed classes and the ruling classes, between the victims of imperialism and its agents. In addition, other political and social factors have contributed to the rise of Islamist ideologies in the Arab world. These include support from the national states (especially oil-rich states) and also from external forces (including the US of course) in an attempt to confront leftist forces and progressive forces in general.

It is in this complex and evolving social, economic, cultural, and political framework that the ideologies discussed in the present book unfold. It is in this framework that the work of Laroui, Al-Jabri, and Yassine to be discussed below should be situated.

Conclusion

Throughout their modern history, colonial and post-colonial, Arab world countries have evolved within a framework familiar to nations on the periphery of the world capitalist system: dominance of foreign capital inhibiting national capital accumulation, investment, and industrialization, adherence to a growth model complementary to that of the capitalist metropolis, inadequate development of the forces of production with consequent structural deformities, and inadequate industrialization and modernization.

Despite all their claims, Arab nationalist, liberal, and statist ideologies failed to achieve true social development and change. They did not represent the interests of society as a whole; they represented the interests of only one social class or another, without due consideration of other sections of society. They spoke on behalf of the modernist national bourgeoisie and neglected the expectations and wishes of the poor peasants and the working classes. Instead of bridging the gap between the national bourgeoisie and the modernist elite on the one hand and the working classes and poor peasants, on the other, they in fact made it wider and wider. But the crucial question is: Are Islamists capable of providing such an alternative without destroying themselves, without destroying some of their basic foundations and views about humanity and society?

NOTES

1. It is very ironic that the French are referred to as the *black men* because they dress in dark colors!
2. The notion of dualism is very ambiguous, for in reality, we see very specific forms of articulation between very specific modes of production, all of which are dominated by the logic and laws of capital.
3. External forces—global economic and political forces—also played a crucial role in the decline of the nationalist and revolutionist movements in the Arab world in the 1960's and the emergence of the Islamic movements. What is ironic is that the very same forces are now playing the same role to defeat the same movements they have created. The first Gulf War between Iraq and Iran, civil war in Algeria, the so-called war on terror, led by the United States, all should be at least partly understood in this context.

· CHAPTER TWO ·

Arab Liberalism: Abdallah Laroui and the Politics of the End of History

The present chapter provides a critical reading of the work of Abdallah Laroui, a major contemporary Moroccan cultural critic and historian, at various stages of his career. Laroui is widely recognized as one of the most eminent Arab social historians and cultural critics writing in Morocco and the Arab world today. Since the publication of his first book *L'ideologie arabe contemporaine* on Arab nationalism and Arab intellectuals in 1967, Laroui's work has been at the center of many academic and intellectual debates in the Arab world and elsewhere. Laroui is quite well-known in the West, maybe more in France than in the English-speaking world. This is understandable, given the fact that his work is written mainly in French and published in France and that only very little of his work has been translated into English.[1] Before discussing Laroui's work, it would be very useful to provide my reader with a brief sketch of his life and work.

An Intellectual Biography

Abdallah Laroui was born into a middle-class family in the small Atlantic town of Azemmour (southwest of Casablanca) in the west of Morocco in 1933. His father was an army officer and his grandfather a *qaid* [literally a local leader], a high-ranking government officer. His mother died when he was two. Laroui attended religious school, and at the age of seven, he went to a public primary school in Azemmour, where he studied between 1941 and 1945. There was no high school in Azemmour then, but Laroui managed to get a grant from the French colonial government to pursue his high school education at Sidi Mohammed High School in Marrakech. Before 1945, it was very hard to get a grant from the government to help fund one's high school or university education, but after that date, the situation was changing both inside and outside Morocco, and the French were pressured to respond to some of the natives' basic demands, mainly demands for more schools and educational opportunities. Laroui stayed in Sidi Mohammed High School for four years, and in 1951, went to Casablanca in order to prepare for the high school *baccalauréat* final examinations. Immediately after receiving his *baccalauréat*, he enrolled in Mohammed V University in Rabat, where he started his undergraduate studies in natural sciences and medicine. At the time, access to the Moroccan public administration was still limited to the French, and the only careers open to young Moroccans were business and trade related jobs for those belonging to the upper classes and medicine or law for those belonging to the middle class.

In 1953, Laroui went to Paris to pursue his studies at the Institut d'Etudes Politiques, where he worked under Charles Moraze and Raymond Aron. In 1958, Laroui completed his *diplôme d'études supérieur* [Master's degree] and wrote his thesis on the commercial relations between Morocco and Europe in the Middle Ages, which was later incorporated into *Mujmal Tarikh Al-Maghreb [History of the Maghreb]*. Later that year, Laroui returned to Morocco, where he worked for the Ministry of Foreign Affairs. In 1960, he became the Ministry's cultural attaché to Egypt, where he met a number of Egyptian and other Arab intellectuals. Reflecting on this experience, Laroui writes:

> It was the last year of unity with Syria. I admired the Egyptian people, but not the intellectuals, whom I found ignorant and arrogant. This was by the way the opinion of Taha Hussein. But I met some fine people, the late George Henein, for instance, who emigrated later to Paris and worked as a journalist, the playwright, Numan Ashur, and the noted intellectuals, Lutfi al-Khuli and Khaled Mohyeiddine (*Muhawarat* 80).[2]

It was in Egypt that Laroui started writing his first book on contemporary Arab ideologies, which he did not finish until 1964.

In 1962, he was appointed cultural attaché in Paris, and a year later, he decided to resign from Foreign Service and devoted all his energies to writing. In 1963, Laroui finished his *agrégation* in France and became an assistant professor of History at Mohammed V University in Rabat, Morocco. Between 1967 and 1971, he taught North African history at the University of California, Los

Angeles. *The History of the Maghreb* was a collection of the lectures that Laroui gave at UCLA. In 1971, he returned to Morocco and finished his doctoral dissertation on the social and cultural origins of Moroccan nationalism. In the early 1970s, Laroui gave a series of lectures at Mohammed V University and wrote several articles on Arab political ideologies, which were subsequently published in his *La crise des intellectuels arabes: traditionalisme ou historicisme* in 1974. This collection of articles, along with Laroui's earlier work on contemporary Arab ideologies, drew the attention of many Arab scholars and intellectuals. It is here where we encounter Laroui's fully developed critique of contemporary Arab thought and intellectuals. Laroui continued his work on Islamic history, and in 1987, he published a collection of articles entitled *Islam et modernité*. This work, where Laroui discusses what he considers to be the foundational concepts of modernity—ideology, freedom, state, and reason—could be considered as an introduction to Laroui's serial books on these concepts: *Mafhum Al-Idyulujyya [Concept of Ideology], Mafhum Al-Huriyya [Concept of Freedom], Mafhum Al-Dawla [Concept of State], Mafhum Al-Aql [Concept of Reason]*, which were written between 1980 and 1996.[3]

A Collective Problematic

Let me ask the following question: What concept (or concepts) of modernity emerges from Laroui's oeuvre? Early in *Mafhum Al-Aql*, Laroui declares:

> All what I have written, so far, constitutes chapters of a single volume on the notion of modernity, and it is possible for the careful reader who reflects critically on the earlier chapters to have insight into what would be said in the chapters that would come later (14).[4]

It is clear that Laroui conceives of himself as a theorist of modernity, as a *modernizer*, and so do many Arab intellectuals who write about the Arab world today.

Mafhum Al-Dawla, first published in 1981, can be treated as marking a point of transition from the "young Laroui" to the "older Laroui"—the former being a vaguely humanist "Marxist" historian, while the latter being the Hegelian proponent of liberal capitalism. This transition, however, does not represent a total break in Laroui's thought, through which one theoretical paradigm is replaced, subsumed, and displaced by another. There has always been an underlying, deep continuity in the ideas and issues discussed in all his work. One way to interrogate this work is to ask the following question: How did the young Laroui see the modern and modernity around 1965, a decade after Morocco's political independence from France? Laroui first experienced modernity as a whole at a moment when Morocco was still under French and Spanish colonial rule.

Laroui's early work and language are informed by a hybrid Marxism, where Hegelianism is already at play. Early in *L'idéologie arabe contemporaine*, Laroui writes that:

> [This study] is the outcome of a reflection on a specific situation: that of Morocco today. No one can help being surprised by the political powerlessness and cultural stagnation that have characterized the Moroccan elite for ten years now. To account for the current state of affairs, we can certainly conduct a political or social analysis; but we can also start with a cultural inquiry, and it is the latter approach that we adopt in the following pages (3).

As the title of the book suggests, the "cultural inquiry" that Laroui has in mind is nothing other than ideology critique, a critique of the dominant ideologies in the post-colonial Arab world. Implicit in Laroui's statement above is the claim that an ideology critique can be conducted independently of the social, economic, and political situation which both the ideologies and their critique inhabit. As I mentioned earlier, one of the central epistemological foundations of this intervention is that any ideology critique is always useless, and at best incomplete, if it does not explore the interconnections and articulations amongst all the mutually constitutive social realms, economic, political, ideological, and cultural.

At the outset, Laroui's book begins with a methodological criticism of two dominant approaches deployed in the study of contemporary Arab societies and of societies in general. The first is the naïve-empiricist approach, which immerses itself in the culture under study, and limits itself to describing in great detail what exists empirically, without due consideration of history. The second is the external-positivist approach, which limits itself to a thick description of what appears to be taking place in society, without due consideration of its origins or genesis. In a way already prefiguring his later work, Laroui rejects both approaches and reveals his own which would enable him to maintain some level of theoretical abstraction in order to situate the work of different thinkers in a certain system, while at the same time understanding the inner logic of each particular writer (5-7).

Laroui's intervention emerges from a reflection on a very specific situation, that of contemporary Morocco. Then, what is it that justifies this move from Morocco to the whole Arab world? According to Laroui, Arab intellectuals have a "collective problematic," a preoccupation with the same questions and problems. Laroui rightly notes that Arab intellectuals, in fact Arab people, share common concerns and that a study of Moroccan ideology will also entail a discussion of the broader context of the Arab world, but what is missing in his analysis is a treatment of the origins of this collective problematic. The emergence and development of these concerns is precisely the product of very specific historical circumstances, mainly Western imperialist interventions in the Arab world and elsewhere during the late nineteenth century and the early twentieth century, and the new socio-economic realities that came with colonial imperialism. In addition to these elements, the Arab world shares other historical circumstances and cultural traits: the earlier Islamic conquests and Ottoman rule, a dominant language (Arabic) and a dominant religion (Islam).[5]

What is this "collective Arab problematic"? In Laroui's view, for over a century, Arab intellectuals have always been longing for four ideals: authenticity, continuity, universality, and an artistic style to express the present social ills (*L'ideologie* 4). First, the major concern of Arab intellectuals is to define their Self, which necessarily involves a definition of their Other, the West. The second preoccupation is with the past: How do Arabs conceive of their long, yet vague past, a past full of successes and failures, of victory and defeat, and of darkness and enlightenment (4)? The third concern is a methodological one, both at the intellectual and scientific levels. What mode of action and analysis will guarantee to the modern Arab intellectual subject equality with the Western Other? The fourth and last preoccupation relates to the expression of this transitory situation, full, as it is, with uncertainties and contradictions. What kind of artistic or literary style is capable of depicting the current situation and diagnosing the present crisis?

There are two major criticisms that can be addressed to Laroui. First, all these common preoccupations are interrelated and are not independent of one another. It is impossible, for example, to grasp the dialectic of the Arab Self and the Western Other without at the same time describing the history of the encounter between the two, just as it is impossible to separate the methodological question from the processes of identity formation, history-writing, and artistic expression. Second, are these concerns limited to Arab intellectuals (in Laroui's limited sense) alone? How do other people and collectivities, Laroui's "non-intellectuals" fit within this scheme?

The Intellectual Elite and Social Change

Laroui sees the role of the intellectual elite as a crucial one in the context of creating a counter ideology, without which there can be no true modernity. In his view, social change is implemented only by an elite group of dedicated intellectuals through a critical look at their past.

What kind of intellectuals does Laroui have in mind here? Is he referring solely to the boffins and academics that sit in their ivory towers or write erudite pieces only read by others of the same ilk? Throughout his work, Laroui uses the words elite and intellectuals almost interchangeably, and it is not always clear whether the word "elite" refers to the intellectual or political elite, or both. Laroui's earlier reference to "the political powerlessness and cultural stagnation that have characterized the Moroccan elite" suggests that he has both intellectuals and politicians in mind. At the historical conjuncture and context Laroui was writing this work, this is somehow understandable. At around the time Laroui was writing *L'ideologie*, say between 1961 and 1967, there were between 12 and 13 million Moroccans, more than 90 per cent of whom were illiterate (*North Africa* 65/82). Most teachers and academics came from France or from other Arab countries, especially Egypt.[6] After all, Laroui chose to write his book in French, and not in his native Arabic. He was addressing the young French-educated and French speaking intellectuals like himself, most of whom were sent to France and other European countries to pursue their education immediately before and after independence in 1956. And it was these very intellectuals who dominated politics and the political scene, especially in urban areas.

Laroui's distinction between "elite" and "non-elite," his division of society into "the enlightened intellectuals" and the "ignorant masses" is not only elitist, but also misleading, as it mystifies the true nature of the processes of social change and says nothing about the social class of these intellectuals. In a much later work, *Islamisme, modernisme, liberalisme*, Laroui does not seem to be bothered by this "natural" division. As he puts it, "It is not society in its totality that becomes capable all at once of self-analysis, of self-critique; it is only an [elite] group more or less limited that fulfills this function" (26). It is impossible, Laroui adds, to carry out a social analysis, to determine whether a society is modern or not, without analyzing the ideas of its intellectual elite (24). Historically, he argues, intellectuals always were the true agents of social change and modernity, and will always be. That is why, Laroui concludes, "*Naturally*, modernity will always appear as if imposed by a minority on a majority, and everyone will be able to attack it as a colonial or imperialist project" (27) [My italics].

Historical Role of Intellectuals

Laroui wants intellectuals to reflect critically on their past and tradition, as well as on their role as agents of social change. He contends that intellectuals can play, at least in theory, a radical role in social critique and change. And to do so, they must subject their mental tools, inherited from the past, and mainly from religion, to a thorough critique, to a rigorous process of deconstruction. They must break with the concepts and tools of their predecessors. Laroui finds the root of social "backwardness" in the realm of ideas, independently of the other levels of the social totality: the economic and political. This view fails to see the links between cultural and ideological backwardness on the one hand, and economic and political crisis on the other.

Laroui suggests that intellectuals must first emancipate themselves from the "slavery of inherited epistemology" before they can effect any social change. So far, Laroui's argument can hardly be distinguished from idealistic determinism, according to which change in ideas will automatically lead to a change in society. What should be stressed here is that it takes more than good will to break away with one's past. What Laroui conceives of as inherited epistemology can be dissolved only when conditions for its dissolution are created. As Marx observes in *The Eighteenth Brumaire of Louis Bonaparte*, "[People] make their own history, but they do not make it just as they please; they do not make it under circumstances chosen by themselves, but under circumstances directly found, given and transmitted from the past" (*Collected Works* 11: 103). What radical intellectuals can do is help create conditions that will make tradition obsolete. Laroui assumes that internal "mental backwardness" is somehow responsible for the current social crisis. But are not our "mental backwardness" and our "material backwardness" mutually constitutive of one another? Are not they two sides of the same coin? And is not it impossible to change one without changing the other?

Laroui remains silent about the indispensable role of mass participation in social change. At best, Laroui's conception of social change would amount to an organized party leadership and would ultimately mean the substitution of one form of domination by another. What Laroui fails to realize is that social change does not come from a decision by an organized party leadership and that there cannot be any social change without the formation of a historical bloc among all the marginalized classes and groups and all the progressive forces, including intellectuals, in society. Laroui does not trust the masses to contribute to social change, arguing that they are incapable of effecting social change in a backward society that lacks, among other things, industrialization. For him, the proletariat, in a backward unindustrialized society such as Morocco, is not capable of fulfilling its historical mission. While I agree with Laroui that the role of intellectuals is crucial, but less in effecting change outside the involvement of the masses, than in developing mass consciousness.

Laroui's distinction between "intellectuals" and "non-intellectuals" is problematic, and even untenable, because it is based almost exclusively on comparative evaluations of the mental activity involved in any act. On this basis, everyone is an intellectual to a certain extent. As Gramsci puts it:

> When one distinguishes between intellectuals and non-intellectuals, one is referring in reality only to the immediate social function of the professional category of the intellectuals, that is, one has in mind the direction in which their specific professional activity is weighted, whether toward intellectual elaboration or towards muscular-nervous effort. This means that, although one can speak of intellectuals, one cannot speak of non-intellectuals, because non-intellectuals do not exist (*Selections* 9).

Gramsci further adds that "Each man," regardless of his or her profession, "participates in a particular conception of the world, has a conscious line of moral conduct, and therefore contributes to sustain a conception of the world or to modify it, that is, to bring into being new modes of thought" (9).

Gramsci identifies two types of intellectuals—traditional and organic. Traditional intellectuals see themselves as autonomous and independent of the dominant social groups and are seen as such by other people. Usually it is this group of people whom we think of as intellectuals. They only seem to be autonomous and independent, but in reality they tend to be essentially conservative, thus serving the interests of the ruling class. The whole notion of traditional intellectuals as a distinct social category independent of class mystifies the true nature and position of intellectuals in society.

Organic intellectuals, on the other hand, are more directly related to the socio-economic structure of society, and they are of two kinds, conservative or radical. On the one hand, conservative organic intellectuals belong to the dominant social group, the ruling class, and are its thinking and directing element. It is through this group that the dominant classes maintain their hegemony over the other classes in society. On the other hand, radical organic intellectuals belong to the working class and are its thinking and guiding element. The role of radical intellectuals is to help develop the consciousness of the working class of their historical mission.

In addition to Gramsci's distinction between traditional and organic intellectuals, it is clear that class origin provides another general basis for classifying intellectuals. In the case of the Arab world, differing types of intellectuals derive from the urban bourgeoisie, the rural bourgeoisie, and the petty bourgeoisie. Generally, the rural and suburban middle classes produce state functionaries and members of the liberal professions, including teachers, while the urban bourgeoisie produces technicians for industry. Hence, traditional intellectuals of rural and suburban origin are usually traditional, whereas urban intellectuals are mostly organic. Although every social group develops its own organic intellectuals, historically, the urban and rural working classes have relied mostly on "assimilated" petty bourgeois traditional intellectuals for leadership. This has always been one of the chief problems and weaknesses of the working classes in the Arab world and the Third world in general.

Dialectical Marxism, which is different from the kind of "dialectics" advocated by Laroui, is the first major step toward the intelligentsia's self-examination of itself. It reveals the socially based nature of knowledge. All intellectuals, whose role it is to create and preserve knowledge, act, consciously or unconsciously, as spokesmen for different social classes and articulate contradictory class interests. Laroui, more than anyone else, is probably aware that the notion of intellectuals as a distinct social category independent of class is itself a myth. Given the historical juncture during which he was writing, to which class do these intellectuals belong, if not to the Moroccan bourgeoisie or the petty bourgeoisie?

Laroui belonged to the new intelligentsia, a new group of intellectuals, mostly of petty bourgeois origin, who were emerging after independence as a result of the need to replace the newly-departing French professionals (teachers, bureaucrats, lawyers, administrators...etc.). Indeed, the Moroccan petty bourgeoisie would soon constitute, along with the national bourgeoisie, the ruling class in Morocco, replacing the colonial "masters."

Three Kinds of State

Laroui divides modern Arab political history into three kinds of state, the colonial, the liberal, and national. Why does Laroui use the word "state" instead of the more empirical word "society"? Can one even speak about an Arab colonial, liberal, or national state? As Laroui puts it, "The notions *colonial state*, *liberal state*, and *national state* are used to avoid the notions of *colonial society, independent society,* and *socialist society*, which, being too empirical, are useless in cultural analysis" (8) [My italics]. I have to disagree with Laroui's conclusion that the notion of society is "too empirical" and therefore, "useless in cultural analysis." In fact, what is empirical is always useful for and implicated in what is cultural, and vice versa. But Laroui's statement is important in another respect; it contradicts his claim, as developed in his later writings, that the state is the embodiment of society's general interest, standing above particular interests, and able to overcome the division between civil society and political society, the split between the individual as private person and as citizen.

Laroui focuses on the national state, rather than on the colonial and liberal states. The colonial state was the result of imperialism, and the liberal state accepted and reinforced imperialist exploitation. But unlike the liberal state, the national state struggled against that exploitation, but in vain. It is very hard to determine what Laroui really means by the liberal and national state, especially within the context of Morocco. Liberalism and nationalism might have referred to ideological, partisan, or even political tendencies that in turn might have influenced the way people saw the state, but in reality, the state always remained structurally dependent on the imperialist project and was unable to break away from it. Regardless of the way the state chooses to brand itself, as either liberal or national, it remains, first and foremost, a structurally dependent state, primarily economically, and to a large extent, also politically and culturally.

Laroui is much less concerned with the economic challenges facing the so-called national state than he is with the cultural and political challenges. State capitalism failed not only because it failed culturally and politically, but also because it failed to be economically independent. At the economic level, the state was unable to put an end to imperialist exploitation; it instead reinforced it. Despite attempts to stop this exploitation, by nationalizing big businesses and industries, taking charge of external commerce, and industrializing and mechanizing agriculture, it always found itself impeded by the logic of global capitalism, by the law of supply and demand. State capitalism failed not because it did not emancipate itself from the inherited meanings and norms, from the traditional worldview, as Laroui claims, but because colonialism interrupted its natural evolution and, in many ways, led to the proliferation of tradition. Politically, state capitalism failed to achieve Arab unity because each individual Arab state sought to promote its economic interests, without due consideration of the general interest of all Arabs.

Laroui's ideal state types correspond, for him, to three intellectual trends: the religious, political (liberal), and (rational) technocratic. First, the religious scholar disavows Western progress on the basis of the secularism of Western society and deals with Christianity from the perspective of the Koran. The religious scholar cannot distance himself from the ancient polarization and clash between Christianity and Islam. The cleric has developed a dual consciousness. Laroui notes that, "The consciousness of our cleric is religious when he analyzes his own society, but liberal when he criticizes the West" (39).

Second, the liberal politician has developed a completely different consciousness, one whose basic concepts and categories (mainly democracy and *shura* [deliberative consultation]) are supplied by the West. The wording of these concepts is religious. The liberal still appeals to Islamic tradition as both a symbol of legitimacy and indicator of cultural authenticity. For him, modernity means modern political institutions. Third, the technocrat sees the difference between the Arab world and the West not in terms of religious conflict, but in the way science is used and applied. Modernity is nothing other than the technological modernization of society (27).

These remain pure types, however. They do not, in fact, correspond to reality; they are not social classes or entities, but mere ideal abstractions. In reality, the relationship between the cleric, the liberal politician, and the technocrat is much more complex than Laroui seems to suggest. For it is not unusual to find a technocrat who cherishes liberal or even religious ideas, or a cleric who also advocates technocracy. That is why, my focus on the work of individual ideologists, rather than on ideologies themselves, serves, among other things, to shed light on the complexity of liberalism, nationalism, and Islamism.

Two Kinds of Marxism

In *L'idéologie*, Laroui establishes a distinction between what he calls "objective Marxism" and real Marxism, between Marxism as an ideological "guide for action" and Marxism as "a means of understanding social reality" (140). Laroui makes it clear that he is not concerned with Marxism as it relates to social and political practices in the Arab world but rather as an "implicit" ideology among Arab intellectuals and politicians. This distinction is very disturbing and even ironic, especially when made about a body of work that has always rejected this distinction in the first place. As Althusser reminds us, one of the constitutive epistemological assumptions of Marx and the Marxism is that ideology cannot be completely separated from objective social reality; it is already an objective social reality. He writes, "[A]s Marx says, it is in ideology that men "become conscious" of their class reality and "fight it out"; in its religious, ethical, legal and political forms, etc., ideology is an objective social reality; the ideological struggle is an organic part of the class struggle" (11–12). Gramsci goes even further to suggest that ideology is the very realm where the masses are organized; it is "the terrain on which men move, acquire consciousness of their position, struggle, etc," and that only through ideology can dominant classes exercise and maintain their hegemony over the marginalized classes in society (*Selections* 376–7).

Within objective Marxism, Laroui further distinguishes between actually existing Arab Marxism and dialectical Marxism. Actually existing Arab Marxism refers to a ready-made and, in many ways, closed system, without due consideration of questions of method. In the words of the older Laroui, Arab Marxism of the 1960s and 1970s "was a simple political ideology, which far from describing social reality, was content to express the hopes and illusions of a very small fraction of the population" (130). In the context of *L'idéologie*, however, Laroui claims that Marxism is the only ideology that appeals to the religious, liberal, and technocratic Arab intellectual and politician alike. It fulfills a number of functions: it is implicit in all other dominant ideologies and can be used to justify the narrow political ambitions and class interests of the religious, the liberal, and the technocrat alike. Further, it is, more than any other ideology, rational, consistent, and very critical of the West (154). For all these reasons, Laroui concludes that, "Marxism is the logical foundation of contemporary Arab ideology" provided it becomes conscious of itself (146).

Laroui rejects Marxism as political ideology and practice, but embraces it as a method of analysis, a method of justifying and defending liberalism. The latter he calls "dialectical Marxism." For him, what distinguishes "dialectical Marxism" is precisely its universal, and not only Western, character. As Laroui remarks:

> But does not the dialectic, imposed by history as a transcendence of the present contradictions, play the same role [as religion in the past]? It, in fact, recognizes the historical superiority of the Non-Self (the West). It confirms its role but not in its present passing form. As to the Self, dear as it is to the heart, hypostatized in dogma, culture, and language, negation dissolves it, thus ending our fascination with it (163–164).

Should the Arab national state adopt the dialectical method explicitly, it will able to put an end to the harmful contradiction between action and thought, between theory and practice (158). In the same way, Laroui adds, "The dialectic, and only the dialectic, can explain and go beyond the persistent opposition between authenticity and modernization," between identity and modernity (158). The dialectic is the only method by which Arabs can understand their social reality, go beyond the present contradictions, ensure their equality with their Western Other, and achieve liberal capitalism, which, according to Laroui, is the highest stage of human and historical development. As Laroui puts it, the Arab world "can catch up with the West, but can never go beyond that origin of modernity [the West]" (*Muhawarat* 19). If this proves anything, it proves the ideological vacuity and incoherence of Arab petty bourgeois capitalism and its structural dependence on the West.

From the above discussion, it can be concluded that Laroui's early work, and *L'idéologie* in particular, already presents us with a certain vision of modernity. According to this vision, Laroui sees the role of the intellectual elite as a crucial one in the context of creating a counter ideology, without which there can be no modernity. Social change and modernity can be implemented only by an elite group of dedicated intellectuals through a liberal-dialectical look at their past. The dialectical method is central to this vision. It not only describes and analyzes the contradictions and dualities of reality and other ideologies, but it also indicates the means by which these can be transformed and by which liberalism (the ultimate aim and "the end of history") can be achieved.

Dialectics at a Standstill

In his post-1967 work, Laroui sees political defeat, i.e. the collapse of Pan-Arabism, as part of a broader problem: the dominance of old mental and epistemological structures. Such causal explanation is hardly dialectical and at bottom ahistorical. Laroui does not disguise his dislike for Islamism, which he considers reactionary and incapable of effecting any change in the world. Laroui offers a critical reading of the dominant ideologies in the post-colonial Arab world and in Morocco in particular and their role in the "cultural and historical retardation" of Arab societies. He deals less with the effects of colonialism itself, not only in the production and reproduction of these ideologies, but also in the creation of the current social, economic, political, and cultural situation.

Laroui relates the Arab world's social ills exclusively to the Arab-Islamic tradition and religion and calls for their total rejection and the total immersion in Western culture. He is more concerned with the symptoms of the problems than with the problem itself. Laroui says that, "When I speak of the notion of modernity as extracted from the history of others [the West], I speak only about *ideas* and not about their *implementation*. For even in *model* countries, the *actual development* did not match the *idea* of modernity" (*Hiwar* 7) [My italics]. While Laroui correctly identifies the fact that social progress does not correspond to the claims of modernity, he never asks, let alone answers, the question: why did actual development in the most industrialized countries not match the ideological claims of modernity? To ask such a question would have taken Laroui beyond the realm of ideas and ideologies. Laroui, who claims to be a historicist, sees the contradiction between the claims of the ideology of modernity and their implementation in the material world as an established fact, as a fact of nature, and not as a creation of concrete historical forces. He says that, "No country is ever absolutely modern" (27). He takes for granted that modernity can be complete only at the level of consciousness, but never at the level of material reality. But what good is this modernity which remains at the level of consciousness without its due implementation in reality? What good is such incomplete capitalist "model" of modernity? And why does Laroui take this as a model in the first place?

Defending Liberal Modernity

In *Islamisme, modernisme, liberalisme*, a collection of conference papers presented mostly outside Morocco between 1987 and 1996, Abdallah Laroui elaborates a different intellectual and political project, a different vision of modernity, relegating the whole project of Arab Marxism, including his own earlier intervention, to being "a simple political ideology," expressing the hopes and illusions of a very small fraction of the population" (130).

In Laroui's view, liberalism, understood as a specific ideological and political project of capitalism, is the only sound guarantee of true modernity. Liberalism, however, is not completely absent from Laroui's early work. In *L'ideologie*, Laroui draws a distinction between two kinds of liberalism, classical and modern liberalism. His argument, put simply, is that contemporary Arab liberalism is incoherent because it is based on contemporary Western liberal theory, rather than on classical liberalism. He writes in passing:

> In the West, there were two kinds of liberal thought, and it did not cross the mind of anyone to bring Montesquieu to the same level of John Stuart Mill. In the 18th century and from the perspective of France, the greatness of the West, personified in England, consisted entirely in its constitutional liberalism. It was precisely this liberalism which France needed to overcome its retardation. The French drama turned around the absence of this element [the Constitution], when all the conditions of its birth had already existed. In contrast, what ideal could the naïve liberalism of the 19th century embrace? After all, such liberalism has but one pre-occupation: It overlooks whatever puts its universalism into question? (35–36).

Laroui further adds that, "The misfortune of Lotfy Sayyid lies precisely in his inability to see this duality of liberalism in Western history; hence, his style, his character, and his political choices were inconsistent" (36). Laroui, however, does not sufficiently explain how the contemporary variant of liberalism of John Stuart Mill, for example, is at far remove from the earlier, "more powerful, and more energetic" liberalism of people like Montesquieu and Lock (56–57).

In my view, what is important is not the distinction between a classical and a modern form of liberalism, which I find less useful, but rather the similarities between the two. Regardless of what we choose to call it, capitalist liberalism establishes nothing but *formal* rights and liberties while allowing *material* and *structural* inequalities that make those rights and liberties meaningless. Having the right to vote, for example, does not guarantee the exercise of that right in a situation where the very political and economic structures and institutions of liberal modernity produce this contradiction in the first place. What Laroui fails to realize is that under capitalist conditions, formal rights and liberties do not necessarily correspond to their actual implementation at the level of material practice.

Laroui's celebration of classical liberalism is in fact a celebration of its naturalization of capitalism and the capitalist mode of production, thus overlooking the fact that the latter is only a stage, among others, in human evolution. Classical Liberals, like Adam Smith and John Lock, view capitalism as what human nature would lead to. In Lock's understanding, in a state of nature, human beings will eventually understand that the most important thing is profit, and will trade and own property freely. Therefore, according to this logic, capitalism is what benefits humans the most, because it is what their natural propensities lead them to. And even assuming that making profit is the most important goal for human beings—and it clearly is not—it is not clear how one can move from this to the claim that capitalism benefits humans the most.

Laroui develops the same line of argument in *Islamisme*. He writes:

> In the narrower meaning, [liberalism] designates a political ideology, a party-program to solve the actual problems peculiar to such and such state, one which certain people accept because it serves their own interests; hence they call themselves liberals. Others, however, refuse this program, and they call themselves anti-liberals. But in a much broader meaning, liberalism is simply the logic of the modern world, the ultimate result of a series of revolutions, which historians call modernity. How can we be against liberalism, in the latter meaning, and still dream of a democratic society, one that is advanced scientifically and developed economically?...To refuse liberalism in its larger sense without prior reflec-

tion on its deep significance is to reject the modern world in all simplicity (133).

Liberalism, Laroui insists, is nothing but the necessary logic of the present age, and to reject it is to reject modernity itself.

Laroui argues that economic freedom is a necessary condition for political, social, and ideological freedom. In the Preface to the 1999 Arabic Edition of *L'ideologie*, He writes:

> Is not the dream of the free, responsible individual actually fulfilled under this cover [liberalism]? I ask the reader to reflect, in this context, on what the process of privatizing public institutions (what we call privatization in Morocco) exactly means, socially and ideologically, not only politically, considering what I claim is an organic connection between liberalism as an Eighteenth century philosophy and modernity as a social system and historical stage (17–18).

This citation is important in two ways. First, Laroui makes free enterprise, in this case privatization, the foundation of all freedom. He echoes Friedman's claim that "economic freedom is...an indispensable means...of political freedom...and in fact total freedom" (9), and that it is capitalism that brought democracy into being in the first place (10). Second, Laroui's claim about the organic connection between enlightenment philosophy and modernity as a historical stage is misleading. As I mentioned earlier, the dominant enlightenment discourses on capitalism operate with an essentialist, naturalizing logic and end up mystifying the historical nature of capitalism even when they deal with history and historical events.

But precisely, why is it that liberalism has been a weak ideology in the Arab world? Why is it that people question liberalism?

The liberal notions of freedom and democracy are illusory because they cannot be adequately implemented in practice, in reality. Liberalism cannot fulfill its promise to protect individual autonomy from outside interference. Liberalism's freedom is full of contradictions. Rather than focus on emancipation, it tries to rationalize society by creating a set of instrumental and bureaucratic institutions, structures, and procedures. Freedom is here intimately tied to the establishment of specific institutions of liberal democracy: the structure of government, the electoral and party systems, the constitution, so-called civil liberties and human rights, all of which guarantee the sanctity of the individual's private space of freedom. But this kind of procedural freedom is too passive; it falsely assumes that once liberal institutions are in place, individual freedom is automatically protected. It is clear that there is a difference between complete freedom and the liberties promised by liberal democracy—speech, association, market...etc. Having all the necessary liberal institutions and structures does not mean that one is already truly free. What does it mean, for example, to have the freedom to vote when one's choice is already constrained by his or her social class and by the existing structures and institutions, whose ultimate aim is to serve the interests of the hegemonic classes and reproduce the dominant ideologies, thus undermining the very rights and freedoms they claim to uphold? I do not mean to suggest that these formal rights and liberties provided by liberal institutions are not essential. Granted, they represent a great progress, but they are not enough and it would be wrong to equate them with true freedom or complete freedom. They may be necessary for participation in everyday life, as one cannot have public meetings if there is no political freedom to speak or to assemble, for example. But these do not amount to freedom all by themselves.

Liberalism's promise of freedom is too limited. It does not operate on society as a whole; it promises merely to protect the individual from arbitrary interference. It shifts the focus from a social solution onto the domain of the individual. The liberal individual is a private being. He is the autonomous ruler of his own private space of freedom. Such understanding of freedom allows for very little public participation, and does not protect the individual from the exploitation and control he is exposed to as a worker and producer. The liberal individual is a private being, detached from his immediate social context. Liberal freedom is usually defined by the notion of self-rule and self-determination. One is free if no one interferes in his activities. The individual is the sole maker of his own space and the sole agent in his life. But such self-rule only mystifies the role of society in the constitution of the human subject; as Marx reminds us, it is true that people make their own history (though Marx is not here talking about people as individuals but as collectivities), but not in conditions of their own choosing.

Laroui identifies equality as a fundamental liberal value and believes that a liberal regime would be a democracy, which gives each citizen equal voice in the process of governance. What he fails to realize is that without adequate material resources and conditions, the individual (in a society based on class and other corresponding contradictions) would not be able to practice his own autonomy. In other words, there would be no individual autonomy without a just economic and political system, where there is no place for class antagonisms.

Modernity and the State

Between the early 1980s and the early 1990s, Laroui was developing what he later referred to as the "foundational" concepts of modernity, namely: the state, freedom, ideology, reason, and history. He now claimed that only the state, not the intellectuals or the masses, was in a position to reduce the separations, divisions, and dualities by which life in modern Moroccan and Middle Eastern societies was defined, thus taking a decidedly Hegelian orientation. Laroui himself comments on this shift from a celebration of the intelligentsia to that of the state. In an interview with *Afaq [Horizon]* magazine, he claims:

> I start from the necessity of change, the overcoming of underdevelopment and global marginalization. That is why, I must admit that the state apparatus, regardless of its individual orientations and due to its controversial relationship with the West, must maintain some *quantity* of its modernization policies, even when that is done for defensive reasons. The elite, on the other hand, whether from the left or the right, defends tradition in either case.... It ends by rejecting and opposing modernity, based on fabricated reasons.... This is what has led me to focus on the state as a modernizing apparatus. I have lost all hope that intellectuals can become agents of modernization (*Hiwar* 163–4) [My italics].

As will become clearer later, the instrumental and quantitative logic that informs this passage also informs the whole oeuvre of Laroui.

The core of Hegel's theory of the state proper is expounded in Laroui's *Mafhum al-Dawla*. As the title suggests, Laroui insists that it is the *idea* of the state that he is dealing with and that any existing state cannot be anything but a mere approximation to the idea. Laroui's attitude toward the Moroccan state, where he currently holds a position as the official head of the Royal Moroccan Academy of Arts and Sciences, can hardly be anything other than quietistic acceptance, if not celebration.

Laroui has repeatedly spoken of the state as the guardian of the general interest of society and individuals and of law as the embodiment of rational freedom. He considers the state as the only organism in which universal freedom and universal reason can and must be realized. For him, the modern state should be based on rational, universal freedom, organized so as to enable individuals (or rather citizens) to fulfill their freedom in conjunction with others. In civil society, however, one can fulfill one's ends only by acting egoistically, that is, by disregarding the interests of others. Laroui goes even further to suggest that there can be no rational freedom without the state, for "to think of freedom is in essence to think of the state," as well (*Dawla* 145). In a statement strongly reminiscent of Hegel and Weber, Laroui remarks that there "can be no strong modern state without a modern bureaucracy embodying the rationalization of society" (167).

For Laroui, the ideal view of the state is in contradiction with the actual behavior of the actually existing Arab state, not because the latter is an instrument of the ruling classes against the marginalized classes, but merely because it is a traditional state. The contradiction between the state's ideal and actual behavior will be resolved in a rational, modern, liberal state. Laroui views the practices and functions of the state in an abstract fashion, rather than as social functions. While Laroui recognizes the distinction between the state and society, between political society and civil society, he asserts their reconciliation in the political society, thus putting the state above society and the political above the social.

In his attempt to critique Arab culture and cultural forms, Laroui claims that the lack of authenticity and universality in these cultural forms stems from the petty bourgeois nature of the contemporary Arab/Moroccan state. For Laroui, the truly universal and authentic Arab culture will spring only from the soil of a progressive liberal bourgeois state, not of a reactionary petty bourgeois state. This is a plea for bourgeois liberalism in its classic form of academic and artistic freedom. For Laroui, the fundamentalist Islamist state, which is "authoritarian, chauvinist, and culturally reactionary," which embraces the "Orientalist caricature of Islamic scripturalism" is a Bonapartist polity, dominated by the class interests of the petty-bourgeoisie. For Laroui, "It is the culture of this class rather than anything inherently Islamic or Arab, which leads to the rejection of a dialogue with the West" (*L'ideologie* 213). If so, then, unless some kind of liberal Islam, representing the bourgeois segments of civil society, challenges the power of the petty bourgeoisie, there cannot be any true modernity. Laroui is ambivalent regarding the role of the bourgeoisie. While he recognizes it as indispensable for economic and cultural development, he is also aware that the bourgeoisie is not inherently liberal and that it *may* rule by itself, without due consideration of the interests of the other classes in society. He, then, asks how it is possible to benefit from the contributions of a vigorous and influential bourgeoisie, without suffering from the self-interested exploitation, the consequence of an unstable and defensive bourgeois hegemony. This is a logical impossibility. For how is it possible for a class whose very existence is based, among other things, on class conflict and class exploitation to defend the interests of the very classes it exploits? For the bourgeoisie to defend the interests of other classes would amount to sentencing itself to death.

Further, Laroui holds that the instrument by which freedom from the illusions of tradition and by which true modernity will be achieved is the bourgeoisie, a class which, according to Laroui, has a noble mission. Laroui rightly asserts that ideological hegemony is a necessity for the rise to power and domination of the ruling class. But unlike Marx, he does not believe that the erosion of bourgeois ideology and its replacement by a realistic mass consciousness is necessary for social change. Instead, he calls for the erosion of petty-bourgeois Islamist ideology and its replacement by a more vigorously revolutionary bourgeois ideology to effect social change. In many ways, he calls for the replacement of one form of domination with another, one form of injustice with another.

What is ironic is that it is not only religious and metaphysical ideas that reproduce false consciousness. Ideas propounded by other intellectuals, like Laroui, at the behest of dominant classes or within the framework of a given historical era, have the same effect. The ideas produced from within the dominant classes are nothing but expressions of the latter's needs, aspirations, and interests, even when they seem to be of universal significance to those who frame them, as well as to others who consent to them.

Laroui expects a large part of the solution to the social ills of Arab societies to emerge from a cultural and philosophical dialogue between Arabs and the West. In particular, he contends that Arabs can contribute to a much more universal tradition by being critical of the parochial character of Western thinking. The emergent universal perspective will necessarily transcend national and regional authenticities, without completely obliterating them. He never asks himself if Arab states, like all structurally dependent postcolonial states, are even in a position to be equal participants in this dialogue.

A New Vision of Modernity

What concept of modernity does Laroui's later work provide? In his attempt to define modernity, Laroui writes:

> First of all, what is modernity? It has been given multiple definitions: historical, economic, sociological, artistic, etc. What is important, in my opinion, is what I call the sense of the sequence of the aspects I have just mentioned. With which aspect do we start and with which do we finish? (*Islamism* 23).

Thus:

> The problem [of modernity] is seen, felt, understood, and presented differently as we move from one discipline to another, from economics to sociology, or from literature to philosophy. In fact, it is not the same to reflect on modernity starting from Marx as it is to start from Michelet, Nietzsche, or even Proust (23).

So according to Laroui, modernity is a highly complex and multifacetted concept, one that has a large number of connotations and can be approached from a variety of disciplinary angles. As a historical phenomenon and experience, however, modernity, Laroui argues, has taken a "unique" trajectory in the Arab world and the Third-World in general. Unlike the West, modernity in the Third-World was first confronted as a psychological and literary phenomenon, and only later was it confronted as a socio-economic phenomenon.

Laroui makes a distinction between modernity as a historical process and modernity as a mere ideological phenomenon. He writes:

> In fact, we should not confuse modernity as a process and modernity as ideology, the social movement itself and the actions of those who are conscious of it. There are those who analyze it in order to either critique and block it, and these are the traditionalists. On the other hand, there are those who seek to accelerate and spread it, and these are the modernists. We can not truly understand the history of a society, decide whether it is actually modernizing, or, as a reaction, is traditionalizing, if we do not describe with precision the action of this group [of intellectuals] (24).

As I have pointed out earlier, it would be very difficult to defend a clear-cut distinction between modernity as a process and modernity as ideology. Modernist ideologies cannot be seen in isolation from the social reality in which they emerge. They do not emerge in a vacuum, but are themselves expressions of very specific social and historical circumstances formations, which they also help to constitute. Not only do these ideologies spring from the contemplation of the societies that produce them, but they also shed light on the historical process as a whole.

Maybe Laroui's greatest contribution to modernity lies in his ability to identify its dynamic and dialectical nature. Laroui is right to point out that modernity is best understood as an ongoing process. He writes that, "For a long time, we have spoken about modernity and tradition, but here we have a static vision. In a dynamic vision, it is better to speak of modernization and traditionalization, two concomitant movements in every society" (24). It is true that modernity is best understood as a set of social processes, but it is also important to distinguish between modernity as a set of *dominant* processes and practices that exist alongside *residual* (so-called traditional) and *emergent* processes and practices and also set the rules for the latter.

Laroui further argues that:

> [M]odernity is dialectical by nature. It is at the same time universalization and differentiation, both inside every society and in relation to the outside. In Europe the ideology of modernity was not concomitant with the phenomenon itself. It was either pre-modern, and it was the philosophy of the 17th century, notably Cartesianism, or postmodern as in the case of England, and it was the liberalism of the 19th century. At the moment modernization occurred, the dominant ideology was Romanticism, in its broad meaning, which looked up to nothing other than the Middle Ages (26).

Part of the dialectic of modernity is that pre-modern, as well as post-modern, ideas and ideals, past experiences and future visions, which are challenged by modernity, also provide the very condition and justification for the present and the future of modernity.

But while Laroui identifies the dialectical and dynamic nature of modernity, the overall vision emerging from his own work is neither dynamic nor dialectical. Laroui claims that just as in Europe, modernity in the Arab World will be "imposed on the majority of people by a limited group, and here we discover the social victor of change, that is, the intelligentsia, that inspires and guides change, regardless of whether it is political, military, or religious. *There is no exception to this rule....* There will always be a movement more or less powerful, more or less violent, against this process [of modernity]" (25-27) [My italics].

So, in his later writings, Laroui's thought produces another concept of modernity, one that is different from the one he developed earlier. This concept is primarily but not exclusively political. It presents a vision and form of a liberal state, the state and the ruling class elevated above society.

Historicism and History

In the Preface to the English translation of *La crise des intellectuels arabes*, Laroui reminds us that "The central thesis of this book is that the concept of history—a concept playing a capital role in "modern" thought—is in fact peripheral to all the ideologies that have dominated the Arab world till now" (viii). According to the same logic:

> To understand the historical process is to understand both oneself and others in a temporal perspective...To the extent that Arab intellectuals, a good number of whom are also political leaders, have a non-evolutionary conception of reality, so will all collective action in the Arab milieu be deprived of a constant and definite orientation, and so will politics, in the noble sense of the word, be reduced to the level of short-sighted tactical maneuvering subservient to egotistical interests (ix).

As far as history is concerned, Laroui wants to settle accounts with two kinds of history: the traditionalist and orientalist. To do so, he relies on historicism, relativity in history. What is historicism? Historicism is the view that the all social and cultural phenomena are historically determined, that nothing can be understood outside its development. To be sure, the basic concepts of historicism formulated in the writings of Laroui—the ideas of individuality, individual development through time, universality, and universal values—contain some elements of the idealism of Hegel and Enlightenment philosophers before him. In contrast to many nineteenth century historicists' focus on the particular and specific, Laroui emphasizes the general and universal. Only in the universal and general can the individual and specific have any meaning. For Laroui, it is impossible to realize a "pure Arab authenticity," as there can be no understanding of the Arab Self unless it is also an insight about the Western Other. Laroui says that, "To recognize the universal is to become reconciled with oneself" (*L'ideologie* 10). But where does that ideational content come from? It is supplied by the liberal worldview. Given Laroui's preference for the realization of "Arab authenticity-within-universalism," it is not surprising that he finds the parochial nation-state inauthentic. It is, after all, a setting in which the alien *techne* of the West, the *non-moi*, stands in opposition to the Arab self. Laroui's philosophical generalizations about "human nature" are at bottom ahistorical and politically conservative. Laroui assumes that history is governed by universal laws, that its evolution is inevitable and cannot be otherwise. Laroui's assumption that history pursues its own course, unfettered by human involvement, that it is the linear progression of fixed, immutable events does not in the least clarify our understanding of historical change; it has the opposite effect of obscuring it.

Conclusion

In his Preface to the Arabic edition of *L'ideologie*, Laroui reminds us:

> What was the reason behind the criticism of this book when it first appeared? Was it because I called for the embracement of Marxism in the same way communist parties and progressive Arab intellectuals did? No, the opposite was true. Many were offended because I denied Marxism its scientific and universal nature, and also because I did not say, like many others, that it is absolute truth useful for all ages and places. My critics did not like what I said and confirmed, namely that, the Arab intellectual, regardless of whatever he might say about himself, resorts to Marxism only as means to achieve an incessant and temporary end. He sees in Marxism a concentrated summary of modern history; thus, he prefers to comprehend the summary very quickly instead of being lost in the details...What this means is that once the end is achieved and the backward society embracing Marxism digests the origins of modern thought, then Marxism loses its attraction and runs out of its historical use (16).

Here, it is clear that Laroui is trying to distantiate himself from his earlier Marxism. Laroui emerges as the theorist of Arab liberal modernity par excellence. For him, there can be no modernity without liberalism, without "a system based on private property, free initiative, on the generalization of the logic of competition in all levels of society" (16).

The transformation from an "objective" Marxist to a liberal Hegelian is very interesting, and in many ways, reflects the historical fact that Marxism was never taken seriously by the Arab intellectual. It also demonstrates the success of repressive policies of the Arab states, supported by capitalist states (usually former colonizers), to combat Marxism and Marxists. This transformation further reinforces the fact that Marxism was never popular among the masses, and that it was primarily an academic phenomenon, popular among students and academics. Laroui's transformation from a "Marxist" into a "Liberal" corresponds to the transformation from a young teacher to a privileged official of the state. Laroui's work has emerged as a reflection on the Moroccan, and more generally the Arab, social and cultural situation respectively. When Laroui first started writing, the Arab political scene was different. At that historical juncture, there was a growing adoption of Marxist and socialist phraseology among Arab leaders and intellectuals alike. This ideology appealed to the petty bourgeois classes because they saw in it a tool to gain the trust of the masses, without which access to power was impossible.

Laroui belongs to a specific generation, a generation of intellectuals that lived under colonialism and also witnessed Morocco win its political independence. Their lives have been deeply affected and shaped by French colonialism. They lived in a colonial society that relegated them to the periphery, even in their own country. And their struggle against colonialism was at the same time a struggle for recognition, for an independent and nationalist state, where they could play a central role. They used Marxism and Marxist phraseology as a tactic to gain political power, and they did. The struggle for political independence was accompanied with economic dependence, as well as intellectual dependence on Western thought systems and categories in their different manifestations, especially liberalism, and nationalism, and even Marxism.

Like the work of any postcolonial writer, the work of Laroui (this is also true of the work Al-Jabri and Yassine discussed later, as well as of my work) raises a legitimate question, one that has been at the center of much post-colonial theory: Will the Master's tools ever dismantle the Master's house? The adoption of any Western theory or ideology—liberalism, nationalism, state capitalism, or even Marxism—requires justification. I would argue that the master's tools can be liberatory, and it would be naïve to call for their wholesale rejection.

I concur with Laroui that the master's tools are now part of our post-colonial world, and instead of blindly rejecting them—which would be ahistorical and undialectical—we should be critical of them. What we need to ask ourselves as post-colonial subjects is: what remains of the Master's tools? Which particular tools will bring about the fall of the Master's house? It is my contention that the Master's tools can be liberating only if they are capable of responding to the needs of society as a whole. Liberalism, nationalism, and Islamism carry with them the seeds of their own failure, because instead putting an end to social antagonisms, they replace colonial Masters with local ones, thereby making the master's house even stronger and longer-lasting. To replace old masters with new masters is to reinforce domination and betray the goals of true liberation and true modernity. In *The Wretched of the Earth*, Frantz Fanon predicted the defeat of third world nationalism and state capitalism as espoused by many post-colonial leaders, especially in Africa. Indeed, without solving the social question, the post-colonial bourgeoisie and the nationalist petty bourgeoisie have ended up reinforcing Western capitalist and imperialist domination.

So the question now before us as postcolonial subjects is: Can Marxist tools be liberatory? As will become even clearer in the course of my discussion, the work of Marx does indeed provide us with a set of tools and categories that are indispensable for the development of any liberatory project in the Arab world, and it would be wrong to conclude, as Audre Lourde does, that "the master's tools will *never* dismantle the master's house," that "the master's tools will *never* enable us to bring about genuine change" (103). Such statement would probably make more sense if it were rewritten to read: "The master's tools [neo-liberal policies] have been unable to destroy the master's house [imperialist countries' economic domination of the postcolonial world]". Indeed, this is precisely how the founding figures of colonial studies, namely Frantz Fanon and Aime Cesaire, understood it.

Even when Laroui devotes much of his work trying to prove that capitalist liberalism is much more progressive than traditionalism and that intellectuals and politicians should not fail to utilize it in their struggle out of the present crisis, he is telling only half the truth. The other half is buried in one form or another in his earlier work.[7] Laroui takes from Marxism what is acceptable to the liberals, to the bourgeoisie (the criticism of the pre-capitalist modes of production, and the progressive historical role of capitalism in general and of capitalist modernity in particular), and discards those elements of Marxism which he deems unacceptable to the bourgeoisie (the criticism of bourgeois capitalism, class struggle, and the antagonisms inherent in capitalism). That is why, by virtue of his objective position and irrespective of what his subjective convictions may be, he inevitably becomes the spokesman of the bourgeoisie. No one can deny that bourgeois modernity is a great historical improvement over traditionalism and absolute rule, but it nevertheless remains formal, and at best limited, based as it is on inequality and exploitation. No one puts it better than Laroui himself when he writes:

> Marxism is born, as it appears to be, to liberate the spirit of individuals, but on one essential condition: that it should be understood as a critique that accepts and goes beyond liberalism; otherwise, it becomes an element of regression, not of progress (*L'ideologie* 131).

I agree with the essence of what Laroui claims here, that Marxism accepts and goes beyond bourgeois liberalism. I can even go further to say that Marxism is a critique of bourgeois liberalism from within bourgeois liberalism itself. What must be underlined, however, is that Marxism affirms liberal capitalism only to negate it. The act of affirmation cannot be distinguished from that of negation. Marxism is Marxism not because it praises liberal capitalism, but primarily because it seeks to interrogate it, go beyond it, and ultimately transform it.

NOTES

1. Two of Laroui's major books are available in English translations: *The Crisis of the Arab Intellectual* (1974) and *History of the Maghreb* (1977).
2. Unless otherwise noted, all the direct citations from the work of Laroui, Al Jabri, and Yassine are my translations from either the original Arabic or French.
3. Laroui is also a novelist. Between 1984 and 1998, he wrote the following novels: *Al-Ghorba [Homesickness]*, *Al-Yatim [The Orphan]*, *Al-Fariq [The Team]*, and *Awraq [Papers]*.
4. This is my translation from the Arabic original.
5. Morocco was the only Arab country not to be under direct Ottoman rule.
6. By 1964, Morocco had ousted many Egyptian teachers and technicians who had stirred up left-wing opposition.
7. The early work of Laroui was very popular among leftist university students in the 1970s and 1980s, who used it to critique and—they hoped—to change Moroccan society.

· CHAPTER THREE ·

Tradition, Rationality, and Nationalism: Al-Jabri's Critique of the "Arab Mind"

The present chapter provides a critical analysis of the major work of Mohammed Abed al-Jabri, one of the most important living Arab cultural critics and philosophers, at various stages of his intellectual development. My major concern in this chapter is to address the following central question: What conception or theory of modernity and modernization does the work of Al-Jabri produce?

The work of Al-Jabri has attracted a lot of attention in the Arab world and has been at the center of many academic and intellectual debates there since the early 1980s. He is widely recognized as one of the most eminent and impressive Arab social philosophers and cultural critics at the current historical conjuncture. In a long career as a committed intellectual, he has made contributions in a variety of fields: politics, education, journalism, history, and, above all, philosophy.

Surprisingly enough, despite his reputation as one of the major thinkers in the Arab world, Al-Jabri is almost unknown in the English-speaking world. Although he has written some thirty books and over one hundred essays on a variety of issues—ranging from Islamic philosophy to contemporary politics, from education to economics, and from human rights and democracy to globalization—almost none of his work has been translated into English.[1] How is one to account for this lack of attention to Al-Jabri's work in the English-speaking world and in the West in general? Why has his work, popular as it is in the Arab world, resisted translation? To be sure, this partly has to do with the character of the work itself. Most of Al-Jabri's major work deals with medieval Arab-Islamic philosophy, with such philosophers as Ibn Rushd

(Averroes), Ibn Sina (Avicenna), and Al-Farabi. In addition, Al-Jabri writes exclusively in Arabic, and in many ways, the Arabic language he uses makes translating his work into standard English prose a hard task.

That is why, before discussing Al-Jabri's work in further detail, I think it would be very useful to provide my reader with a historical background on his life and work, as well as on the historical formation within which his work has emerged and the intellectual debates to which it responds and contributes.

An Intellectual Biography

Who is Mohammed Abed al-Jabri? Al-Jabri was born into a comfortable middle-class family in Figuig (Ouajda region) in southeastern Morocco on December 27, 1936. His family, religious and nationalist, was politically engaged in Morocco's struggle for independence from French occupation. Al-Jabri attended religious school, and at the age of fifteen, he enrolled in the Mohammadia School in Casablanca, and, two years later, joined the same school as a primary school teacher. In 1956, the same year Morocco gained its political independence, he received his middle school diploma, as well as a *License* to practice as a primary school teacher. A year later, in 1957, he received his high school *baccalauréat* and joined the Ministry of National Education as a permanent teacher. In the same year, Al-Jabri came into contact with the leftist Moroccan leader Mehdi Ben Barka, who led the leftists in the *Istiqlal* [Independence] Party and later broke with it to found the *Ittihad Al-Watani Lil-Quwwat Al-Shaabiyya* [National Union of Popular Forces] party in 1959. This party, which included young radicals and leftists, launched a radical attack on the conservative forces in the *Istiqlal*. At around this time, Al-Jabri, in addition to teaching and studying, had already moved into journalism and, in the summers of 1957 and 1958, he worked for *Al-Alam* newspaper, which was then the official publication of the *Istiqlal*. In 1958, Al-Jabri went to the University of Damascus in Syria to study philosophy, but came back to Morocco a year later. At the age of twenty-two, he enrolled in Mohammed V University in Rabat, where he pursued his undergraduate studies in philosophy. After the 1959 split of the *Istiqlal*, he became one of the editors, in Casablanca, of the influential *Tahrir*, the official newspaper of the leftist *Ittihad* party. In 1960, Al-Jabri went to Paris to pursue his studies at the Sorbonne, but soon changed his mind and returned to Morocco, where he received his Bachelor's degree in philosophy in 1962 and continued his political activities and ambitions. On July 16, 1963, he was arrested, along with many of his comrades in the *Ittihad*, under the pretext of conspiring against the Moroccan monarchy, but was soon released. Since 1964, Al-Jabri has contributed to a number of left-leaning newspapers and magazines, including *Aqlam* (1964–1983) and *Al-Muharrir* (1964–1973). Between 1964 and 1967, Al-Jabri taught philosophy in Moulay Aballah High School. Meanwhile, he was also involved in education-related research, and between 1966 and 1967, co-authored (with Mustafa Al-Omari and Ahmed Sttati) two high-school text-books: *Durus fi Al-Falsafa Li-Tullab Al-Bakaluriya [Courses on Philosophy for Baccalaureate Students]* and *Al-Fikr Al-Islami Li-Tullab Al-Bakaluriya [Islamic Thought for Baccalaureate Students]*. These publications were quite well-received among students and teachers alike, for they emphasized the role of education in social change, as well as the interaction of the social and the cultural realms. The books were especially popular in the 1970s. Al-Jabri's academic experience as an educator had a major impact on his career as a thinker and writer. He devoted a good portion of his writings to education; in 1973, he published a book on the problems of education in Morocco, entitled *Adwaa Ala Mushkil Al-Taalim Bi-Almaghrib [Focus on the Problem of Education in Morocco]*. More than ten years later, Al-Jabri would return to the same subject. In 1988, he devoted an entire book to the evaluation of current educational policies in the Maghreb.[2] Issues of education would also resurface in his later writings, especially in his most recent work on globalization, democracy, and cultural identity.

In 1967, Al-Jabri completed his *diplôme d'études supérieur's* [Master's] thesis on the philosophy of history in Ibn Khaldun at Mohammed V University in Rabat, Morocco, and became a lecturer at the Department of Philosophy and Islamic Studies there. In 1970, he finished his doctoral dissertation on the thought of Ibn Khaldun.[3]

In the mid-1970s, Al-Jabri gave a series of lectures at Mohammed V University and wrote several articles on Islamic philosophy, which were subsequently published in his now well-known *Nahnu wa Turath [We and Tradition]* in 1980. This collection of articles drew the attention of many Arab scholars and students, and it would not be an exaggeration to say that Al-Jabri was hardly known in the Arab world (except in Morocco) before the publication of this book. At about the same time, Al-Jabri was still actively involved in politics and in 1975, he was elected as an official member of the political bureau of the *Ittihad*. In 1981, Al-Jabri left party politics and devoted all his energies to writing.[4] However, he never broke with the party; he maintained good relationships with its leaders and continued to contribute to the party's official newspaper, *Tahrir*.

Al-Jabri continued his work on Islamic philosophy and tradition, and in 1982, he produced a book on contemporary Arab thought, *Al-Khitab Al-Arabi Al-Mouasir [Contemporary Arab Discourse]*. This critique of contemporary Arab ideologies could be considered as an introduction to his multi-volume work, *Naqd Al-Aql Al-Arabi [Critique of Arab Reason]*, which was written between 1984 and 2001.[5] It is here where Al-Jabri's fully developed critique and reinterpretation of Islamic thought and tradition is to be found.

Historical Context

As I mentioned earlier, the 1967 Arab defeat in the war between several Arab states, led by Egypt, and Israel dealt a serious blow to the nationalist and revolutionary movements of the 1950s and the 1960s and to Arab petty bourgeois state capitalism and Nasserism in particular. It became clear that state capitalism was unable to resolve the contradictions and antagonisms of Arab society. In their search for a way out, many people were turning back to Islam and Islamic tradition, calling for the dismissal of all other ideologies: liberal, nationalist, and even socialist. Throughout the Arab world, it became commonplace to relate defeat to dismissal of tradition and religion. The proponents of the new ideology called for the return to Islam and Islamic tradition, not as religion, but as a political system, in which "authentic" Islam was presented as the only way to "salvation" and development. This ideology, which would become the dominant ideological logic all over the Arab world, became known, especially in the mid-1970s, as the "Islamist awakening." The 1979 Iranian Revolution was both a significant result as well as a major contributing factor to this "awakening."[6]

It is within this historical context of "Islamist awakening" that the work of Al-Jabri and the concern with *turath* [Islamic tradition] in general should be located. The concern with Arab-Islamic tradition has been central to contemporary intellectual discourses; it lies at the heart of the work of many contemporary intellectuals, including such thinkers as Hassan Hanafi in Egypt, Taha Abderrahman in Morocco, and Mohammed Arkoun in Algeria.[7] For these "reformist" intellectuals, Islamic *shari'a* [law] needs to be largely reinterpreted in a way that emphasizes Islam's message of social justice, egalitarianism, rationalism, and tolerance. This reformist trend could be seen as a reaction against two major trends in the Arab world: on the one hand, it is directed against the more fundamentalist Islamists, such as Hassan Tourabi in Sudan, Rashid Al-Ghannushi in Tunisia, and Mohammed Said Ramadan Al-Buti in Syria, and Abdessalam Yassine in Morocco (the latter to be discussed in the next chapter), all of whom seem to insist on strict and rigid adherence to and application of Islamic law as it is preserved in the Koran and *sunna* [the prophetic tradition]. On the other hand, it is a critique of more liberal and leftist thinkers, such as Abdallah Laroui in Morocco, Adonis (Ali Ahmed Said), and Sadiq Jalal Al-Azm in Syria, who totally reject Islamic tradition and consider it a hindrance toward progress and modernity.

But probably more than any other Arab intellectual, Al-Jabri has written extensively on Arab-Islamic philosophy and tradition. Most of his work speaks to, reinforces, and also critiques this concern with *turath*. Al-Jabri's work on Islamic tradition has been the subject of numerous discussions throughout the Arab world since the early 1980s.[8]

Like Laroui, Al-Jabri conceives of himself as a social philosopher and a political intellectual who is critically engaged in the problematic of national renaissance, modernity, and modernization in the post-colonial Arab world in general, and in contemporary Moroccan society in particular. Let us start with the following question: How did Al-Jabri, as a young academic, see the modern and modernity at around 1975, two decades after Morocco's political independence from France?

"Fundamentalist" Approaches to Tradition

The critique of Islamic tradition, and especially philosophical tradition, is indeed key to Al-Jabri's project of modernity, particularly in his four-volume *Naqd Al Aql Al Arabi*. But even relatively shorter works like *Nahnu wa Turath*—a collection of conference presentations written in the mid-1970s—and *Turath wa Al-Hadata [Tradition and Modernity]* speak to this concern. Al-Jabri claims that if Arab subjects do not practice rationalism in their tradition, they will never be able to achieve modernity. For him, rationalism and democracy are two essential aspects of modernity. As he puts it, "modernity is, before anything else, rationalism and democracy" (18). In *Nahnu*, Al-Jabri examines some of the myths associated with Islamic philosophy and the transmission of the Greek tradition during Europe's Middle Ages. Contrary to the claims of some scholars, who have followed the lead of Ernest Renan in the last century, Al-Jabri claims that Medieval Arabic-Islamic philosophy is not a mere replica of Greek philosophy, lacking on that account any measure of originality.

At the outset, Al-Jabri's book begins with a methodological criticism of three dominant approaches to Arab-Islamic tradition: the fundamentalist, the liberal, and the Marxist.

The Fundamentalist Approach

Al-Jabri claims that the fundamentalist approach seeks to answer two interrelated questions: How do Muslims revive their tradition? And how do they regain the greatness of their past? This approach, according to him, is characterized by a blind celebration of the past, without due consideration of the present. The past is so powerful that it extends to the present and absorbs it; it replaces, displaces, and consumes the present and becomes the only path towards achieving one's authenticity and identity, individual and cultural.

The fundamentalist intellectual and political formation, which initially took the form of a religious reformist movement with such thinkers as Jamal Eddine Al-Afghani and Mohammed Abduh, calls for a new understanding of religion and the past, without falling "prey" to Western thought. It is based on a religious conception of history, a conception which makes the past extend into the present and treats history as a continuum. As I have argued elsewhere, "The orthodox Muslim conception of history declares that human society is created to fulfill a divine scheme," and "the whole historical process is the working out not of man's desire but of God's will" (Aksikas 18–19). This vision of history is based on a very peculiar view of time, where history constitutes a continuum and time is eternally present (19). Al-Jabri concludes that, "the fundamentalist reading of tradition is ahistorical, and can result in only one understanding of tradition: the traditional understanding of tradition. [It is] tradition repeating itself" (*Nahnu* 13). For the fundamentalist, it is faith—and faith alone—that moves history and determines identity, and any other factor should be considered "secondary," "subservient," or even irrelevant (13).

The Liberal Approach

The liberal understanding of tradition, Al-Jabri argues, addresses two interrelated questions: How do we Arabs live in the present era, and how do we approach our tradition? Unlike the fundamentalist, the Arab liberal celebrates the present, without any due consideration of the past. Unfortunately, instead of directing his attention to the Arab present, he celebrates the present of the West and presents it as the only path possible for all humanity. The liberal view, which is largely shaped by the Western frame of reference, sees in tradition only what the Westerner himself sees in it. As Al-Jabri puts it, "The Arab liberal looks at the Arab-Islamic tradition from the perspective of the lived present, the present of the West. He, thus, interprets tradition in a Western spirit, that is, he views it from the Western system of reference and sees in it only what the Western subject sees in it" (14).

While the liberal adopts the orientalist's tools and categories, he insists that he rejects their ideology. But as Al-Jabri points out, it is not possible to separate the two, the method from the ideology. From a methodological perspective, Orientalism is based on opposing cultures, on reading one tradition through another. It adopts a philological approach, one that takes "every" particular thing back to its "origin." Thus, the study of Arab-Islamic tradition is limited to the exploration of its Judeo-Christian, Persian, Greek, Indian and other origins. The major concern of the orientalist, according to Al-Jabri, is to understand not Arab tradition itself, but rather the extent to which "Arabs" understood the heritage of their predecessors. The merit of Arabs and Arab tradition is limited to their historical role as intermediaries between ancient Greece and the modern West, between the Greek and modern Western civilizations. If the "future" of Arabs in the past lied in the assimilation of a foreign culture, namely Greek culture, then, according to the same logic, the "future" of Arabs today is conditional upon assimilating the European past and present alike (15). Al-Jabri concludes that "the call for "modernity" in contemporary Arab liberal thought reveals *a dangerous denial of Self*, not only as reactionary at present, but also—most dangerously—as a reactionary history and civilization" (15).

The Marxist Approach

In Al-Jabri's view, the Marxist critic asks the following questions: How will revolution be achieved? How does one reconstruct tradition and approach the cultural past? In doing so, he establishes a dialectical relationship between the future and the past, where both are mere projects yet to be fulfilled. The major concern of the Marxist critique, according to Al-Jabri, is to discover a method through which revolution can be fulfilled and also through which tradition can be reconstructed so that it can play a major role in that very revolution. In other words, the revolution must contribute to the reconstruction of tradition, and tradition, in turn, has to help fulfill the revolution.

Al-Jabri does not object to the dialectical method itself, but rather to the way it has been used by certain Arab leftist intellectuals. As he puts it, Arab leftist thought "does not adopt—in our assessment—the dialectical method as a method *to be applied*, but as an *"already applied" method"* (15). For the Arab leftist:

> Arab-Islamic tradition has to be a reflection of class struggle on the one hand, and a realm for struggle between "materialism" and "idealism" on the other. The task of the leftist reading of tradition, then, becomes one of determining the parties and spots involved in this "double" struggle. When leftist thought realizes its inability to achieve this goal in a satisfactory manner, it, troubled and worried, blames this on the "unwritten Arab history" or on the difficulty of analysis in the face of such complexity that characterizes the events of our history. And even those who insist on taking a further step are unable to go beyond fitting historical reality into theoretical frameworks. In this case, if "class struggle" does not work, they would use "historical conspiracy" and if they cannot find materialism, they would resort to "heretical materialism" (15).

Thus, the "leftist" approach to Arab-Islamic tradition, according to Al-Jabri, turns into a form of what he calls "Marxist fundamentalism." It turns out to be an "unproductive" attempt to prove the validity of the dialectical method as it was employed in the foundational texts of Marxism, rather than applying it (16).

Al-Jabri rejects all three of these readings, because, in his assessment, they are all fundamentalist readings of tradition. They are based on a "naïve" form of analogical reasoning. In his attempt to provide a solution to the reactionarism of the current historical conjuncture, the fundamentalist intellectual (traditional, liberal, or Marxist) looks back to the past for solutions. He looks back to the past for what is analogous to the present. Such mechanical reasoning, according to Al-Jabri, cancels time and blocks development, and is at bottom ahistorical (19). He writes:

> As a whole, modern and contemporary Arab thought is ahistorical, and lacks minimum objectivity. That is why, its reading of tradition is fundamentalist. It treats the past as if it were sacred, seeking to find in it ready-made solutions to all the problems of the present and the future. And if this is clearly true about religious thought, it is no less true about the other currents of thought, given the fact that each current has and seeks refuge in its own founding fathers. Thus, all Arabs model their renaissance project on some kind of past, be it the Arab-Islamic past, the European past-present, or the Russian or Chinese experience...etc. It is the mechanical mental practice that seeks ready-made solutions to all emergent problems in some origin or another (19).

In his attempt to critique this kind of "fundamentalist, analogical" rationality, Al-Jabri develops a new approach to tradition. But does not Al-Jabri's reading fit within this framework? Otherwise, why would he give such importance to tradition in the first place?

Toward a New Approach to Tradition

Al-Jabri's major concern is to provide a systematic deconstruction and critique of Arab rationality. According to him, rationalism, which is the organized habit of critical deconstruction and reconstruction, reveals the nature of the undercurrents of the Arab and Muslim past, thus allowing us to reconstruct the rational foundations of contemporary Arab society and culture. In other words, a past reconstructed in an enlightened, rational, critical manner is a vital part of any true modernity. In a manner reminiscent of Foucault and later Said, Al-Jabri seeks to reveal the underlying epistemological and ideological underpinnings of Arab and Islamic thought. In Al-Jabri's view, the dominant understanding and treatment of the Islamic tradition is characterized by *all'aqlaniyya* [irrationality]. What is needed, then, is the development of a rational and critical interrogation of it. Such new interrogation should be based on a method that deconstructs the texts and reconstructs them, by giving them a modern reading. Al-Jabri seeks to investigate the historical genesis and development of Arab rationality in an attempt to reveal its underlying and hegemonic concepts, methodological tools and presuppositions, and its political and ethical imperatives.

A modern philosophical, rational understanding of medieval Islamic philosophy, Al-Jabri argues, should displace the seemingly rigid, fundamentalist understanding of the Arab-Islamic tradition and philosophical tradition in particular. This would allow tradition to be contemporary with the present, so that its positive aspects are put to use for the purposes of contemporary aspirations. For Al-Jabri, Reading *turath*, or tradition, where it is more than blind consumption, is neither mere appreciation nor mere explication, although apparently both elements are indispensable for criticism. Critical reading implies a rational critique of the text, as well as recognition of its historical nature and limitations. What distinguishes Al-Jabri's method is the submission to the act of historical empathy and the attempt at critical reconstruction. Reading entails the element of critique. Al-Jabri writes:

> In my view, the correct approach to address the problematic [of liberal modernity] should be: How can contemporary Arab thought regain and assimilate the rational (liberal) dimensions in its tradition, as well as employ them anew in the same direction they were initially employed, the direction of combating feudalism, Gnosticism, and fatalism and of founding a republic of reason and justice, a free, democratic, and socialist Arab republic (*Nahnu* 53).

According to Al-Jabri's logic, to achieve true renaissance, true modernity, Arab intellectuals must first revive the philosophical rationalism of earlier medieval Arab philosophers. Between the 9th and 13th centuries, rationalism constituted a robust philosophical-political movement against the irrationality and dogmatism of Muslim scholastic theology and politics. Eleventh century theologian Imam Al-Ghazali, along with many other jurists and theologians, argued that revelation was by nature superior to reason, given its divine source and nature. Human rationality is limited and should always be subservient to the divine text. The central claim of *Tahafut Al-Falasifa [Incoherence of Philosophers]*, Al-Ghazali's most famous attack on philosophers and rationalism, is that it is impossible to know "truth" by reason alone. He writes:

> Now, I have noticed that there is a group of people who believe in their superiority to others because of their great intelligence and knowledge. They have abandoned all duties Islam imposes on its adherents...They defy the injunctions of the Sacred Law....Our present-day heretics have heard the names of people such as Socrates, Hippocrates, Plato, Aristotle...etc. They have been deceived by the followers of these philosophers—who claim that the ancient masters possessed extraordinary power, that the principles they have discovered are unquestionable, that

the mathematical, logical, physical, and metaphysical sciences they have developed are the most profound...and that with all the subtlety of their intelligence and the originality of their discoveries they repudiated the authority of divine laws... (2) [My translation].

Al-Ghazali was directing his attack on rational philosophers, like Al-Kindi, who argued that revelation and reason were not necessarily opposed, and that they instead complemented each other. In the 9th century, Al-Kindi wrote, "We should not be ashamed to acknowledge truth from whatever source it comes to us, even if it is brought to us by former generations and foreign powers. For him who seeks the truth there is nothing of higher value than truth itself" (qtd. in Albert Hourani, *A History of the Arab Peoples* 76). Three centuries later, Ibn Rush went even further to suggest that in case reason and revelation seemed opposed, the Koran has to be reinterpreted in a way that makes it in conformity with reason, thus establishing the primacy of rational reflection over the Koranic text.

For Al-Jabri, it is only by reconstructing the rational elements in Islamic tradition that we can preserve our uniqueness and secure a place in the modern world. In many ways, this is an equally narrowly nationalist position, one that ends up by blindly celebrating the past (or at least some aspects of the past), without due consideration of the accomplishments of other traditions. This position is not that different from the fundamentalist position, but while Al-Jabri glorifies philosophy, the fundamentalist glorifies theology. Much of Al-Jabri's early writing is best seen as a struggle to confirm the continued validity and relevance of philosophy in a world that does not need philosophical interpretation any more, but cries badly for change. It is an attempt on the part of a young teacher to secure a place in academia and a role in the political life of Morocco. What Al-Jabri fails to explain, however, is how we can move from rationalism in philosophy to rationalism in reality? For what is needed, after all, is rationalism in society not in our philosophical tradition.

Towards a New Method

Al-Jabri presents his reading of tradition as a self-consciously ideological reading, one that "goes beyond documentary research and analytical study" and "proposes candidly and consciously an interpretation that gives to the object "a meaning" that makes it at the same time of significance for its ideological-social-political context, and also for us as readers" (*Nahnu* 11). For him, "it is better one thousand times to try to read our tradition ideologically, but self-consciously, than to continue an unconscious ideological reading, a false and reversed reading" (7).

Al-Jabri claims that any call for the renewal of Arab rationality and thought will remain mere futile rhetoric if it does not, as a first step, aim at deconstructing the modes of reasoning and thinking inherited from the so-called "dark ages." This cannot be achieved without a systematic critique of its foundational structure: mechanical analogical reasoning. The reconstruction process of a critical rationality must start with a decisive epistemological break with the analogical mode of Arab reason in the dark ages and its extension into modern contemporary Arab thought (20).

What does Al-Jabri mean by an epistemological break? He writes that:

> We should point out that such epistemological break does not include the object of knowledge. Thus, it has nothing to do with the pernicious thesis, calling for locking up our tradition in museums or for confining it "there" to its place in history. Such mechanical rejection of tradition is neither scientific nor historical, and is itself a result of traditional thinking in the dark ages. The epistemological break deals with the "reasoning act." The reasoning act is an activity performed in a certain way and by certain tools or concepts, within a certain epistemological field. The object of knowledge may remain the same, but the way of its treatment, the mental tools used and the problematic guiding this treatment, as well as the epistemological field where it is conducted, all this is subject to change. When the change is deep and organic, that is, when it reaches the point of no return to the previous method, we can then speak of an epistemological break (20).

So, Al-Jabri is not calling for a break with tradition in a Larouian sense, where tradition is rejected all at once. Instead, he calls for the dismissal of the traditionalist understanding of tradition. As he puts it, "The break we are calling for is not a break with tradition, but rather a break with a certain kind of relationship with tradition, one that transforms us from "traditionalist beings" into beings with a tradition" (21).

But what kind of method should we adopt to achieve this break from tradition and traditional modes of thought? Al-Jabri claims that:

> The question of method for our object is not a question of choice between the historicist, the functionalist, or the structuralist method...etc. One approach might be adequate in one area and not in another. But all

these methods cannot become suitable, except when the object is independent from the self-subject (21).

This statement further supports our claim about the confused incoherence of Al-Jabri's thought and practice. The absence of a consistent method reflects the absence of a consistent ideology in Al-Jabri and in the petty bourgeois intellectual and politician.

The statement raises other questions: Is not tradition part of one's self? How can one separate the two? The search for a method that allows one to separate the knowing self from the object and the object from the knowing self is impossible. Al-Jabri's claims that to "disjoin the subject from his tradition is a necessary first step towards objectivity" is untenable. What this fails to realize is that the researching subject is already inside his or her object of study, and that to deny our biases instead of consciously engaging them is just another way of allowing them to operate behind our backs with even greater vitality and force.

Al-Jabri claims that he adopts a combination of three approaches:

1. The Structuralist Approach
In Al-Jabri's view, the aim of the structuralist analysis is twofold; first, it treats the thought of a certain author as a whole; second, it links the thought of one thinker around a single problematic.

2. The Historical Approach
For him, this approach links the thought of a certain author to its historical context in all its dimensions, cultural, ideological, political, and social. Such historical perspective does not only provide us with a historical understanding of the object under study, but enables us to know what a text can possibly contain and what it cannot possibly contain. In other words, the historical perspective helps to determine what is historically possible and what is not, what a text could have potentially said, but was silent about (24).

3. The Ideological Approach
Historical analysis, according to Al-Jabir, remains incomplete, abstract, and formal without due consideration of the ideological (socio-political) function of the work in question. As he puts it, "To reveal the ideological content of a certain thought is the only way to make it contemporary to itself, and to link it to the world to which it belongs" (24).

Methodological Assumptions

Al-Jabri notes that his approach to tradition is based on three major methodological assumptions: the unity of thought, the historicity of thought, and the specificity of Islamic philosophy.

The Unity of Thought or the Unity of Problematic

Al-Jabri starts from the assumption that, "theoretical thought in a given society at a given time constitutes a distinct unity," where different tendencies come together (27). He further adds that, "the truth here is the whole, not the parts, for each part is nothing but a one-dimensional expression of the whole itself" (27). The unity of thought, however, does not refer to the unity of thinkers or objects under study, but rather to the *unity of their problematic*. According to the same conception, "A problematic is a system of relationships—in a certain thought system—created by a set of interconnected problems that cannot be solved independently of each other, and that cannot be—theoretically—resolved except within the framework of an all-inclusive solution" (27). Thus, it becomes possible, for example, to speak about Greek thought or contemporary Arab thought, despite all the diversity and the multiplicity of their schools and movements.

Al-Jabri gives the example of 19th century Arab *Nahda,* or Renaissance thought. Throughout the renaissance era, all thought has been, in one way or another, preoccupied with one problematic, that of revival, and from here its unity. While it is true that Arab intellectuals were preoccupied with a set of problems, and not only one, these problems could not be solved independently of one another, as they included, among others, Western imperialism, Ottoman totalitarianism, poverty, illiteracy, education, language, status of woman, and national division. Thus, a critique of one problem or phenomenon necessarily involves a critique of the other problems or phenomena. In fact, what is important is not the problem itself, but rather the function it plays as an element within the whole problematic (28).

What is ironic is that Al-Jabri deals a blow to this very methodological assumption in the same book. He describes the essays collected in *Nahnu* in this way:

> These are "contemporary interpretations" of some central aspects of our philosophical tradition that I have conducted as a humble contribution to the ongoing effort by modern and contemporary Arab thinkers to find an "appropriate" approach in dealing with *turath* (tradition) (11).

Al-Jabri argues that he uses the word "interpretations" in the plural form, not because these interpretations differ from one another in terms of methodology or perspective, but simply because each was conducted independently of the others. He goes even further to suggest that, "there was no preconceived assumption organizing all of them, an assumption making each study "subject" to the influence of the others and to the domination of the totality. The opposite was true. Each study was conducted independently of the others, far from any outside influence. We prefer to start from the part in search of the whole, quite convinced that the ready-made "totality" misleads the reader and distorts the object under study" (11). Once again, Al-Jabri reveals his methodological vacuity and inconsistency. Part of the problem can be attributed to Al-Jabri's attempt to reconcile contrasting, even irreconcilable traditions, in a manner reminiscent of Ibn Rushd's attempt to reconcile philosophy and theology, faith and reason. In Al-Jabri's view, Ibn Rushd is the embodiment of Arab rationality, and any true modernity project must start with Ibn Rush's philosophy.

Al-Jabri's claim about the necessity to start from the part is undialectical. It is misleading and leads at best to fragmentary knowledge. Ollman puts it very nicely when he writes, "Unlike nondialectical research, where one starts with some small part and through establishing its connections to other such parts tries to reconstruct the larger whole, dialectical research begins with the whole, the system, or as much of it as one understands, and then proceeds to an examination of the parts to see where it fits and how it functions, leading eventually to a fuller understanding of the whole from which one has begun" (14).

The Historicity of Thought

The second assumption that informs Al-Jabri's reading of tradition is the historicity of thought, that is, "its connectedness to the political, social, economic, and cultural realities that produced it, or at least, where it evolved" (29). Immediately afterwards, Al-Jabri, however, contradicts this statement and, thus, produces a most ahistorical understanding of historicity. Al-Jabri argues that a given problematic is not confined by history, and that it remains open for any subsequent generations to take as long as it has not become obsolete. As he puts it:

> The historical space of thought is not necessarily history whose development and stages are determined by the succession of nations or the development of economy, or the breakout of wars, or any other measures

that thought does not submit to necessarily. The relative—but nevertheless very often real— autonomy of thought compels us to resort to the constitutive elements of thought itself in order to determine its historical space (29).

What is implied here is that thought exists outside social, economic, and political history.

In Al-Jabri's understanding, the historical space of a given thought, of a given problematic is determined by two factors, the epistemological field and the ideological content. The former refers to homogenous "epistemological material," that is, to the conceptual apparatus (concepts, assumptions, method, and vision...etc.) that is employed or could be employed by those who think from within the same problematic. The latter seeks to explore the ideological function (socio-political) for which the epistemological material is employed.

The Specificity of Islamic Philosophy

In Al-Jabri's view, the distinction between the epistemological and ideological aspects of thought is especially valid when it comes to Islamic philosophy, which was a reading of Greek philosophy, namely of Plato's and Aristotle's philosophies. In the words of Al-Jabri, "Islamic philosophy was not a continuous and renewed reading of its own history as has been the case with Greek philosophy or Western philosophy since Descartes. Rather, it presented independent readings of another philosophy, Greek philosophy, readings that employed the same epistemological material for different and contrasting ideological objectives" (31). Based on the epistemological material that Islamic philosophers employed, it appeared as if they were merely repeating each other. That is why, according to Al-Jabri, the distinction between the epistemological and ideological aspects of Islamic philosophy is necessary so that we can understand its dynamism and variety and also relate it to society and history (31). Al-Jabri concludes that:

> What is new in Islamic philosophy should be sought, not in the epistemological material that it invested and reproduced, but rather in the ideological function that each philosopher gave to this material... That is why, the distinction between the epistemological content and ideological one in Islamic philosophy is necessary so that we can discover its variety and dynamism, and thus, relate it to society and history (7).

It is clear that there is no logical cause-effect relationship between the two parts of this passage. The distinction between what is epistemological and what is ideological is not a prerequisite for a historical understanding of Islamic philosophy.

Al-Jabri criticizes orientalist and Arab historians of Islamic philosophy alike on the grounds that they looked at Islamic philosophy in terms of the epistemological material it employed alone, without due consideration of the ideological role. While this critique is tenable, the distinction between the epistemological and ideological is questionable on a number of grounds. In fact, a distinction of this kind will only blur our understanding of Islamic philosophy. Part of any historical understanding of Islamic philosophy would be to explain precisely why Muslim philosophers chose to translate or comment on Greek philosophy and not any other philosophy, as well as why they chose to emphasize certain Greek philosophers and not others.

Role of Philosophy in Social Change

Central to contemporary political and intellectual discourses on modernity in Morocco, and in the Arab World in general, is the status and role of the Islamic *Turath* (cultural tradition or heritage). Like many other Arab intellectuals, Al-Jabri sees himself as engaged in the critical study of the past for the sake of the present. However, being a philosopher by training, Al-Jabri advocates a stronger emphasis on the philosophical aspects of the Islamic cultural tradition, which is central to his concern with Arab nationalist renaissance and modernity. In the "Introduction" to the Second Edition of *Nahnu*, he writes that:

> [These studies] present themselves to all those who write on Arab-Islamic philosophy as a result of a reading that aims to open the path for a new approach to our philosophical tradition, one that meets at the same time the scientific expectations of the present era and the ideological concern that takes us back to tradition, our concern with a nationalist renaissance....Consensus over a new way to deal with tradition cannot be achieved without debate or revision (5).

Implicit in this passage are two major questions: First, how should the Arab cultural past be understood, and how relevant is it to the present? According to Al-Jabri, concern with Medieval Islamic philosophy reflects a concern with Arab society at the present and its renaissance. In Al-Jabri's understanding, philosophical renaissance is a precondition for the renaissance of the entire Arab culture and civilization. It is a project of "intellectual emancipation," which leads to social emancipation. It is part of the cultural decolonization project that began in post-independent North Africa with people like Franz Fanon. Unlike Laroui, Al-Jabri does not dismiss tradition as irrelevant, nor does he accept any particular Western school of thought. Philosophical thought and politics are interconnected and philosophy is indispensable to any project of cultural decolonization. It is philosophy not politics that can lead to liberation. Arab renaissance requires the development of a critical, philosophical rationality, as opposed to religious, fundamentalist rationality. Critical philosophy can free contemporary Arab culture from the one-dimensionality and parochialism of the fundamentalist rationality and serve to revive the Arab nationalist project.

Unlike Laroui, who insists on a break with, and even rejection of, traditional culture for the sake of modernity, Al-Jabri consistently rejects this as a dangerous regression to a position close to that taken by the traditionalists themselves. He introduces a completely different concept of modernity, one that is firmly based on the idea that tradition is part of modernity, that the past is indispensable for the present and future alike.

What role did philosophy play? Al-Jabri claims that throughout Islamic history, philosophy was politically motivated from the very beginning and was not just a futile exercise in rationalism. It was engaged in all sorts of ideological and political struggles. As he puts it:

> If we look at Arab Islamic philosophy, through its function within the totality of social contradictions and struggles, we find that it was a militant ideological discourse committed to the service of science and progress, and to a dynamic vision of society. This means that the opponents of philosophy were always reactionary and conservative elements in society, whose ethnic or class interests lied in moving history backwards (35-36).

Al-Jabri notes that the translation process of Greek philosophy into Arabic, which started at the beginning of the Abbasid era, especially during the reign of caliph Al-Mamun, was not an autonomous cultural process, but rather a vital part of a larger strategy, developed by a newly-established dynasty to confront hostile forces, mainly the Persian aristocracy. The latter, following their political defeat, were determined to launch a large-scale ideological attack against the Abbasid, "employing a religious-cultural heritage based on Gnosticism, the belief in the existence of a source of knowledge other than reason" (36). Thus, they introduced the notion of divine inspiration in an attempt to question the legitimacy of the newly formed dynasty. The reaction of the new state was two-fold: on the one hand, it adopted the Mu'tazilite doctrine as the official state doctrine; on the other hand, it encouraged the translation of the scientific and philosophical works of the Greeks, the historical foes of the Persians. Al-Jabri concludes that, "The function of Arab-Islamic philosophy was, thus, determined from the time it was a mere project with the early translations. It was to become a weapon against the ideological attack on Gnosticism which was aimed at the foundations of the state" (36). What one might find striking in Al-Jabri's analysis is the compliance of philosophy and the state, the instrumental use of philosophy as a means to an end. The rationality of philosophy reflects the rationality of the state. Is the rational state, then, a precondition for the emergence of rational philosophy and critical thought? Is not Al-Jabri giving assurances to the Moroccan, and with it the Arab state, about philosophy's pro-state stance, about the role it can play to reproduce dominant ideologies?

Al-Jabri's discussion of the role of philosophy in society raises a number of questions. Is not his celebration of philosophy itself a regression to a position similar to that of the very fundamentalists he criticizes? Is Al-Jabri's philosophy irrelevant and perhaps socially harmful through its tendency to distract us from real problems? And more importantly, how is Al-Jabri's critique relevant to contemporary Arab society? I am going to come back to these questions later.

Two Philosophical Traditions

Al-Jabri distinguishes between two major traditions in the history of Arab-Islamic philosophy: the philosophy of the *Mashriq* (Islamic East) and that of the *Maghreb* (Islamic Spain and Morocco). He further suggests that there is an epistemological break between the two traditions. According to this understanding, Ibn Sina emerges as the representative of Arab irrationality, while Ibn Rushd is the ideal embodiment of Arab rationality. While Ibn Sina represents the domination of irrationality, Ibn Rushd represents the victory of Arab Reason. As Al-Jabri puts it, "Islamic philosophy in the Orient was of a metaphysical episteme and orientation because of its concern with harmony between religion and philosophy, while Arabic philosophy in the Maghreb and Andalus (Islamic

Spain), and with Ibn Bajja in particular, was of a scientific episteme and secular orientation because it liberated itself from that problematic" (9). Thus, the history of Arab thought emerges as a dialectical relationship between rationalism and irrationalism, between enlightenment and myth, between religion and philosophy.

The aim of Al-Jabri is to redeem the rational aspects of Islamic tradition and Islamic philosophy in particular. He asks: What remains of our tradition? What elements of our philosophical tradition are likely to contribute to our modernity? He writes:

> What remains of our philosophical tradition, what of it can live into modernity can only be Rushdian (Averroist). So let us look at what of Averroism is likely to be invested in our contemporary intellectual life (49).

He further adds that:

> Averroism broke with the very Avicennianism that Ibn Sina (Avicenna) had reinforced through his oriental philosophy, which was also adopted in one form by Al-Ghazali and by Suhrurdi of Aleppo in another.... Let us take from Ibn Rushd this break. Let us break in our turn completely and once for all with the [irrational and Gnostic] spirit of oriental Avicennianism, and launch a decisive battle against it (50).

So it is possible, in the critical spirit of Ibn Rushd, to reconstruct a new relationship between our tradition and universal thought, in such a way that guarantees our authenticity and modernity all at the same time (51). But, as mentioned earlier, what Al-Jabri fails to explain is how we move from rationality in thought to rationality in society, let alone, explain why we need to go back to medieval philosophy, and to the philosophy of Ibn Rushd in particular, to look for rational elements there.

Privatization, Liberalism, and Socialism

Al-Jabri claims that the failure of the practical application of socialism "everywhere" dealt a major blow to the socialist ideology itself. Socialism, which was once a powerful ideology both in and outside the West, is in decline, a thing of the past. Throughout most of the twentieth century, and in the middle of the dramatic changes at the various realms of the social—economic, political, historical, and ideological—many people were convinced that socialism, and only socialism, could offer a comprehensive solution to social divisions and to class and nationalist struggles. As Al-Jabri puts it, many people thought then that:

> Socialism was the only solution to the social question, to class struggle and capitalist hegemony. Socialism was the only solution to the nationalist question, to the colonial phenomenon, and to the world imperialist competition. At the time, socialism meant at the first level, the social level, the transfer of private ownership to the state. At the second level, it meant the organization of all the workers of the world in what was called the "international proletariat." In one word, between the last part of the last century [19th century] and the last decades of the present century, the path to salvation consisted in two slogans: nationalization and the international proletariat (9).

Now, Al-Jabri argues, socialism is a thing of the past. He further claims:

> Today, those of us who lived in the 20th century—regardless of our age—with the slogans of the nationalization and the international proletariat hitting our ears and minds in every moment, today we see that things are upside down. The application of socialism and communism had failed everywhere, and the international proletariat is now a thing of the past. Immediately, the slogan of "privatization" replaced that of the nationalization, and that of globalization replaced the "international proletariat." Once again, one slogan is raised for salvation, with voices calling: "Liberalism is the solution" (9).

But the question that comes to the fore is: While the socialist ideology has been in decline, does it mean that the questions that it sought to address have been resolved? Or does the "triumph" of the liberalist ideology mean that it provides a better alternative to socialism? Al-Jabri remarks that:

> No one can deny the failure of the socialist experience in what was known as the countries of the communist bloc, an experience which was duplicated, in one way or another, by a number of other states in Africa, Asia, and Latin America. Further, no one can deny the progress accomplished by liberal systems in Europe and North America at the economic and technological levels in particular, or at the cultural level in general. What should not escape our sight and attention is that the failure of certain socialist experiments does not mean that the social problems that socialism initially sought to find just solutions to have found their solutions in the "successful" liberal systems. Nor does it mean that these problems are decreasing or shrinking (13).

In the light of post-Cold War historical and socio-economic developments, we could even go further and say that social problems and inequalities, as well as the class divisions and international conflict, have proliferated. Indeed, the world is more unstable than ever before, and the international gap in wealth between rich and poor nations and the domestic gap between rich and poor people are alarmingly intensifying. According to liberal sources themselves, since 1950, the relative gap between rich and poor countries has widened by 60 percent (World Bank 2003).

Al-Jabri defines privatization as the transfer of ownership of the means of production from the public sector to the private. He insists that he is not interested in privatization as an ideological policy, but rather in its practical and logical results (is it even possible to separate the two?). He wants to know if the liberal system will achieve the same results in the Arab world as it did in the West. He argues that liberalism in the West managed to minimize the intensity of the capitalist crisis. But this would not have been possible without the struggle of the working classes and the flexibility demonstrated by capitalism in adapting to the crisis. Al-Jabri writes:

> Liberal systems had to make significant compromises: they raised the wages and related them to the market prices; they provided significant, wide social services in education, health, retirement, unemployment compensation, and decreasing the labor hours...etc. These Western achievements were made in the context of the nationalist state: the nation-state: the capital and competition were national; and the trade relations with the outside were conducted through protective tariffs, and were meant to serve the economic and strategic interests on "the other side of the ocean" (13-14).

The same achievements were also made in the context of colonialism and neo-colonialism, which played a major role in all these social, political, and historical developments. Through colonialism and neo-colonialism, colonizers have managed to secure the control of resources and markets in the colonies.

Al-Jabri sees post-colonial Arab society and state as mere extensions of those of the colonial era. He writes that:

> One of the main features of the modern Arab state is the fact that it inherited the colonial state or was based on its model, imitating its structures and functions: a central state puts itself on top of society as a whole, supervising and leading it, if not, consuming it completely. European colonialism in the Arab world distinguished from the very beginning between the countries that served its economic and strategic interests and those that did not (11).

The same instrumental logic was applied within each country, as well. Al-Jabri further writes:

> And just as European colonialism settled and implanted its structures in the former [countries that served colonial interests], leaving the latter [those that did not] to themselves, satisfied with their supervision and siege from outside, it did the same thing inside each state. It was especially interested in the coastal cities, mining centers, fertile land, administrative capitals, implanting in it the administrative, economic, media, and educational structures of its modern state, in a way that served its colonial, economic, and strategic interests. The rural regions and other less useful areas were left to their own, dragging their poverty and cruelty of life (11).

The logical consequence of such colonial policy was the huge gap at the level of modernization and development between different countries and even within the same country. The division was not limited to the economic, administrative, and architectural aspects only, but included the cultural, intellectual, and personal aspects, as well. Thus, "there was reinforced an inherent duality in the Arab world as a whole and inside each of its countries, the duality of the modern and the traditional sector, the modern elite and traditional elite" (12).

The post-colonial Arab society inherited this duality and division between the modern and traditional, in economy, society, culture, and even thought. That is why, all the measures and policies of Arab governments have failed. Al-Jabri is right when he says:

> And if the Arab governments have tried to generalize the aspects of modernization, to a certain degree or another, by offering some vital infrastructures at the level of transportation, administration, and free health and educational services, and if some of these states have in fact taken major steps in the developmental program, the phenomenon that remained prevalent was the increasing duality inherent in the social body, a duality which reproduces itself endlessly (12).

Indeed, colonization has been one of the most formative experiences in the history and development of post-colonial Arab societies. Even today, one can encounter these dualities and paradoxes at all levels of society: on the one hand, an apparently modern, coastal, urban world; on the other hand, a traditional, land-locked, rural or semi-urban world. However, this gap should not be seen as the difference between a modern and a traditional sector, between a sector integrated into the capitalist system and another untouched by that system. In fact, both sectors reveal different levels of integration into the world system, one relatively well-integrated and the other relatively less integrated.

Modern imperialism, instead of creating a new rationality, used the dominant forms of thought. Al-Jabri points out that,

> Currently the Arab self lacks independence because it draws its actions and reactions from two competing and incompatible frameworks of understanding. Both of these frameworks are independent from the Arab self, that is, they belong to two different worlds that do not express the realities of the Arab world today. The first belongs to the Arab-Islamic past, and the second to the Western present and future. The control these two systems of reference—the traditional Arab-Islamic and the contemporary Western systems—exercise on the Arab self, on orienting its thoughts and views is precisely what I mean by lack of "complete historical independence" at the level of consciousness and thought, as well as at the level of behavior and practice. That is, to the extent that we Arabs are today almost unable to think about any of our problems except from within either one of those above-mentioned systems. In either case, our thought is on one side and our reality on the other. In this way, the "self," the thinking self and acting self, finds itself divided between an alien thought of the past or the Other on the one hand, and a dark prison of a reality, unenlightened by thought and ungoverned by reason (12).

And so "the only path to fulfill historical independence of the Arab Self is to liberate itself from both models—I mean systems of reference—to liberate itself from their "fundamentalist" and "referential" authority (*Takwin* 576). What is ironic is that by calling on the Arab subject to turn to medieval Islamic philosophy for solutions for the present malaise, Al-Jabri serves to reinforce, rather than destroy this fundamentalist authority.

Is it possible for liberalism to achieve the same results in the Arab world as it did in the imperial West? In Al-Jabri's view, the failure of "Arab socialism," or rather of the public sector (what I prefer to call state capitalism), is a well-documented fact. Nonetheless, no one can deny the achievements of the public sector, no matter how limited or "undeveloped" they are. The so-called national Arab state managed to minimize the problem of unemployment, provide important social services (mainly education and health care), and introduce major agricultural reforms and industrial projects. Now two questions need to be addressed: First, what will happen to the hundreds of the workers and employees who are no longer needed as a result of privatization? Second, what will be the future of the public social services that the national state used to provide to its citizens? Al-Jabri writes that, "Only one answer appears in the horizon, supported by the processes of privatization on a daily basis: firing employees in thousands and decreasing or canceling the free public services in education and health, and in other sectors, as well" (14). Al-Jabri concludes that:

> It does not appear that privatization will be able—at least in the foreseeable future—to succeed in what the so-called "Arab socialism" failed to achieve. The private sector in the Arab world cannot—in the foreseeable future—find true and successful solutions to the social problems that the public sector failed to resolve completely. The private sector in the so-called developing countries is not deep-rooted. It is dependent on the global centers of domination. It cannot engage effectively in global competition and cannot play the same role that capitalism played in the West, simply because it lacks independence and the protective and supporting nation-state, as well as external resources. These are the very foundations on which the Western liberal economic system was based (15).

I concur with Al-Jabri here that privatization is incapable of resolving the current increasing and deepening social crisis. Quite the opposite, it is more likely to increase the social contradictions of contemporary Arab society.

Globalization as a New Economic System

But despite his powerful diagnosis and critique of privatization, Al-Jabri seems to have a rather naïve understanding of globalization. Al-Jabri defines globalization thus:

> Globalization is an economic system, run by economic actors of a new kind. From the European renaissance to the middle of the present century (twentieth century), the dominant forces in modern economy were mainly the owners of capital, commercial and industrial capitalists and others, and their activity limited by the borders of the nation-state they belonged to. But outside these borders, it was the state itself, which acted on behalf or through them, that took charge of trade relations with the rest of the world. In other words, the economy was governed by the logic of the nation-state, the logic of the "inside" and the "outside" (15).

He goes on to argue:

> But today, what distinguishes globalization is that economic activity is conducted by enterprises, financial institutions, and private capital— with the help of their states—through multinational corporations and institutions. The aim here is to jump beyond the "internal" and "external" borders and to dominate over the global economic and financial

realms...And since competition and integration governing this kind of economic activity leads to concentration and reduction of the number of actors or "players," the inevitable result of this would be the concentration of global wealth in fewer and fewer hands. In this context, researchers and experts estimate that no more than fifteen somehow integrated global networks constitute the actual actors in the global market. The owners of these networks are the "true masters" of the new world, the world of globalization (16).

I have quoted this passage in its entirety because I would like to take issue with some of the ideas raised here. First of all, globalization is best understood, not as an economic system, but rather as a worldwide process of integration of national economies. As such, this process is not new, but has been an inherent feature of capitalism since its early development. In many ways, we can say that this process of integration of Third-World countries into the world market reached its peak with colonization when individual countries were much more deeply embedded in the world. The conventional understanding of globalization as a post-colonial phenomenon is ahistorical and at best misleading. As Paul Smith and many others in the Marxist tradition have argued, the dynamics of capitalism had a "globalizing" imperative from the very beginning. Also, the contrast of the power of the nation-state with that of business reifies their true relationship, which is one of complacency rather than opposition. The growth of international business and particularly of transnational networks of production, trade and finance has not in any major way rendered nation-states or national contexts irrelevant or less powerful. As Smith puts it:

> In fact most corporations that are pointed under the rubric of globalization are in fact heavily concentrated in and dependent on particular national contexts. Some of this dependence is played out in relation to legal factors such as taxation... Another way in which such corporations remain essentially tied to a given national base is in terms of their complex relation to the bodies of corporate and international law—legal ownership is still an important localizing factor, for instance. Or else – and to their own benefit – they protect their own patents and technologies through the benefits offered by national domicile, and equally by taking advantage of the protections offered by most Northern nations regarding technology transfer (39).

So it would be wrong to oppose global to national economies. In many ways, they complement and complete each other. According to Al-Jabri, "the first aspect of globalization consists in the concentration of global economic activity in very few hands, and thus, marginalizing and distancing the rest once and for all" (16). This leads to an international gap in wealth between nations and to a domestic gap in wealth between different classes. He gives the following example:

> Thus, for example, the holders of the same academic degree do not receive the same salary. And so is the case for those who belong to one sector or the same generation. In certain cases, in many cases in fact, the income of two or three top managers of a banking institution equals that of half of its small and middle employees. And if this phenomenon, that of the huge differences, used to be considered peculiar to "underdevelopment" in the "developing countries," if not the Third world as a whole, the same phenomenon is becoming conspicuous in the developing countries themselves, mainly the United States and other European countries (16).

In Al-Jabri's view, the economic logic governing global economy is to produce as many commodities as possible with the fewest workers possible. And it is the same logic that leads to unemployment. He claims that, "If in the past economic growth created jobs, economic growth in the era of globalization and savage liberalism leads to—and is based on—reducing jobs" (17). But has unemployment not been attached to capitalism throughout its development? In my view, to claim that economic growth in the earlier stages of capitalism created jobs is to read history upside down and to have an ahistrocial view of the habits and dynamics of capitalism.

It is clear that the process of capitalist globalization will not be able to achieve true, stable, deep-rooted development and modernity in the Arab world. Nor will it decrease the growing gaps between nations and classes. Quite the opposite, it works to "develop underdevelopment," by widening and deepening the gap between the poor and the rich: the poor become poorer, and the rich richer. As Al-Jabri rightly points out, such phenomena as religious, ethnic, and separatist movements cannot be understood completely unless we take into consideration the fact that, in part at least, they are reactions against the growing social inequalities created by capitalism.

Social Justice and Democracy

According to Al-Jabri, questions of social justice and democracy did not emerge as a response to internal problems in the Arab world itself per se, but were rather, and in large part, a consequence of contact with the West, as well as its liberal and socialist traditions. The confrontation of the modern Arab elite, especially in Egypt, Lebanon, and Syria, with the West and Western liberal and socialist thought, played a crucial role in the development of consciousness of such issues. In the early part of the twentieth century, there emerged several ideas and theories, echoing liberal and socialist thought and their concern with "socialist democracy" and "scientific socialism."

Because these ideas, concepts, and theories were transferred from one ideological and social setting to another, they could not easily attract enough people and become "material forces" in history. What happened was that these new ideas, calling for socialist democracy and raising questions of class division and class struggle, "remained at the periphery" throughout the early part of the 20th century and even until the end of the Second World War (138).

In Al-Jabri's view, there are several reasons why socialist and Marxist ideologies failed to attract the masses in the Arab world. He writes that,

> This situation, the situation of remaining at the surface or living in the periphery of the ideas and views "extracted from" the theories of socialist-democrats or from "scientific socialism" was due not to the fact that the masses had a false consciousness of their exploitation alone. Nor was it due to the fact that the main concern of the masses and the elite was with the nationalist question, the question of independence alone. We must add to these two factors that the ideas and theories which raised the socialist problematic in the Arab world did not speak in the name of Arab social reality, nor did it express its specificity. Such ideas and theories carried with them all the issues and specificities peculiar to the West. In the best cases, it spoke in the name of the "possible"–what may or may not happen in the Arab world—and not in the name of actual reality itself (138).

Al-Jabri's point is well-taken. Arab socialist ideologies did not speak the language of the societies they were supposedly helping to change. They were mere extensions of the very same debates and issues in the West, without any consideration of the social realities in the Arab world. In many ways, this is still true of the Arab world at the current historical conjuncture. Arab leftists are partly responsible for this state of affairs; for example, they have thus far failed to produce a comprehensive analysis of Arab hybrid and dependent capitalism.

The problem was not with the Marxist tools of analysis themselves, but rather with the mechanistic application of those tools. As Al-Jabri points out:

> In one word, we can say that, in the Arab world, the socialist problematic was treated, not based on the circumstances of Arab society as a whole, and not based on the specificities of each of the Arab states, but was rather based on the invocation and importation of concepts and ideas expressing the social realities of the West as a whole, and the specificities of each Western state, to which was related the thought of a certain Arab intellectual or politician. Thus, the modern Arab elite would prescribe for their society, not by analyzing its reality, but based on the results of the analysis of another reality, the reality of one Western state or another. That is why there was a gap, a huge gap, between thought and reality, between the elite and the masses in the Arab world (138).

In the context of the West, the theories of social justice and democracy emerged as a response to a very specific historical context: the existence of the nation-state; increasing industrialization; the existence of a liberal bourgeoisie; the emergence of an expanding working class; the existence of political parties, as well as the decline of the leading role of the church; the decline of feudalism; and the disappearance of tribalism (138).

The situation was different in the Arab world when these ideas first surfaced on the Arab scene. In the absence of solid industrial structures and a deep-rooted liberal bourgeois tradition, the Arab proletariat could not live up to the same historical mission prescribed by the Western proletariat for itself. As a result of the decline of nationalist and socialist ideologies (due to internal and external factors), the "repressed" allegiance to tribe and religious fractions, returned to the fore of individual and social consciousness to guide thought and practice. What is important, according to Al-Jabri, is not to predict whether this state of affairs will or will not last long, but rather to provide "an ongoing analysis of the current Arab situation and a critique of Arab thought" (140).

The Arab Bourgeoisie, the State, and Alternative Modernity

According to Al-Jabri, an ideological division characterizes the current Arab social reality. On the one hand, there are modern economic, social, and ideological structures that find their expression in the ideas and aspirations of "the modern elite". On the other hand, there are also "traditional" economic, social, and ideological structures that find their expression in the "traditional elite" and its dreams and hopes. For Al-Jabri, there can be no successful social movement without starting from Arab reality as it is, taking into consideration all its constitutive structures, modern and traditional, elites and masses, minorities and majorities, workers and students. This should not be based on false and temporary political alliances, of an opportunistic nature. What is needed is the creation of a historical bloc, based on one objective political project, moving all the political currents, towards freedom, authenticity, democracy, socialism, justice, and the upholding of human rights.

Al-Jabri maintains that there are at least two contrasting referential systems informing Arab ideologies at present, the modern Western system and the traditional theological system. Neither the traditional perspective nor the modern one can adequately resolve the social problematic. The traditionalist analysis is based on concepts and practices that are unable to put an end to exploitation, while the Western concepts and tools of analysis do not apply to Arab societies.

The social question consists in "the existence of a public sector including the strategic sectors in the national economy, being exploited by a group of intermediaries, functionaries, entrepreneurs, and "businessmen" in the private sector, which makes it subject to exploitation by a minority of a "fortunate" group in society" (153). Al-Jabri further adds that:

> Now it has become clear throughout the Arab world that class exploitation, or pseudo-class exploitation, is exercised by a group of entrepreneurs, businessmen, and go-betweens, who use, in one way or another, the state and its apparatuses to extract the surplus value produced by the public sector....And since all the Arab states are dependent on the centers of global imperialist hegemony, the above-mentioned group deepens and develops its exploitation of the belongings of the state by functioning as the go-between, the servant of those centers of hegemony (153).

This hybrid bourgeoisie does not constitute a "bourgeois class" in the historical sense of the word. On the one hand, it is not independent from the state apparatuses, but is their extension. On the other hand, it is not totally independent from the traditional tribal, regional, religious social structures. In addition, it is not a bourgeoisie because it lives off mediation. It does not have a specific futurist project peculiar to it. It does not have any liberal values. In fact, it does not have any "static values." At times, it adopts the values of modernization and modernity, and the values of fundamentalism and "authenticity" at others, in a rather superficial and opportunistic manner, corresponding to "what's hot" in the market. One can say the exact same thing about the imperialist bourgeoisie, for did not the colonizers deploy both tradition and modernity to reinforce their interests and reproduce their hegemony? In most Arab countries, including Morocco, most people work in the public or semi-public sector, and so the direct opponent facing the working class is the state. The latter is main owner of the means of production, especially in the most strategic sectors. Al-Jabri writes that:

> In this case the state stands in the way of the working class demanding its rights, not as a class, but as spokesman for society and as representative of "national interest"...and it intervenes in this way to protect its very existence, which means the protection of the exploitation exercised by the mediating group, the group of mediators, entrepreneurs, businessmen of the private sector, those who live off the state, I mean the means of production that it owns legally, but manages only "theoretically" (154).

According to Al-Jabri, the only path towards true modernity in Morocco and in the Arab world "has to start from what a Moroccan opposition leader once called "the nationalization of the state," referring to the protection of the state and its means from the group we talked about [the national bourgeoisie] and delinking—I mean the state as owner of means of production and the market—from the global imperialist centers of domination" (155). It is clear that the nationalization of the state in this way requires the transfer of political authority from those who hold it now on behalf of the local bourgeoisie to those who work on behalf of the working classes and the poor, in particular, within the framework of a futurist project, putting the satisfaction of the needs of the masses at the top of its agenda. But, "in order for the new ruling class not to become an unbearable bureaucracy and therefore a manifest or hidden dictatorship, whether "reactionary" or "progressive"," Al-Jabri insists that, "political rule should be subject to popular supervision within the framework of plurality of voices, because one voice, be it based on the single party or "the heroic leader" "the just dictator," there is nothing that prevents its perversion—and as we say authority corrupts" (155).

Al-Jabri calls for some kind of liberal democracy (155). In the underdeveloped world, "political democracy, when applied with the least degree of freedom," writes Al-Jabri, "can become the means of true change, at the service of true development and at the service of the interests of the masses at present and in the future" (155). That is why, the call and struggle for democracy should be the crucial mission of the national forces working for progress and change (155). As experience in Morocco and elsewhere has shown, would not this kind of liberal, pluralistic democracy lead in the end to the single voice, the voice of the class that owns the means to communicate its message, the means that pressures the masses, materially and ideologically, and result in fraudulent elections and other forgeries?

Al-Jabri's work offers a strategy for renewing the left that avoids the free-market liberalism of Laroui and the state socialism of the new left. But such "third-way" politics, as recent experience has shown, has also failed. In fact, the mid-left Moroccan government of the 1998 continued the neo-liberal policies of its conservative predecessors. It promoted the interests of the multinational corporations, privatized areas where even conservatives dared not go, followed the prescriptions of the WB and IMF to the letter, and allowed social and economic inequality to continue growing. The mid-left does not have any coherent strategy for achieving greater equality or reconciling the interests of individuals and collectivities.

Conclusion

Many criticisms can be addressed to Al-Jabri's project. As historical experience shows us, there are good reasons for being critical of the illusions of the Enlightenment and of rationalization. Part of the dialectic of rationalization is that the retreat of "dogmatism" and "superstition" has been accompanied by fragmentation, discontinuity, and loss of meaning. Technical progress has not been an ambiguous blessing; and increasing rationalization of social and administrative organization, while leading to efficient organization, has also meant the end of freedom and self-determination. The decline of religion and tradition has gone hand in hand with anomie and alienation, unstable identities, and existential insecurities. This does not mean, by any means, rejection of modernity and rationalization as desired ends. What is called for, instead, is a reasoned/rational critique of rationalism itself, a critical reconsideration of the profits and losses of "rationalization" and "progress." Rationalization must include a rational critique of reason itself.

Indeed, Al-Jabri's work in its totality reflects the anxiety and the desire to construct a new way of seeing tradition and its role in society. What is at stake is the search for the elements of a new approach and a new methodology in dealing with cultural tradition in general, and Islamic philosophical tradition in particular. How can we understand tradition in its historicity? Al-Jabri has discovered that the problematic of tradition is central to Arab thought at present. That is why, all the studies conducted after his 1975 study on Al-Farabi focused on philosophical tradition in an attempt to provide a foundation upon which a new view of tradition will be built. The central aim was to provide a new interpretation of tradition.

Why did the project of Arab modernity fail? For Al-Jabri, it failed because it was not an overall critical analysis of Arab rationality. Arab reformists bitterly criticized the stagnation and reaction of their societies; however, their criticism was bereft of philosophical rationalism. In their attempt to understand and move beyond the social realities of the Arab world, they either used inadequate theological methods, in the case of religious thinkers, or borrowed Western methods, in the case of liberal and leftist thinkers, without stirring the rational passion of the people. Reason and only reason is capable of ending the social and cultural chaos in contemporary Arab society. In this respect, rationalism has a dual function; first, it liberates people from the deeply ingrained shackles of tradition and at the same time enables them to understand the challenges of the present and live up to them.

NOTES

1. Maybe the only English translation available is that of his short overview of Islamic Philosophy: *Arab-Islamic Philosophy: A Contemporary Critique*, originally published in French in 1994 as *Introduction a la critique de la raison arabe*.
2. The book in question is *Al-Siyyasat Al-Taalimiyya Fi Al-Maghreb Al-Arabi*.
3. This dissertation, which was the first dissertation in philosophy in Morocco, was subsequently published as *Al-Asabiyya wa Al-Dawla: Maalim Nazariyya Khalduniyya fi Al-Tarikh Al-Islami [Group Solidarity and the State: Towards a Khaldunian Theory of Islamic History]*.
4. Between 1994 and 1997, Al-Jabri wrote several books on a number of other issues and subjects. Titles of his books include: *Al-Masaala Al-Taqafiyya [The Cultural Question]* (1994), *Al-Din wa Dawla wa Tatbiq Al-Shari'aa [Religion, the State, Application of Islamic Law]* (1996), *Al-Dimuqratiyya wa*

Huquq Al-Insan [Democracy and Human Rights] (1997), and *Qadawa fi Al-Fikr Al-Muaasir [Issues in Contemporary Thought]* (1997).

5 This is a four-volume work: *Takwin Al-Aql Al-Arabi [Genesis of Arab Reason]* Vol. I (1984), *Bunyat Al-Aql Al-Arabi [Structure of Arab Reason]* Vol. II (1986), *Al-Aql Al-Arabi Al-Siyyasi [Arab Political Reason]* Vol. III (1990), and *Al-Aql Al-Akhlaqi Al-Arabi [Arab Ethical Reason]* Vol. IV (2001).

6 There is no doubt that external forces—global economic and political forces—played a crucial role in the decline of the nationalist and revolutionist movements in the Arab world in the 1960's and the emergence of the Islamic movements. What is ironic is that the very same forces are now playing the same role to defeat the same movements they have created. The first Gulf War between Iraq and Iran, civil war in Algeria, the so-called war on terror, led by the United States, all should be at least partly understood in this context.

7 Mohamed Arkoun currently lives in France, where he holds the position of Professor Emeritus at Sorbonne.

8 The work of Al-Jabri has generated numerous responses, some of which more critical than others. See George Tarabishi's *Nazariyyatu Al-Aql: Naqd Naqd Al-Aql Al-Arabi [Theory of Reason: Critique of the Critique of Arab Reason* (Dar Saqi, 1999) and *Ishkaliyyatu Al-Aql Arabi: Naqd Naqd Al-Aql Al-Arabi [Problematic of Arab Reason: Critique of the Critique of Arab Reason* (Dar Saqi, 1998). See also *Naqd Al-Aql Arabi fi Al-Mizan*.

· CHAPTER FOUR ·

Islamism and Modernity: Abdessalam Yassine and Islamizing Modernity

Probably the most recognized and powerful ideologue and activist of contemporary Islamism in North Africa is Abdessalam Yassine, the so-called "spiritual" *murshid* [guide] and political leader of *Al-Adl wa Al-Ihssan* [Justice and Spirituality], which is Morocco's largest and most significant Islamist opposition movement. While an Arab liberal like Laroui rejects tradition, and an Arab nationalist like Al-Jabri seeks to "modernize" Islamic tradition, Yassine wants to "Islamize modernity." The present chapter provides a critical analysis of Yassine's major work in an attempt to address the following interrelated questions: How does he perceive the modern and modernity? What are his thoughts about modernism and modernity, and how does he conceptualize them? And what kind of alternative Islamic modernity, if any, does his work present?

An Intellectual Biography

Abdessalam Yassine is a well-known Islamist scholar, political activist, and religious preacher. But most importantly, he is the political leader of one of the largest and most powerful Islamist opposition movements in North Africa and the Arab world.

Birth and Early Years

In 1928, Abdessalam Yassine was born into a poor peasant Berber family in Marrakech, in southwestern Morocco. At a rather late age, he attended a traditional religious school in Marrakech, where he finished his primary school. In about 1940, he joined Ibn Youssef School, the biggest religious school in the region. He stayed there for four years. In 1945, he joined *Madrasat Takwin Al-Muaalimin* [Teacher Training School] in Rabat. Immediately after his graduation in 1947, he joined the Ministry of National Education, where he worked as a French teacher and later as an educational inspector for some twenty years. He was particularly interested in French literature and culture. In 1968, he was suspended from his job most probably because of his religious affiliations and activities. He was granted the status of retiree in 1987.

In 1965, Yassine had joined *Al-Zawiyya Al-Butshishiyya*, a religious, Sufi brotherhood, an experience that was to have a major impact on his thought and practice. His decision to join the brotherhood resulted from his disillusionment with Western (especially French) culture and a renewed interest in Islam. During this period, he wrote two books[1] in which he rejected the contemporary dominant Islamic practices in Morocco and the Islamic world in general, and called upon "all Muslims" to return to "true" Islam. He called for the development and propagation of new, oppositional forms of Islam.

Yassine's dedication to the development and propagation of new, oppositional forms and practices of Islam has put him at odds not only with *Al-Zawiyya* itself but also with the pro-Western regime of King Hassan II. In 1974, he sent an open letter to the late King Hassan II, entitled "Al-Islam aw Toufan [Islam or the Deluge]", calling upon him to either return to the "true" values of Islam and to establish a "true" Islamist state, a "true" Caliphate, characterized by justice and equality, not tyranny and oppression, or to step down. As a result, Yassine was sent to a psychiatric hospital where he spent more than three years. In 1978, the very year he was released, he gave a speech in a Marrakech mosque, calling on all Muslims to return to the "authentic Islam" of the Koran and the *sunna* [the prophetic traditions] and unite against tyranny and oppression, but he was soon banned from preaching in public places, including mosques.

Between 1978 and 1979, Yassine called for the unity of all Islamist movements in Morocco within the framework of an Islamist political party. Yassine had already attracted the attention of many people when in 1979 he launched *Al-Jamaa [The Group]* magazine, which was to become, "the loud voice of Islamists" in Morocco ("*Jamaat Al- Adl wa Al-Ihssan: Taarikh [Justice and Spirituality: A History]*" 2). Meanwhile, in 1980, he wrote his book *La revolution à l'heure de l'islam* and a long letter, "Pour un dialogue avec l'élite occidentalisée." In both of these works, written in French, Yassine presents himself as engaged in an open dialogue with the French-educated Moroccan elite.

Organized Activism

In 1981, Yassine founded an Islamist organization, *Usrat Al-Jamaa* [Family of the Group], which was renamed *Al-Adl wa Al-Ishan* [Justice and Spirituality] in 1987. The organization has never been recognized by the Moroccan state. In July 1981, Yassine wrote his book *Al-Minhaj Al-Nabawi [The Prophetic Method]*, which is considered the official constitution of the organization, and in 1983, he launched a new magazine, *Al-Subh [The Dawn]*, to which he was the major contributor. His articles on political issues of the day assumed a manifest oppositional and anti-government stance and attracted much attention. In November 1983, the Moroccan government banned the magazine and Yassine (along with several other members in the organization) was arrested and spent two years in prison.

House Arrest

In 1985, Yassine was released, and a year later, the Executive Council of *Al-Adl wa Al-Ihssan* was established. Sub-executive committees included committees in charge of high school students, university students, cadres, and teachers. A process of mass of Islamization through education and activism began, and the work of Yassine and his organization became very popular, especially among university students. The success was swift, and between 1985 and 1990, the organization had several branches all over Morocco, with hundreds of registered members. The organization established mosques, schools, clubs, and a welfare service network that distributed free meals to the poor and needy. Currently, there are more than a half million active members registered, in more than one hundred branches. In 1989, Yassine was seen as a threat to the government and was put under house arrest in December of the same year. During this period, Yassine wrote several books in which he presented a detailed outline of his vision of a "true" Islamist state, based on justice and spirituality. These books, all of which were published in 1989, included: *Al-Islam wa Tahaddi Al-Marxiyya-Lininiyya [Islam and the Challenge of Marxism-*

Leninism], Rijal Al-Qawma wa Al-Islah [Exemplary Men in Islam], Muqaddimat fi Al-Minhaj [Introductions to Method], and *Al-Islam wa Al-Qawmiyya Al-Ilmaniyya [Islam and Secular Nationalism].*

House arrest was a great boost to *Al-Adl wa Al-Ihssan*, which accumulated increasing influence in poor urban neighborhoods and universities, and did well to exploit the great disappointment of the Moroccan masses in light of the first US-led attack on Iraq and the subsequent Iraqi defeat in the second Gulf war in 1991. The socio-economic situation also heightened the feeling of frustration among the masses as the gap between the poor and the rich increased. Yassine continued his attack on the corruption and immorality of the Moroccan state, devoting much of his intellectual production to religion and politics in Morocco and the Muslim world.[2]

Release from Arrest and the 2003 Terrorist Attacks

Immediately before his release from house arrest in 2000, Yassine addressed a rather highly publicized open letter to King Mohammed VI charging the late King Hassan II and the state with embezzlement of billons of dollars in public funds. Yassine called on the new king and the royal family to use their inherited wealth to pay off the heavy national debt of Morocco. Just after his release, Yassine started a series of organized trips all throughout the country, calling on his supporters to continue asserting themselves against oppression and the injustices of the system, as well as against Western ways of life.

Despite the 2003 terrorist attacks in Casablanca, which certainly had a great impact on all Islamist movements and parties in Morocco, *Al-Adl wa Al-Ihssan* still maintains a strong presence on university campuses. In the last few years, it has succeeded in organizing a number of public protests. The movement has also been heavily involved in social and charitable activities and practices. The Moroccan state, however, has never recognized the organization and has even rejected its recent demands for party status and parliamentary access, even denying it the right to participate in the 2002 elections. Yassine is still under close police surveillance. Since 2000, he has written several books, articles, and letters on various Islamic themes, including a book, entitled *Al-Adl: Al-Islamiyyun wa Al-Hukm [Justice: Islamists and Power]* (2000), in which he confirms his status as the spiritual and political leader of *Al-Adl*. In the last two years, Yassine has turned his attention to human rights issues and abuses in Morocco and elsewhere. Meanwhile, several of the movement's leaders and activists are still in jail, and all of its magazines and newspapers are banned.

On the Historical Formation

Islamist movements and ideologies emerged in the wake of the failure of modern Arab nationalist, liberal, and socialist political movements and ideologies in achieving true social development and true modernity. Many factors contributed to the so-called "Islamist revolt." These included, among others, social marginalization, class divisions, economic deprivation, and state oppression. Class tensions and widespread poverty contributed to the rise of nationalist-statist movements all over the Arab world during the 20th century. But the decline of these statist movements, the failure of so-called modernization and development ideologies, the international reorganization of capitalist production under the notion of "flexible accumulation," along with the collapse of the Soviet Union, ultimately reduced the influence of leftist ideologies. Thus, Islamism has emerged as the only remaining revolutionary ideology in Arab societies. Rather than a mere reaction against the modernization of Arab societies and the complete integration of their already structurally dependent economies in the world capitalist market, Islamism should also be understood as the very product of these new shifts and developments.

Subaltern classes found themselves subject to a system that, despite all its claims, only deepened their suffering and marginality, at the material and individual levels. As a reaction to such oppressive circumstances, which the liberal and nationalist ideologies could not address, the oppressed masses—lost, disorganized, and uneducated—found a refuge in the one thing they had: religion and tradition. Islamist fundamentalism was, thus, one way of resisting a system that has relegated them to the margins of their society. In *The Terrorist*, a rather well-known Egyptian film produced in 1994, Nader Jalal provides us with an interesting examination of Islamist fundamentalism. The film takes us to the world of a young Islamist terrorist. Ali Abd-El-Zaher, a young man in his late twenties, is part of an underground Islamist radical group which has been launching attacks against, among other targets, government officials and clubs, under the orders of the spiritual leader Brother Seif. Ali belongs to the poorest segments of his society, where the experience of social injustice, oppression, poverty, and even humiliation are part of his everyday life and world. The cause which he espouses is driven by the necessity of a more egalitarian system, by a sense of injustice of a social system, where he and the overwhelming majority of people like him feel that some of their most basic rights—their rights to food, shelter, education, and work are ignored. Even the right to marriage is denied to Ali. In the course of a conversation between Ali and Brother Seif, the latter suggests that "The best way to give you peace of mind is for you to get married." To this Ali half ironically responds: "And do I have a shelter that I may seek a bride?"

In the same film, Fouad Massoud, supposedly a progressive intellectual and journalist, claims that Islamist fundamentalism is primarily a "struggle of ideas before anything else." What such view overlooks is the fact that it is also a struggle against and a product of social injustices and class contradictions. Sayyed Qutb, one of the leaders and of the *Islamic Brotherhood* of Egypt, used to say: "If Islamists are unwilling to fight for their religion, they should fight for their daily bread."

At the core of Islamist fundamentalism is a class struggle between the oppressed classes (workers, poor peasants, and some traditional intellectuals), who represent the overwhelming majority of the society, and the ruling classes (foreign and national capital and the political elite). In addition, other political and social factors have also contributed to the rise of Islamist ideologies and movements in the Arab world. These included support from the state and also from external forces in an attempt to confront the leftist forces and progressive forces in general. The Iranian Revolution in the late 1970s, which was in a sense a product of all these factors, was also a major force in the development and rise of Islamist movements all over the Middle East and North Africa.

It would be wrong to conclude, with Al-Jabri, that the rise of Islamism was due purely to ideological-cultural factors, namely the deeply ingrained irrationality of the Arab mind. Otherwise, why were other ideologies popular in the first place? And why did Islamism emerge precisely at the current historical conjuncture and not before? In the case of Morocco (and this is also true of some other Arab states, especially Egypt), in the light of the post-independence wave of modernization, the traditionalist intellectual elite found itself marginalized in education and at work. The best jobs required a modern education and were thus limited to the "Westernized elite."

What caused the decline of Arab nationalist, liberal, and statist ideologies? Why did they fail to achieve true social development and change? To be sure, they did not represent the interests of society as whole; they represented only the interests of the hegemonic classes, without due consideration of the other sections of society. They spoke on behalf of the modernist national bourgeoisie and neglected the expectations and wishes of poor peasants and the working class. Instead of bridging the gap between the national bourgeoisie and the modernist elite on the one hand and the working class and poor peasants, on the other, they in fact made it wider and wider. Unless Islamist movements realize this and unless they develop a comprehensive alternative to the social system that perpetuates social inequality and oppression, they will repeat the same mistakes of previous political ideologies. And so the crucial question is: Are Islamists capable of providing such an alternative without destroying themselves, without destroying some of their basic foundations and views about life and society?

What is Modernity?

What does Yassine understand by modernity? It would certainly be interesting to put his writings on the subject back into their historical context. In one of his later writings, *Mihnat Al-Aql Al-Muslim [The Muslim Mind on Trial]*, written in 1994, Yassine presents us with a Western modernity in decline. As he puts it:

> The modern age is in crisis. Let us not be deluded by what others have built, such as scientific skyscrapers strewn all around and unrelated to any human project. For them, the human being has no meaning except the egoism of the strong, the wasteful consumption of the wealthy, the pleasure of the rich and the death of the poor in the Somalia of starvation and civil war, or in the Bosnia of annihilation, savage slaughter and ethnic cleansing (*Mihnat* 91).

The image of modernity that emerges from this passage is very bleak, indeed. It is a world where human beings have no value, a world full of contradictions and dualities: a world where the rich and the poor, pleasure and death, scientific progress and human degradation stand in sharp contrast with each other. It is a world plagued by war and violence, by "savage slaughter" and "ethnic cleansing."

In a later work, *Islamiser la modernité*, written in 1998, Yassine returns to the same theme, that of a modernity and a modern world in crisis. I should point out that this is one of the very few books that Yassine, an ex-French teacher, has written in French. He comments on this when he says:

> So far, I have been writing in Arabic, addressing myself to a very limited Arabic-speaking audience. Now, I have decided to write in French, a Western language engaged in a fierce struggle in order to survive in a linguistic landscape where the fight over universality is limited to powerful languages such as dominant English, proud Japanese, and Chinese, a language rich in its prestigious history and ambitious future.
>
> I hope that the language forced upon me will not veil my primary objective: to make known the message of the Koran, a message of peace for a violent world, a message of meaning for a lost world, a spiritual message to a modern man sick in his modernity (7).

Yassine's stated objective in this book is to "shed light on the path towards an individual-personal spiritual quest" (9). But as the title of the book itself suggests, there is another concern: to *Islamize modernity*.

At the outset, Yassine associates modernity with the West. He writes:

> "Modernity" came into use with the literary quarrel between the Ancients and the Moderns in seventeenth-century France. Since that triumphant era, and as a prolonging of the Renaissance that awakened Europe from its medieval slumber, modernity has become for Europeans a way of being, thinking, living, governing oneself, and taking one's bearings in the world (40).

He continues:

> It is a socio-cultural and political manner of being, in contrast to the autochthonous Middle Ages, to an outer world given over to barbarity, and, ultimately, to colonization, predation, and underdevelopment, and to public contempt. Central to the notion of modernity is a reference to historical memory, and the perception of having progressed from medieval Europe (40).

There are some important ideas in these passages which need to be interrogated further. Yassine associates modernity with a time, the seventeenth century, and a place, the West and conceives of it as a literary, social, political, and cultural break not only with the Middle Ages, but with the rest of the world, as well. Central to his conception of modernity is a division between two worlds, that of the modern West and that of the pre-modern non-West, between the superior West and inferior non-West, between the world of progress and that of underdevelopment, and between the world of wealth and that of poverty and dispossession.

Yassine does not stop at this rather too general dichotomy between the West and the non-West. He wants to know where Islam, as a culture and as a religion, fits in all of this. Yassine writes:

> [Modernist] ideology, by far the most dangerous weapon of the lot, fires at everything that is ancient, decreeing it archaic, supported merely by the irrational, to be rejected as fraudulent because it claims its basis in some "revelation" or "superhuman" volition. *Islam* thus provides a direct target for modernism: it rests upon a sacred revelation, and its authority is that of the Messenger of God—exalted be His name (47).

Yassine, thus, constitutes the "West" as the "other" against which an Islamist social order must be constructed. In fact, he goes even further as to make Westerners the very absolute Others of Muslims, based on a falsely assumed atheism. As he puts it:

> In this perspective, they are *jahiliya* [ignorance] and we are Muslims. That is an essential difference, because someone who believes in God and the Last Day is not like someone who does not. The unbelievers and the *jahiliya* civilization are superior in the means of strength and the adornment of worldly life, but they remain on the scale of eternity in loss and bankruptcy (79).

So even though Yassine admits the scientific and technological superiority of the West, he believes that the West lacks God. This leads him to the conclusion that, "Islam is true and *jahiliya* is false" (80).

Yassine then moves to a repudiation of modernity and what it stands for. He deplores many aspects of modern society and modernity. For him, Western modernity is the cause and the incarnation of immorality and secularism. He attacks not only the sexual practices and the financial institutions (and the banking system in particular) of the West, which he finds contrary to Islamic law, but also the total devotion to the consumerist ethic and concern with material commodities.

Yassine conceives of modernity as an ideology that eradicates the sacred, the divine, and the purportedly irrational, while at the same time celebrating the "natural law of reason" (41). According to such triumphant modernist logic, whatever stands in the way of reason and rationality is insignificant, "fraudulent," and irrational, and must be resolutely discarded, combated and even destroyed.

And this, according to Yassine, is the very logic of the imperialist project. As he puts it, "This is the pretext invented for the military and economic colonization of the world of the South, thus turning it into a mere market and depot of the commodities of modernity, where material, cultural, and residual waste—all of it harmful and polluting—has been thrown around willy-nilly" (40-41). Modernity, according to Yassine, was equally responsible for so many evils and calamities throughout the twentieth-century, particularly the two world wars and the rise of fascist ideologies. "Hitlerism," Yassine writes, "is nothing but the decisive manifestation of a modern notion of progress founded on reason and committed entirely to efficiency" (46).

The overlap between Yassine's critique and the critique of capitalist modernity coming from the left is very striking, indeed. But for Yassine it is the absence of God and the relegation of religion to the periphery, and not any concrete materialist forces, that lie at the root of all this evil. The modernist ideology has relegated God to the periphery, replacing Him with society "as the principle of moral judgment" (43). As Yassine puts it, "To be modern, it is supposed, we have to rebel against the sacred, against the divine" (41).

However, Yassine insists that the major concern of his book is not to provide a critique of Western modernity, but rather to explain Islam to a modern world, "to a modernity deafened by the noise of the new, blinded by the sheen of colored images, dazzled by incessant flashbulbs, seduced by the magic of the "electronic superhighway," dumbfounded by bursts of virtual reality" (8). What Yassine objects to most is the separatist logic and secularist character of modernity. He sees a major danger in the fact that "it wants religion to be confined to the private sphere, while the public sphere is left to politics" (61). Yassine, like other Islamists, is opposed to the separation of religion and state. He sees religion as a total system, covering all realms of social life.

Yassine attacks secularism because it seems to him the principal premise of modern society; everything he dreads seems to spring from it: the life of pleasure, materialism, parliament and the parties, moral decay, and lack of true political leadership. Even more he senses in secularism the source of his inner suffering and alienation. His one desire is for a new faith, a new community of believers, a world with clear standards and no doubts, a rebirth of Islamic religion that would bind all Moroccans and all Muslims together. All this secularist modernity denies. Hence he deplores and blames it for making outcasts of true believers, for uprooting the Muslim from his glorious past, and from his faith.

Part of Yassine's critique on secularism and secular thought is his critique of philosophy. Yassine rightly objects to Al-Jabri's philosophical project, not because such rationalization of thought remains abstract and futile, but because it is "a search for a predecessor in secularism" (*Mihnat* 66). Yassine raises a rather interesting question. He writes:

> By the way, why should we perform postmortem examination of stiff corpses? Aristotelian philosophy is dead and gone. Other subsequent philosophies equally died, refuted as they were by advances in the sciences. Whenever the scientific mind discovers a new horizon of knowledge, the philosophic mind sees its original horizon eclipsed. Whenever the discoveries establish a new continent for the sciences, the edifice of philosophy collapses (66).

All these claims are fine, but what Yassine does not realize is that the same charges could also be made about religion. Here again we see the modernist bias in the argumentation of Yassine, who is quite content to invoke science as his authority in refuting the views of his adversaries, or to invoke democracy as means to an end. The reference to "science" here further supports the interpretation that fundamentalists are not traditionalists; their worldview is fundamentally modern.

But it would be wrong to conclude, as Laroui does, that Yassine (and other Islamists) rejects modernity as a whole and is therefore anti-modern. This may be true of more extremist Islamists. The Qutbist groups of the 1970s and the 1980s, namely *Al-Tkfir wa Al-Jihad [Excommunication and Holy War]* (founded in 1971 by Shukri Mustapha) and *Jama't Al-Jihad [The Group of the Holy War]* in Egypt, are examples of two extremist, anti-modern Islamist movements. In an address to his followers, Mustapha Shukri preaches: "The Muslim is obligated to seek his path and knowledge before God alone, and so-called knowledge, which is actually no knowledge at all because it is not founded in the Lord, is forbidden."

Unlike more extremist Islamists, Yassine does not totally reject modernity. If he can be described as anti-modern for his attacks on certain aspects of modern life and modern society, he was very modern in his commitment to such ideas as change, democracy, and even progress. According to him, the ultimate aim of Islam is the progressive fulfillment of the potential of human beings. But since spirit distinguishes man from other creatures, progress should be measured not only by material but also spiritual criteria as well. To understand why he does this leads us to the core of his thought and political project.

Yassine's essential argument begins as follows:

> We should appropriate to ourselves whatever positive aspects of modernity are useful to us, without letting ourselves be fooled by the glitter of post-modernity, without letting ourselves be overshadowed by modern advertising that tries to fob off what is false at an exorbitant price (49-50).

He continues:

> Thus we will embrace modernity, but on our terms. We will need to conduct ourselves as canny purchasers of modernity. A shrewd buyer examines the merchandize in order to uncover damages and spot the cheat. It is along these lines that we ask such questions of modernity and *insist that the past be taken into account*. And it is with the intention of requiring justice and equity from modernity that our plan of *making modernity Islamic* must begin, by posing such questions and exploring meeting points (50) [My italics].

So, Yassine makes it very clear that he rejects certain aspects of modernity, while at the same time being ready to appropriate others. He presents us with a two-fold project: first, to appropriate the positive aspects of modernity and to reject its negative aspects; second, to take the past into account. This is what Yassine means by "Islamizing modernity," by "making modernity Islamic."

The problem with Yassine's analysis, and Islamist discourse in general, is that it reduces everything to a mere religious, ideological struggle, a struggle between Islam on the one hand, and secularism and atheism, the other faces of Christianity, on the other. It is as if all the history of humanity were the history of religious struggle. Such analysis emphasizes the exclusive role of religion, and denies the role of social factors in social and historical change.

Social Change, Politics, and *Qawma*

As a political leader of an opposition movement, Yassine is naturally concerned with issues of social and political change. He sees Muslim society currently living in a state of *fitna* [conflict] or *jahiliyya* [ignorance], a state characterized by the following elements: crisis, reactionarism, instability, anarchy, and atheism. How do we move from the state of conflict to a state of *adl* [justice]? He writes,

"Among Islamists is raised—very sharply—the following question: where does change begin? Does it begin with a coup from the top, through which people in power impose the laws of the Koran, or does it come about by a gradual, patient preparation of generations so that change emerges from below" (*Hiwar maa Al-Fudalaa [Dialogue with Honorable Democrats]* 109). Yassine makes it clear that his political project is based on the Prophetic method and that it aims to re-establish an Islamist caliphate. The first step toward change is the preparation of an organized elite group, capable of leading society on the day of *qawma* [uprising].

What does Yassine understand by "*qawma*"? He distinguishes between revolution and *qawma*. As he puts it, "We use the word *qawma* to avoid the word revolution" (9). In Yassine's view, the notion of "revolution" implies violence, and violence is mere use or rather misuse of power to satisfy one's desires and whims, while the notion of *qawma*, which Yassine derives from Islamic history, implies power, and the use of power for legitimate purposes. In *Rijal*, he writes, "Muslims in earlier eras would distinguish between "*al-qaim*" [the riser] and the revolutionary. They used the former to refer to whoever stands up against unjust rulers, while they used the latter to whoever fights the *sultan*, [regardless of whether he was just or not]" (7). Yassine further adds that he rejects the notion of revolution because it was employed to describe "ignorant" social movements (9). This distinction is hardly convincing. For violence is not inherent to revolution; there are historical examples of non-violent revolutions. Also, as will become clearer later, the distinction contradicts Yassine's own description of the Islamist *qawma*, where violence does play a major part.

What kind of uprising does Yassine have in mind? For him, it must be a radical movement, whose ultimate aim is to transform society from a state of *fitna* and *jahiliya* into a state of stability and glory, into a state of justice and spirituality (9). To achieve a total social transformation, Muslims must undergo a strict process of disciplined religious education, which teaches every member of the Islamic community what exactly his mission and role is. While violence should be avoided as much as possible, it can become part of the natural process of this uprising of liberation. Yassine writes that, "When the huge wave [of revolutionaries] is ready, believers can put an end to corruption by total disobedience, total strike in the streets" (10-11). This goes counter to his earlier claim about the non-violent nature of the Islamist *qawma*.

The idea of a revolutionary vanguard of militant believers does not have an Islamic origin. The truth is that this is a projection of the modern Marxist notion of revolution. Not surprisingly, Marx's name does not occur in Yassine's list of references. Here, Yassine, despite his claims to "authenticity," is projecting a modern notion onto Islam.

Yassine makes it clear that for such a movement to be successful, three major obstacles must be overcome. The first obstacle has to do with the herd-like mentality of the Muslim masses today. This passive mentality turns people into mere dupes to be exploited, thus depriving them from any ability to act. The second obstacle has to do with the dominant tradition of dependency characterizing contemporary Muslim societies. This dependency on the West and Western systems in all aspects of life makes it difficult to see things from a purely religious perspective.[3]

The third obstacle lies in the existence of a small group of Muslims who are filled with destructive selfishness. This group of people, who inflict harm on themselves as well as on others, will naturally find it difficult to join the movement because they are greedy and selfish. But who exactly constitutes this group? Yassine remains silent about this, just as he is silent about issues of material and social exploitation of the oppressed classes. Not only that, in some of his later writings, he makes it clear that he is not opposed to the class that produces and reinforces that exploitation: the bourgeoisie. In *Al-Ihssan*, he writes, "The major difference between us [Islamists] and leftists is that they are enemies of the bourgeoisie and tribal political systems based on their attack on injustice, while we are enemies of unbelief, atheism, and whatever is related to them" (503).

But what Yassine overlooks are the causes for which leftists fight for. It is clear that Yassine does not see the would-be uprising in terms of class struggle or social exploitation. In the last few years, Yassine and his group have organized a number of major public protests and campaigns, the last of which was an unsuccessful campaign in 2000 to institute gender segregation on some beaches in Morocco. It is very surprising—or maybe not—that not even one of these protests were aimed at such social issues as structural poverty and unemployment. Yassine's writings are full of assurances to capital and capitalists, regarding their continued importance, should the so-called *qawma* be successful. In *Al-Adl*, Yassine makes it clear that the would-be caliphate cannot do without the national bourgeoisie, given "their expertise, competence, and knowledge of the inner workings of the world market" (418).

Prophetic Method

In Yassine's view, for Muslims to achieve success in spiritual and material life, they need to re-discover the Prophetic method. The latter, derived from the career of prophet Mohammed, is propounded by him as a strategy "of clarification, planning, coordination, and execution" of an Islamic vision of society (*Minhaj* 1). It is the only way that will help reconcile man with his Creator and will lead Muslims out of their current cultural, economic, and military state of crisis. Once again, Yassine reveals his preoccupation with the authenticity of his concepts when he claims:

> The word *minhajiyya* [methodology] which is a translation of a foreign concept refers to a system of thought, to a practical approach in an ideological, scientific, or applied analysis meant to control people's life. We prefer to use the Koranic-Prophetic word *minhaj* [method] to not only express its mediating role as a scientific bridge between truth in scripture and the life of Muslims. It also refers to the adherence to God's commandments and to the Prophet's way of life at all levels of (private and public) individual and group behavior: psychological, ethical, religious, social, political, and economic (4).

The Prophetic method emerges as an inclusive method, covering all facets of life, but with specific focus on people's spiritual life. The Prophet provides us with a method to be followed, but not blindly. Yassine adds that:

> This does not mean that we should raise and organize a group that looks at our glorious past during the era of Mohammed and his rightly guided caliphs, and then confine ourselves to the world of dreams. Quite the opposite, it means that we should prepare a generation, if not generations, after him [the Prophet] capable of acting on behalf of God and his Prophet on earth. To do so, we need to base ourselves on the Prophetic model and struggle. Our goal is to reestablish the caliphate [Islamic state] on the Prophetic model, as well as to destroy the hereditary and absolute rule that has lasted for so many centuries (4).

The Prophetic method is not there to be celebrated blindly but should rather serve as a guide in the search for true change. It is "a method of combative education and organization" (1).

In *Mihnat,* Yassine further develops his analysis of the Prophetic method. Here, he writes:

> The Prophetic Method of the Koran was sent down as a Law by the One Who created the human being, shaped him and set him in order. It was applied with wisdom and in a timely fashion by a Prophet endowed with grace and solicitude in all his movements.
>
> The Prophetic Method, purifying and instructive, came from the very same source from which came the body of the human being, his mind and his soul. The Method that purified and instructed the first faithful generation will do the same for all generations to come, on the condition that it remains Koranic and Prophetic (22).

The Prophetic method is a method of *fitra* [human nature], not an ideological method, a method of practice, not of argument (33).

As is clear from the conceptual tools employed by Yassine, he is very much concerned with the question of authenticity and authenticating his concepts. In his attempt to do so, Yassine develops a set of concepts, drawn from the Koran, the Prophetic tradition, and the Islamic tradition. He claims that authenticity, not blind imitation, is the only way out of the impasse of Muslims. To overcome their present malaise, "The Muslim people who have to this point been resigned and made to consume the products of others—including cultural products—must break the yoke of docile vassalage to imported modern norms in order to embrace the normative principles of Islamic law" (*Islamiser* 310).

The problem with such claims to cultural and conceptual independence and authenticity is that they become entangled in an essentialist position in fixed cultural practices. Thus, certain concepts are iconized as authentic, while others are readily dismissed as foreign or imported. Such metaphysical approach to Islamic tradition and identity is not new; it echoes the orientalist approach, which, as Edward Said argues in *Orientalism,* reduces Islamic culture (as well as other cultures) to a set of fixed, stereotypical cultural practices, denying them the possibility of change. As Aziz Al-Azmeh puts it:

> [This discourse] was taken for granted in classical orientalist writing on the present condition of the Arab world, a discourse in which antiquarian erudition provided the material on which continuity and identity were established on bases which were ostensibly firm, and which proffered knowledge which enracinated the future, as well as the actually existing present—in contradistinction to the merely visible, in the Hegelian

sense—in what it took to be its proper bearings, that is to say, in the past, in the vehicle of the invariant *Geist* (19).

This essentializing discourse on identity and culture might have very dangerous implications, indeed. It ignores the historicity of cultural practices and concepts; it ignores the fact that culture and concepts undergo change to satisfy changing circumstances and conditions.

Commitment to the Movement

Yassine's recurrent references to the responsibility of the individual before God on the Day of Judgment, individual reward and punishment, are very misleading, indeed. The duty of the individual is not only to submit to God, but also to join the community of believers, to give his or her freedom for the sake of the good of the community. In *Al-Minhaj [The Prophetic Method]*, Yassine claims that commitment to the political community is the secret to Prophet Mohammed's success and the key to any contemporary effort to follow God's path. The fulfillment of the divine plan on earth is not, and cannot be, the result of individual preaching or divine intervention. He writes:

> Muslims need badly to unify their word, thought, direction, and method. Some Muslims limit their appeal to religious knowledge. Others limit their education to individual devotion. Some concern themselves only with Islamic thought...What divides us is the existence companionships that do necessarily lead a group.... We need to appoint a sheikh [spiritual and political leader], a good educator, suitable for *jihad* [holy fight], who has, among other traits (...), a distinctive trait: unifying the group and maintaining that unity (1).

Yassine considers lack of commitment to the *Al Adl* movement a danger, an obstacle to the fulfillment of the ideal Islamist state and community. He writes:

> There are corresponding dangers to be avoided. One of the dangers is that the newcomer and his hosts may concentrate on the improvement of their own souls, the enjoyment of the warmth of love, the air of serenity and the intimacy of companionship. In so doing, they become disengaged from the missionary function, shrink together and retire into a closed circle (*Mihnat* 45).

In Yassine's view, the major function of an "organized" Islamist movement is to give guidance to society as a whole. The movement should strive to integrate its members into society, to ensure that their activism is appreciated, to ensure that spirituality is central to other people's lives, and to gain support for their mission and leadership. Otherwise:

> If the small group withdraws into seclusion, goes on the offensive, or issues charges of unbelief, it will cut itself off from the body of the *umma* by an abominable and blameworthy attribution of purity to itself. It will turn sterile and condemn itself to perdition (46).

> Outside the educational nursery is the scorching heat of a society of hatred, and the danger of melting in an environment flooded with the clamor of life, the ideas of the *jahiliyya* and the obstacles of deviations. Entering into the turmoil of the clamor, conflicting ideas and furious upheavals, is part of the training of those engaged in *jihad*. It is one of the obstacles on their path, and a test to demonstrate the extent of their patience to assume responsibility for the welfare of the entire *umma* (46).

Yassine makes a very dangerous claim about Islam and Islamic history. He projects onto Islam the same imperialist civilizing mission of the West, thus somehow justifying what he claims to refute. He writes:

> Islam was victorious in the battlefield, and it quickly gained popularity among peoples of different races from the borders of China to North Africa. After the political victory, it was essential to incorporate the peoples, to codify the Law, to establish the methods of sciences, to civilize the nomads, to teach the illiterates and to respond to opposition (60)

In such concentration on the movement, on the political community, Yassine reveals his modernity once again.

Toward an Islamist State

For Yassine, Islam is a political system as much as it is a religious one. Politics lies at the very heart of Yassine's project. Like many other Islamists, he holds that political power is indispensable to the establishment of the ideal Islamist state and society. The concept of an Islamic political system is a recurring theme in Yassine's work, but perhaps the most detailed analysis of such concept is to be found in his book *Al-Adl*. Here, Yassine claims that Islam provides the first authentic political and legal system of state in the history of mankind. The concept of caliphate, which Yassine borrows from the Islamic tradition to describe the Islamist state-to-be, is not only religious but essentially political. Yassine firmly believes in the supremacy of Islamic civilization. According to him, the Islamic caliphate has to be regained, and there is no doubt that such vision will be re-fulfilled, as it was once fulfilled during the life and times of prophet Mohammed and the *rashidun* [rightly guided] Caliphs after him.

Drawing on Prophetic tradition, Yassine divides Islamic, in fact human, political history into two major kinds of rule: just caliphate rule and absolutist rule. He draws on a rather famous *hadith* [saying] by Mohammed, according to which the latter prophesies that Islamic political history will pass through four major systems of rule: the prophetic, the caliphate, the compulsory-hereditary, and the absolutist. After the collapse of absolutist rule, Mohammed prophesies a second caliphate, characterized by justice, and it is the latter that Yassine seeks to establish.

In his interpretation of this prophetic vision, Yassine writes:

> Imposed monarchy, established by heredity and compulsory allegiance, is now gone, a thing of the past. Today, Muslims are under absolutist, or to adopt a modern term, dictatorial rule. And it is even worse than hereditary rule: Like the hereditary system, the absolutist uses religious banners, but unlike it, it has emptied all state institutions, media, education, and laws from all Islamic elements. This oppressed *umma* is in need of those who can raise and organize a generation capable of liberating it from the atheist absolutist rule that hides under the banner of Islam. The *umma* is in need for those who can reestablish the caliphate-state, long-promised in the Koran and in the context of this prophetic saying [the above-mentioned prophecy]... (*Minhaj* 2).

So, Yassine makes it very clear that his ultimate objective is to reestablish an Islamist caliphate, an Islamist state. This echoes the view of an extremist Islamist like Ali in *The Terrorist*, where he claims that, "There is no solution other than reestablishing the Islamist *caliphate* [state]." However, according to someone like Yassine, "the Islamic caliphate is not an alternative to the civilization of materialism in terms of its industrial, social, and political achievements, but is rather a continuation, in a new form, of the same materialist civilization" (1).

At the center of the Islamist vision of an Islamist state lies the question of the implementation of *shari'a* [divine law]. This vision revolves around the advocacy of a political order that goes back to the time of Mohammed and his immediate successors (known as the rightly-guided Caliphs). This order is, in large part, based on an extra-Koranic tradition; it is an accumulation of pronouncements and practices from not only the Koran but mainly from the *sunna*. The prophetic tradition is immense, and only certain practices and statements are included, while others are excluded. This act of selection is political through and through and is further complicated the complex system of coding and classifying these pronouncements and practices on the basis of their authenticity or lack thereof.

While Islamic doctrine obliges the caliph to comply with *shari'a* at the normative level, the questions that come to the fore are: what will the caliphs choose to include or exclude as far as *shari'a* is concerned? What will guarantee the ruler's compliance with this authority? What kind of institutional authority is there to control the ruler's compliance with this obligation? There is ample evidence in Islamic history, especially during the Umayyads and the Abbasids, that supports the fact that the authority of the caliph went unchecked and unquestioned. Such political system can very easily turn into *another* absolute monarchy. In *Al-Muqadima [The Introduction]*, Ibn Khaldun, the well-known fourteenth-century Islamic philosopher, shows how the caliphate did indeed turn into absolutist monarchy throughout Islamic history. Like many other Islamists, Yassine dismisses history and historical facts. He gives primacy to the Holy Scripture, without the least consideration of historical events and processes. Islam, as a pure principle expressed in the scripture, is immutable, regardless of history, time, culture, or place. In Yassine's view, only people and circumstances can change, but not divine laws. Any deviation from the laws set forth in the Koran and *sunna* is a deviation from the right path. Yassine goes even further as to suggest that the current state of malaise is a result of this very deviation from the right path.

However, Yassine has very little to tell us about the nature of the political system he so zealously seeks to institute. What specifically is an "Islamist state"? The question of the nature and character of such state remains largely unanswered, and from the very little that can be inferred from the work of Yassine itself, the model of state presented by Yassine could very easily be—and historically has been—a form of totalitarian rule. According to this vision, the caliph is beyond questioning.

The Islamist caliphate is not a hereditary monarchy; it is not an absolutist monarchy. Let us then ask the following question: Who chooses the caliph? The word *khalifa* (caliph), the title given to the political and spiritual leader of the Islamic *umma* [community], literally means successor or deputy. The primary obligation of the caliph is to implement divine law, which simply means that the caliph is answerable to no one, but God.

So whatever the caliph does is unquestionable, since only God can assess the Caliph's intentions. Who has the power to choose and, if need be, remove the caliph? To be sure, it is not the people who have this power, but rather a very limited group of scholars, *ahl al-hall wa al-'aqd* [literally, the people who have the power of binding and unbinding]. These people give their *bay'aa* [allegiance] to the caliph in return for his promise to apply divine law. But who appoints those scholars? Not the people, but the caliph. If this is not a vicious circle, I wonder what is!

Islam is unquestionably a political religion, although not in the sense of providing a concept for a specifically "Islamist state," but in clearly outlining a political ethic for governing a polity. Islam is political only in the sense of providing the ethics for governing but not the technical instructions for establishing a government in an "Islamist state." Why did Mohammed resist providing a set of static laws about the organization of the state? If this resistance means anything, it simply means the impossibility of providing eternal laws, without due consideration of history. Otherwise, how can we explain the changes in the laws in the Koran itself, as well as the differences and shifts in major issues between the caliphate during Abu Bakr and that of Omar, the two "rightly guided" caliphs after Mohammed?

The idea of an "Islamist state," then, is a vague concept based on politicizing and reviving various arbitrarily selected components of Islamic doctrine while unwittingly projecting modern concerns into classical Islamic history and thought. The notion of Islam as *din wa dawla* [religion and state] and the contention that *shari'a* is the constitution of an Islamist state are purely modern phenomena with little content and no real background in classical Islamic history or in the authoritative sources of the scripture.

In a civilization largely determined by Islam, there maybe nothing wrong with basing the ethics of government on Islamic morality (which do not contradict other moralities after all), *except that shari'a provides ethical guidelines, but not the system itself.*

What Yassine's analysis reveals—and very clearly—is a projection of modern political systems and forms into earlier phases of Islamic society. According to such ahistorical perception, secularization in modern Islamic history is not simply a deviation from divine law, but actually the product of a well-organized conspiracy directed against Islam and Muslims. Thus, Yassine reduces socialism into a mere ideology, whose aim is to "deal in the business of Islam" (*Minhaj* 13).

One of the major weaknesses of Yassine's Islamic modernity lies in his inability to address the most important question in any theory of social change: What kind of alternative socio-economic system does he propose? In other words, how does one move from the current stage of *fitna* characterized as it is by oppression and tyranny to the stage of an Islamist caliphate characterized by social justice and spirituality? What is, for example, a Yassinian policy of economic change and development, one that would be based on Islamic values? What kind of institutions would take charge of this role? Unfortunately, but predictably enough, Yassine remains silent about all these issues.

Shura or Democracy?

The relationship between political Islamism and democracy is very complex indeed. The conventional distinction between extreme Islamists who deny any correspondence between Islam and democracy and more moderate Islamists who argue that Islam requires a democratic system or is inherently democratic is of little use. What such distinction overlooks is the ambivalence, complexity, and even contradiction characterizing the views of many Islamists regarding Western democracy and the relationship between Islam and democracy.

The views of Yassine on the subject illustrate this complexity. Like many Islamists, such as Turabi in Sudan and Al-Ghannushi in Tunisia, Yassine advocates democracy as a tactic to gain political power, while still believing that democracy is a foreign concept and practice, one that emerged in secular Western society. He writes that:

> The functional and efficient truth of democratic procedure, when democracy is well propped in its native habitat, is undeniable. Whatever the criticism one would address to democracy as it developed and to its losing speed in the "advanced" societies, it *remains the least evil way of running the commonwealth* (*Islamiser* 314).

So is democracy a mere means to arrive at power? Yassine uses the same instrumental logic that he criticizes in modernity and capitalism.

After all, democracy, in Yassine's reading, is not incompatible with Islam and the Koran, and "[d]emocratic forms and methods, applied with precaution and discernment, cannot harm *shura*" (310). Not only that, *shura* needs democratic methods and procedures for it to be implemented in the modern world.

But while Yassine does not reject the "virtues" of Western democracy, which he considers a great advance in human political history, he also argues that, "the other face of democracy—the religion of secularism—is unacceptable" (310). For him, the concept of popular sovereignty denies the fundamental Islamic affirmation of the sovereignty of God and is, therefore, a form of idolatry. In other words, the idea of the sovereignty of the people contradicts the sovereignty of God. But this does not mean that Islamists should not make use of democracy, or should limit themselves to futile intellectual debates. In addition, democracy cannot live up to its own claims. As Yassine puts it:

> It is not our intention to initiate the trial of democracy. It is enough that we note here that democracy is, by birth, freedom from every absolute except its own, an enemy to every ethic that differs from its own. This radical exclusivity that democracy hides behind democratic tolerance, pluralism [etc.] is a virulent mechanism that turns democracy against itself and drives it to destroy its own ethical basis (307).

Yassine argues that once a democracy encourages its citizens to denounce every truth, including the truth of the idea of general interest, democracy itself becomes a relative political and social ideal, a mere non-truth (307). What democracy produces is a world full of doubt and uncertainty. Only religious faith can restore certainty.

In a rather sarcastic tone, Yassine ridicules the conventional celebration of democracy as the only political system that is capable of solving the problems of Islamic societies. Yassine scorns the "cosmetic" nature of political democracy in the Islamic world, which, according to him, is nothing but a hidden form of oppression and tyranny (310). He asks: Can Western democracy as a political mechanism respond to our need of exercising power without making us lose our soul, without taking us to the same state of "advanced" modern societies, where relativism and moral decline reign supreme? Yassine presents *shura* as an alternative form of Islamic democracy, as "the name of our kind of democracy" (309).

First of all, what is *shura*? What is the difference between *shura* and democracy? Yassine explains:

> *Shura* and democracy belong to radically different reference points. The historical itinerary of democracy, a Greek word and practice, is utterly other than that of *shura*. The first begins at pagan Athens and ends in "advanced" modern societies as a secularist practice, atheist and immoral, while the second has its beginning at pious Medina and remained a dead letter for nearly fourteen centuries. Today it is both a vital need for Muslims and a divine system that forms a part of our Islamic plan. *It remains to be put back into practice by means of a process yet to be found or borrowed from the wisdom of the people* (310).

In the Scripture, God commands the prophet to consult all Muslims in affairs of war and politics (*Koran* 3:159), and the righteous are described as those people who, among other things, manage their affairs through *shura* (*Koran* 42:38). The actual practices and actions of Mohammed and the rightly guided caliphs after him, namely Abu Bakr and Omar, show them to have been actively engaged in one form or another of deliberative consultation in politics and all other affairs of society and state. As Yassine puts it:

> The first Islamic government—I use the term government for lack of a better name—functioned for ten years under the aegis and direction of the prophet. During the prophet's lifetime and under his four successors called "rightly guided," consultation was practiced without ceremony (*Islamiser* 310).

Yassine presents *shura* as the only political practice, the only political system capable of ensuring true development and true unity of all Muslims. He claims that:

> There is no stability without *shura*, and no unity on the basis of nationalistic democracies that are at variance with Islam, and at variance with the course of the material civilization whose peoples are joining together, leaving us to follow the mirage of the nation state that the colonizing snake has worn since the nineteenth century, and is now attempting to slough off so that we may wear it as tattered rags (*Mihnat* 90).

The failure to enforce or adhere to *shura* is a common theme invoked in narratives of oppression and rebellion in early Islamic historical sources. But the concept refers merely to a ruler's *nonbinding* solicitation of opinions from *ahl al-'aqd*, the very people who choose and are chosen by the ruler. And Yassine is fully aware of this. He writes that, "*Shura* is a decision-preparation stage. Deliberation should go on until consensus or semi-consensus is reached. After that, the emir decides, orders, and is obeyed" (*Al-Adl* 562). Yassine bases his claim on an ideological interpretation of the Koran, according to which "believers should obey God, the prophet, and *those in charge of [them]*" (562) [My italics]. *Shura* can, thus, turn easily into a process of blind, unquestionable obedience, into a tool of political manipulation.

Yassine scorns Western secular democracy, arguing that Islam was the first democracy set on earth, based as it is on the legal concept of *shura*. Unlike many fundamentalist Islamists, Yassine does not totally reject democracy. Yassine bases his contention on the early Islamic practice of *shura* referred to in the Koran, claiming that it is the first theory of democratic government known to humanity.

In the political thought of Islamic fundamentalism, the references to the *shari'a* (and to the *shura* as its political component) are supposed to be the foundation for the call for an "Islamist state." These references do not, however, make the call any clearer with respect to concrete political demands. Clearly, Islamic fundamentalists are not traditionalists; rather, their reading modernity into Islam sometimes bears interesting fruit. But vagueness cannot be overcome by projecting present conditions onto the distant past. The belief that God alone is the sovereign and, hence, the only legislator can have very dangerous implications. This view willy-nilly presents the will of human rulers as the will of God. And this is what history tells us. During the Umayyad and the Abbasid eras, the caliph was no longer the successor of the prophet, but rather the deputy of God on earth. And who could question the authority of a ruler with such divine power?

The Islamist views analyzed here give us little hope that the approach of historicizing one's own history, that is, recognizing the pertinence of historical development and breaking with the naturalizing moves of essentialism, will find its way into Islamist thinking in the foreseeable future.

On Ethnicity Politics

In many ways, Yassine's rhetorical vision of an Islamic society characterized by tolerance of difference and recognition of others falls short of his own acts and those of his movement. This becomes especially clear from the views and actions of Yassine on two major identity politics issues: the political rights of Berbers and those of women.

Whether or not Berbers are the indigenous inhabitants of North Africa, it is a well-established historical fact that Berbers have lived in North Africa and in Morocco in particular for at least 4000 years, well before the early Islamic conquests some 1300 years ago. Since the coming of Islam in the seventh century AD, there has been a continuous process of Islamization and Arabization. To be sure, Islam and Arabic have been very closely linked. (According to Islamic law, prayer must be performed in Arabic, and only in Arabic.) According to the Moroccan Institution, Arabic is the official language of Morocco. The overwhelming majority of present-day Arabic-speaking Moroccans are originally Berber, and a large number of the younger generation of Moroccans who consider themselves to be Berbers can speak only Arabic.

Berbers (who call themselves *Tamazight* [free people]) perceive their cultural identity, and especially language, to be threatened primarily by marginalization and exclusion from access to education and media exposure in the country. In 1991, in an attempt to reinforce the significance of their ethnic identity, several Berber activists and advocacy organizations based all over the country met in the city of Agadir. There, they signed what came to be called the "Agadir Charter" which outlined Berber demands for the creation of a *Tamazight* research center that would provide the impetus and framework necessary for any project to preserve and promote Berber language and cultures. In 2000, Berber activists drafted and addressed what they called the "Berber Manifesto" to the Moroccan state, calling on it to recognize Berber as a national language, teach it in schools, license a Berber language media, and so forth. Before this date, Berbers had made other demands and raised other issues, including the development of a special alphabet and the creation of a Berber Congress.

It was in this general context that Yassine, who is of a Berber origin himself, wrote his rather famous book, *Hiwar maa Sadiqi Al-Amazighi [A Dialogue with my Amazigh Friend]*, which was published in 1997. As the title suggests, Yassine presents himself as being engaged in a dialogue with fellow Berbers. While Yassine addresses the book to a specific person, Mohammed Shafik, a Berber activist and a former colleague of Yassine, the book is in fact addressed to the Moroccan Berber movement as a whole and all who are concerned with Berber identity and politics in Morocco.

Here, Yassine aims his critique at the political project of the Moroccan Berber movement. He criticizes the movement's concern with ethnicity politics and with "secondary" issues of cultural representation, while overlooking the need for a shared commitment to the common ideals of Islam and Muslims. He further adds that the movement is made up of two different groups, with two different projects: the cultural and political. On the one hand, the first group seeks to address purely cultural issues, especially language and cultural representation; on the other hand, the second group seeks to exploit the issue of ethnic identity and ethnicity for political ends. It is true that Yassine's book targets the political group, but he later denies the very distinction he has made between the cultural and political. As he puts it, "Every cultural movement, despite being preoccupied with academic questions, will have, today or in the future, in this generation or the next, political aspirations and ambitions" (*Hiwar* 77).

Unlike Islamic identity, Berber identity, in Yassine's view, is a fake "selfish earthly and worldly" cultural identity, based on tribelike affiliations and loyalties. The call for a Berber identity aims to divide the individual into two entities, the Berber and the Islamic, thus leading to the fragmentation of the Moroccan subject. Yassine makes it clear that he wants only one identity, and one identity only: the Islamic identity. What he fails to explain is: In what way does Berber identity threaten Islamic identity and unity? Why cannot they exist together?

Yassine sees the call for the recognition of the Berber language as a call for a multilingualism that threatens the Arabic language, the language of the Koran. He goes even further as to accuse Berber activists of heresy and atheism. He writes:

> And he who disbelieves in the Arabic tongue also disbelieves in God. The Arabic tongue is God-chosen in the same way Prophets are chosen[4]...If I write that he who disbelieves in the Arabic tongue also disbelieves in God, I mean the language of the Koran and the *surats* of the Koran. And since serving Arabic and its sciences means serving the Koran and the understanding of the Koran, my general statement becomes true (*Hiwar* 97).

What Yassine fails to recognize is the fact that Berber, as language, is one important cultural component of Morocco, just like Arabic and Islam, and to reject it is to reject one's culture and past. By doing this, Yassine destroys his own project of an ideal community founded on tolerance and justice.

On Women and Gender

Issues of women and gender have always lied at the very center of the debate over modernity and modernization in contemporary

Morocco. Since the early 1990s, however, there have been a number of events and changes that have attracted more attention to women issues than ever before, both from pro-feminist and antifeminist camps. In 1991, the Moroccan Feminist Action Union launched a national campaign calling for substantial changes in the Islamic-based *Moudawana*, the Personal Status Law, in order to make it consistent with the Moroccan Constitution, which clearly states that men and women are equal before the law in their rights and responsibilities. The Union would not stop here; a year later, in 1992, it organized a national conference, calling for immediate and urgent reforms in the Personal Status Law. In the course of the same year, late King Hassan II met with representatives of the Moroccan feminist movement and later constituted a royal committee to reconsider the *Moudawana* on the basis of the recommendations of this movement. And this was how the so-called "new" *Moudawana* of 1993 came into being. In fact, anyone who is familiar with the first *Moudawana* of 1957 would recognize that (with the exception of minor changes in the divorce and children custody procedures) there was very little new about the 1993 *Moudawana*, and that it was nothing other than a new edition of an older text for mere political propaganda.

It was in this historical context that Yassine conceived and wrote his so-called guide to the Muslim woman, *Tanwir Al-Mouaminat [Enlightening Believing Women]*. Here, Yassine seeks to clarify his position on the place and role of women in his political project. Right at the outset, he links the decline of the status of Muslim women to the decline of the status of all Muslims. As he puts it:

> The status of the Muslim woman is part of the decline of all Muslims. The decline started with the destructive transformation of the Islamic political system from a *caliphate* on the prophetic model into an oppressive hereditary monarchy....Thus the woman was turned into a commodity in the market and a slave-servant in palaces. She became a neglected object until the age of secularization, the age colonial agents brought the good news that she has entered the era of freedom, an era where she can be like her "perfect" sister in the West a master over her body. Thus, our westernized women blindly imitated the Western victors. Now they are calling and struggling in the name of human rights, that is, in the name of woman's right to be liberated from a world where women are treated as neglected objects, as commodities (1).

For Yassine, "Islam constitutes an indivisible whole" and "The question and social status of the woman is but one battle, among many battles against total contradiction" (1). Yassine is right to point out that issues women and gender cannot be considered outside the problematic of social change as a whole. Yassine's essential argument, however, is that the feminist movement, like the Berber movement, and its demands for woman's equality, is the product of a conspiracy by secular, atheist, and imperialist Western forces against Islam. In *Tanwir*, he writes that:

> Woman in the West has been liberated from the racism of man, a racism that is inherent in the church's view of the woman. Over the centuries, churchmen have been arguing over whether woman has a soul, or over how to burn witches, or over how man can cleanse himself of the evil of his Satan: woman.
>
> The Church is the enemy of the woman. Every religion is a church, and to be liberated from religion is an honorable achievement for every free woman. Those women who call for dependent ...find proofs in the reality of Muslim allowing them to compare the oppression of the church to the injustices to which the Muslim woman is subject to. Thus, Islam is a church from which women must be liberated (2).

Maybe, Yassine is right to question the projection of the relationship between women and the church onto the relationship between women and religion in general. But what kind of alternative does Yassine propose for the liberation of women? He claims that in the West reconciliation between men and women was achieved through liberation from an oppressive church and religion. He proposes another alternative for the Muslim world. In his view,

> Instead of the Western model of reconciliation between the world of man and that of woman which was achieved through the liberation from religion, reconciliation [in the Muslim world] shall be achieved on the basis of the *shari'a* [law] of justice and spirituality. The law of justice and spirituality has called upon both the sexes, men and women, to be united in obeying and worshipping God alone. It has called upon the two sexes and worlds to a life of harmony, cooperation, and mutual support, a life where men and women complete each other... (*Tanwir* 2).

He continues:

> The justice and spirituality of Islam seeks one world, characterized by mutual mercy, affection, and sense of giving, not conflict and enmity [between men and women]. The justice and spirituality of Islam and its *shari'a* are a framework of tolerance between men and women; it is an open entity where the world of men and women are joined in complete harmony" (2).

The Islamic trajectory to the liberation of women will be based on Islamic law and on justice and spirituality, where both men and women lead a life of harmony, cooperation, mutual support, and tolerance. But this world that Yassine envisions soon collapses when he writes:

> The struggle of those who defend woman's rights from the Westernized and immoral perspective is centered on a central demand, the demand for the equality of men and women, and thus, erasing all the specific Islamic laws about the woman, starting by *the denial of the superiority of men over women* (200) [My italics].

According to Yassine, complete equality between men and women is wrong for two reasons. First, it is a claim that emerged in the atheist, secularist West, and is therefore unacceptable. Second, such claimed equality does not conform to Islamic laws, which, according to Yassine, grant woman a "second class status" after man. We should point out here that by making such a dangerous claim Yassine not only destroys the beautiful life of "harmony, cooperation, mutual support, and tolerance" he promises for both men and women, but he also destroys his own so called "egalitarian" political project, which he presents as based on equality and justice for all, regardless of gender, ethnicity or any other identity marker.

Conclusion

I have not, however, selected this ideological work simply to ridicule its author, but rather to introduce a wholly representative work by a renowned Islamist scholar. Yassine is a respected Islamist scholar and political leader. While Islamism appears to be an ideology and political movement that is adamantly opposed to modernity and capitalism, seeking to reestablish the rule of traditional Islamic values and laws, it is in fact the very product of the destruction of the pre-capitalist Arab-Islamic world. As an ideological and political project, it is inherently modernist and capitalist in nature. As a moralist and as a guardian of Islamic tradition, Yassine attacks the progress of modernity—the growing power of liberalism and secularism. He enumerates the discontents of the Muslim world's (with a specific focus on Morocco's) industrialization and warns against the loss of faith, of unity, of "moral values".

Yassine's proposed reforms, his utopias, are meant to overcome this secular world, and his reforms as well as his criticisms reflect the strong subjective element of his thought. He feels that only some outside agent, some conspiracy could have dissolved the ancient unity of the people of faith; hence by stamping out the agents of dissension and by instituting various revolutionary reforms, the older community can be revived and reestablished.

These in brief are the elements of Yassine's thought. Together they constitute an ideology, at once an indictment, a program, and a mystique. The ideas of Yassine (and of other Islamists, mainly Sayyid Qutb in Egypt) have strongly affected the sentiments of the Moroccan youth, and especially students, in the late 1980s and still do. They nurture the idealistic rejection of modern society and the resentment against the imperfections of Western ideals and institutions, but mostly for the wrong reasons. And it is in this sense that he has contributed so greatly to the enfeeblement of socialist ideologies in Morocco. The appeal of Yassine's ideas is heightened by his style. Yassine writes with great fervor and passion. He not only analyses or argues, but also condemns or prophesizes and most of his writing shows that he loves-hates the discourses of intellectuals, appreciates and depreciates reason all at once.

This chapter has addressed the origins, content, and impact of Islamism as an ideology and a political movement. There is another link, admittedly less tangible, in the peculiar tension between the life and the ideological aspirations of the Islamist scholar to anticipate a more dangerous type of malcontent of the masses who might find a safe haven in such fundamentalist idealism. There is a politically exploitable mass discontent which has been embedded in Moroccan culture for a very long time. I am speaking here of a process which is nothing less than a fundamentalist revolution, where the doctrines of arbitrary authority, discipline, obedience, submission, and tradition are more likely to kindle the imagination of the masses than the ideals of social justice and socialism. What we see here is the rise of political passions and Islamist movements against the West and all that the latter represents.

Until a few decades ago, this fundamentalist Islamist movement had escaped Moroccan intellectuals and politicians alike, and only recently is it starting to attract some attention. Its claims have been so elusive and its political manifestations so sporadic that few have recognized the power and pervasiveness of this revolutionary mood. The Islamist movement does embody a paradox: its followers seek to destroy the despised present in order to recapture an idealized past in an imaginary future. But the problem is that these are disinherited fundamentalists who have nothing to return to, because the values and practices of the past do not respond to the present conditions and are unable to address present contradictions.

Liberal capitalist society leaves many people dissatisfied—materially and spiritually. The materially alienated have often taken the easier path; they have often turned to the ideology of conservatism, traditionalism, and fundamentalism. For several decades, this attack has gained popularity and with it political power. Combining cultural criticism with religious fundamentalism, this ideology maintains that the character of modern capitalist society is alien to the spirit and tradition of the people. It would not be an exaggeration to claim that Islamist ideologies are essentially similar in every dominantly Muslim country. The originators of this ideology are themselves the victims of capitalist modernity, writing no longer as critics but as victims and prophets. They appeal to the disorganized masses, who in their resentment of capitalist modernity sought to smash all that it represented. We are at a point when the Islamist revolt could easily erupt into politics. It might take the form of some desperate political force that is able, with the help of this ideology, to exploit the material and psychological grievances of the masses. The recent political achievements of the Islamists in the 2003 Moroccan elections are a further proof of this. Contemporary Moroccan society (and Arab society) harbors many such people, and at moments of crisis, this discontent can very easily turn into political disaffection. The material roots of the Islamist discontent can be found in the social and international division of labor and class contradictions, in a word, in capitalist relations of production.

Islamists half-rightly denounce every aspect of the capitalist society and its materialism. They attack the spiritual emptiness of life in an urban, industrial society, and lament the decline of faith and virtue in a commodified society. They attack the media as corrupt, political parties as agents of the state and their new leaders as ineffectual agents and puppies of the West. At the commencement of *The Terrorist* film, Brother Seif, the spiritual leader of terrorist organization, is shown preaching a group of teenagers. His list of commands includes:

Do not read the newspapers of the infidel state! Nor watch any movies or TV! That is a novelty! And every novelty is a transgression! And every transgression leads to hell! Do not pray behind an Imam who smokes! Never shake hands with a Christian or salute him. Never allow your sister or mother out without the veil! Or else you are doomed to hell and ill fate.

The present seems dark, and the past is more attractive. Most Islamists think this world has been destroyed by evil hands. All these charges, however exaggerated and distorted, have some basis in reality. But for the colonial experience and all that came with it, it would have been impossible to conceive of this indictment of the West. These charges are linked to reality, and that is a precondition of their success. This discontent does not stem from dissatisfaction with life in an urban and industrialized culture alone; it also springs from economic necessity and social inequality—a dissatisfaction that most of Yassine's followers experience on a daily basis.

The direct target of Islamists, however, is not capitalist liberalism, but rather secularism. They blame all the vast undesirable changes in the life and experience of Muslim men and women on the disappearance of religion. They equate socialism with a disregard of human's spiritual aspirations, with the human loss of life and morals. They ignore the utopian aspirations of true socialism, its dedication to freedom, justice, and to the rational, humane, tolerant view of humanity.

As is clear from the categories that Yassine uses, the impact of leftist thinking and politics is undeniable. He reinterprets several classical Koranic concepts and uses them to describe essentially modern practices and processes. Despite all claims to the contrary, Islamist ideology is far from static. While it looks back at the past as a model, many of its concepts and categories are essentially modern.

What can we learn from Islamism? In fact, if there is anything we can learn from Islamism it is its internationalist spirit. Islamism is fundamentally internationalist in its aims and direction, operating across borders as readily as within them. Islamists are participants in a struggle about how the whole world should be.

NOTES

[1] In 1971, he wrote *Al-Islam Bayna Al-Daawa wa Dawla [Islam between the Appeal and the State]* and in 1972, he wrote *Al-Islam Ghadan [Islam Tomorrow!]*.

2   Between 1994 and 1998, Yassine wrote many books and letters, including: *Hiwar maa Al-Fudalaa Al-Dimuqratiyyin [A Dialog with Honorable Democrats], Fi Al-Iqtisad [On the Economy], Mihnat Al-Aql Al-Muslim [Muslim Mind on Trial], Al-Shura wa Al-Dimuqratiyya [Consultation and Democracy],* and *Islamiser la modernité [Islamizing Modernity].*
3   In addition to these major obstacles, Yassine adds "the oppression and persecution of preachers, ignorance of religion, as well as the materialist nature of our civilization" (2).
4   It is very important to point out here that Yassine charges the Jews of ignorance and arrogance on the basis of their claims of being God-chosen.

· CHAPTER FIVE ·

Toward A New Project of Modernity: Marxism and the Arab Left

The present chapter attempts to provide a theoretical foundation upon which a radical project of modernity, an alternative vision of modernity, can be developed. Towards the beginning of his *Introduction to Modernity*, Henri Lefebvre, a French Marxist cultural and social critic, writes:

> If we are to understand our era [in other words, modernity] – and to call it complex would be an understatement – it is absolutely vital that we construct a set of conceptual tools. In our view this conceptual apparatus is still far from satisfactory, despite the efforts of various theoreticians (who call themselves 'philosophers', 'sociologists', 'anthropologists', etc.), and *despite the fact that the theoretical base already exists in Marx and Marxism* [My italics] (3).

I concur with Lefebvre here and argue for the importance of the work of Marx (and of others in the Marxist tradition) and the insights it offers as the foundation for an emancipatory project of modernity.

It might be asked: But why Marx at a moment in which Marx and Marxism are everywhere under attack? Well, the answer is very simple. Marx's work (in fact Marxism in general) is an analysis and critique of capitalism and capitalist society, and as long as the capitalist mode of production exists, and as long as the questions that Marx raised are not resolved, Marx's critique will remain of great relevance and importance, despite all claims to the contrary. However, it would be wrong to conclude from this that Marx provides a complete critique of capitalism. Marx's critique is incomplete in two ways. On the one hand, Marx died, but capitalism continues to exist; and in so doing, it has been growing, developing, changing, and penetrating more and more areas of our life and the world. On the other hand, *Capital*, Marx's major work, is incomplete, and no one knows what a full Marxian critique of capital and capitalism would be like had Marx lived long enough to finish it.[1] The unfinished nature of Marx's project, far from being a flaw, is in fact a metaphor for and a reminder of the incomplete, historical, and dynamic nature of human thought and life in an age where incompleteness, historicity, dynamism of social phenomena are blurred and hidden in our conventional thoughts and practices. Marx's work is best understood as a contribution to the critique of capitalism, and it is not for nothing that several of Marx's works have the word "contribution" as part of their titles.

Much postcolonial studies scholarship fails to take the project of Marx and Marxism seriously, even arguing that it is a mere essentialist narrative complicit with imperialism and colonialism, thereby failing to engage with the enormous contribution such project can make (and has made) to the global South. In *Orientalism*, which is regarded as the catalyst for postcolonial theory, Edward Said argues against what he considers "Marx's own homogenizing view of the Third World" (325). Said explains how:

> Marx's economic analyses are perfectly fitted thus to a standard Orientalist undertaking, even though Marx's humanity, his sympathy for the misery of people, are clearly engaged. Yet in the end it is the Romantic Orientalist vision that wins out, as Marx's theoretical socio-economic views become submerged in [a] classically standard image (154).

What is hidden here is the dialectical nature of Marx's understanding of the imperialist project as a contradictory project, and to claim that it is "the Romantic Orientalist vision that wins out" is simply inaccurate.

This chapter—in fact the whole book—makes a case for the continued relevance of Marx and Marxism for any emancipatory political project in the postcolonial world, and in the Arab world in particular. Marx's work is a critical analysis of capitalist modernity, that is, modern life under capitalism (in its socio-economic, political, and ideological manifestations), and in so doing, goes beyond that to offer *an alternative vision, an alternative project, another modernity*. However, in my view, the importance of Marx's critique lies less in the substance of the analysis itself and more in the methodological, conceptual tools Marx employs. I am not suggesting that the substance of Marx's critique is irrelevant or futile. Quite the opposite, if this work is trying to prove anything, it is the continued relevance and validity of many aspects of Marx's work. After all, it would be impossible to separate *completely* the substance of Marx's work from his method. What I am suggesting is that Marx provides us with a set of conceptual and methodological tools and frameworks that could help us better understand our (Moroccan/Arab) society at this particular conjuncture. These tools demonstrate a certain level of abstraction and universality that makes them useful for the study of Moroccan society, a society which is, to be sure, at a different stage of development from the nineteenth-century English social formation that Marx analyzed.

Let us address the following question: what should be the aim of a Marxist theory of modernity with regard to the Arab world and Morocco in particular?

The aim of this theory should be two-fold: First, it should provide a critique of all ahistorical analyses of the Moroccan society and Arab society in general, that is, the liberal, nationalist, Islamist, and even orientalist analyses of Moroccan society. Second, and more important, it should provide an alternative to such analyses and theories, and also *serve as a guide for political praxis and social change.*

Applying Marxist Tools to Moroccan Society and Ideology

Marx, more clearly in his early work, develops a highly critical, dialectical theory of modern society and modernist ideologies, insisting that cultural and ideological phenomena cannot be fully understood "in terms of themselves" and independently of their socio-economic context. In *Marxism and Philosophy*, Karl Korsch provides the following summary of Marx's method. He writes:

> It is a theory of *social development* seen and comprehended as a living totality; or more precisely, it is a theory of *social revolution* comprehended and practiced as living totality. At this stage there is no question whatever of dividing the economic, political, and intellectual moments of this totality into separate branches of knowledge (57).

The Frankfurt School's theory of modern capitalist society, and its approach to society as a totality and the conjunction of the social, economic, cultural, and political draws on Marx's critique of modern capitalism and in particular of capitalist political economy and commodity fetishism and its later appropriation by Lukacs in his theory of reification. Adorno and Horkheimer provide valuable insights for the critical analysis and study of the relationship between theory and society. They develop a dialectical framework through which one can understand the different mediations that link the social and cultural institutions and activities of everyday life with the logic and commanding forces that shape the larger social totality, as well as the interconnections between the economic sphere and the transformations in the social and cultural realms. They also reject the view of culture as a mere super-structural by-product of collective labor, as well as the traditional view of it as an autonomous entity unrelated to the economic and political processes of everyday life and separated from the social totality. According to them, both views are equally reductive because they abstract culture from its historical context and blur our understanding of its multifaceted nature. Culture is not a "super-structural" by-product, nor is it an independent realm that exists on its own, and any conception based on the autonomy of culture has to be rejected, as well. As Adorno puts it in his classic essay "Cultural Criticism and Society":

> [Such a traditional view of culture], it may be argued, overlooks what is decisive: the role of ideology in social conflicts. To suppose, if only methodologically, anything like an independent logic of culture is to collaborate in the hypostasis of culture, the ideological *proton pseudos*. The substance of culture, according to this argument, resides not in culture alone but in its relation to something external, to the material life-process. Culture, as Marx observed of juridical and political systems, cannot be fully 'understood either in terms of itself...or in terms of the so-called universal development of the mind'. To ignore this, the argument concludes, is to make ideology the basic matter and thus to establish it firmly (29).

Thus, it is impossible to understand culture "in terms of itself" and any claim to that effect is ideological. Such understanding only naturalizes culture and abstracts it from the socio-historical context that gives it meaning in the first place. That is why a critical approach to culture that does not recognize "the latter's position within the whole" is inconceivable (29). Developing this argument, Horkheimer writes that, "A conception is needed which overcomes the one-sidedness that necessarily arises when limited intellectual processes are detached from their matrix in the total activity of society" ("Traditional and Critical Theory" 199). For:

> It would be mechanistic, not dialectical thinking, however, to judge the future forms of society solely according to their economy....

> Economism, to which the critical theory is often reduced, does not consist in giving too much importance to the economy, but in giving it too narrow a scope. The theory is concerned with society as a whole, but this broad scope is forgotten in economism where limited phenomena are made the final court of appeal ("Postscript" 249).

Society constitutes a unified whole which emerges, develops, and changes ceaselessly. The economy, culture, and politics are part of this whole and one of the greatest merits of Marx, Lukacs, and the Frankfurt School is to have emphasized the dialectical nature of this social whole.

Marxism thus recognizes the centrality and all-pervasive nature of the capitalist mode of production in modern societies. Its approach to and analysis of modern society, complex and challenging as it is, can have immediate effects on and implications for any emancipatory modernity project in Morocco and elsewhere in the Arab world. Marxism's emphasis on the position of all aspects of society within the social totality could lead to a much more profound critique and a much more active sense of revolutionary activity in contemporary Moroccan society than the persistently abstract models derived from the liberal, nationalist, and Islamist theories of Laroui, Yassine, and Al-Jabri.

As I have argued earlier, the various Moroccan liberal, nationalist, and Islamist discourses and ideologies are in essence ahistorical and hardly dialectical. They are ahistorical because questions of social underdevelopment are not examined in their specific historical context. In different ways, consciously or unconsciously, what emerges from their analysis is a worldview that regards Arab society, and Moroccan society in particular, as (almost) unchanging. Al-Jabri's emphasis on the role of Islamic tradition in underdevelopment and the tracing back of irrationality to medieval times; Yassine's relating backwardness to abandonment of a certain form of Islam; Laroui's celebration of liberalism and liberal capitalism as the highest stage of social and human development, all tend to reveal the fundamentally ahistorical nature of their thought. In many respects, the approaches of Laroui, Al-Jabri, and Yassine to Moroccan society are nothing but extensions of the orientalist approach to Arab society. Like the orientalists, they lay excessive emphasis on the importance of Islam in defining Arab society and culture. Laroui's call to break with tradition altogether, Al-Jabri's call to revive elements of medieval Islamic tradition, and Yassine's call to reestablish and implement Islamic laws to the letter, all make it seem as if the problem of Arab society lies somewhere within Islam and Islamic tradition. It is true that Laroui, Al-Jabri, and, to a lesser extent, Yassine discuss the role of social forces in defining Arab society, but such discussion is only of secondary importance. In Laroui's work, the role of imperialism in the development of Arab-Islamic society is almost absent. The attention that Al-Jabri gives to the analysis of Islamic tradition is so substantial that other important social factors are ignored or dealt with only in passing.

What these discourses seem to ignore are the interconnections between cultural and political underdevelopment on the one hand and the economic side of it, on the other. Such reductive accounts serve—either consciously or unconsciously—as instruments for the validation and naturalization of the discourses and practices of the dominant classes in society, thus hiding the very historical and political nature of these discourses and practices.

The question of underdevelopment in Morocco and the Arab world, and elsewhere, cannot be addressed or resolved outside its historical context in the social totality. Marxian dialectics understands social phenomena as constituting a connected and integral whole, and not merely as a set of unconnected events, without any interaction whatsoever. The dialectical method insists that no social phenomenon can be properly understood without proper consideration of its interconnections with other phenomena in the social totality. What is needed, therefore, is an analysis of contemporary Moroccan and Arab societies and their world context, as well as of the social processes of change at all levels: economic, cultural, political, and social.

Early Marx and the Project of Radical Democracy

In Marx, we have "the beginnings of a reflective process, a more-or-less advanced attempt at critique and auto-critique, a bid for knowledge," a critique that "bear[s] the mark of [its] era and yet goes beyond the provocation of fashion and the stimulation of novelty" (Lefebvre 1-2). In addition, the Marxist vision of modernity goes beyond the theoretical itself to the realm of political practice, making the two inseparable, not because one cannot exist without the other, but because one is meaningless without the other. Marx's eleventh thesis on Feuerbach, stating that, "The philosophers have only *interpreted* the world, in various ways; the point, however, is to *change* it" (*Marx-Engels* 145), further illustrates this.

Now let us ask the following question: What did the modern, modernity, and modernist ideology mean for Marx? How did he conceive of modern society which was still in its infancy? Marx used the term "modern" to refer to the emergence of industrial capitalism, to the ascendancy of the bourgeoisie, to their political and ideological manifestations, as well as to the critique of all of these processes of social, economic, political, and cultural change in their totality. For Marx, the origins of modernity are to be found in the emergence of industrial capitalism as a socio-economic system and the new patterns of labor and life propelled by it. The ideology of modernity, as a phenomenon of consciousness, as an abstraction, does not exist in a vacuum; it is nothing other than the manifestation, the reflection of certain economic, cultural, and political processes and social relations.

The work of Marx, at different stages, produces two *complementary*, *interconnected* (and I insist that these are inseparable) political projects in an attempt to overcome the contradictions of modern capitalist society: a project of radicalizing democracy of the younger Marx and a project of socialist revolution of the older Marx. These two projects, I would argue, provide us (the Arab left) with two critical strategies of political practice. In other words, the young Marx and the older Marx develop two strategies in an attempt to go beyond the problems and contradictions of capitalism. These two incomplete[2] projects, if developed properly, could provide the Arab left with two effective political projects, one short-term and the other long-term.

In early Marx, we have a certain concept of modernity. As Lefebvre puts it:

> [B]etween 1840 and 1845, Marx's thought produces a concept of modernity. This concept is primarily but not exclusively a political one. It designates a form of the state, the state elevated above society, but also the relation this form has with everyday life and with social practice in general. The form of the state is defined as one which separates everyday life (private life) from social life and political life.... As a result, private life and the state—that is, political life—fall simultaneously into identical but conflicting abstractions. And everywhere, in every area, the irrational and the rational become separated and yet confused, the one hiding the other in a single contradictory reality which is a rational (social and political) unity in appearance only: generalized unreality (170).

But what Marx presents us with is not a mere concept, but a whole project of radical democracy and modernity. In the manuscripts of 1844, Marx had already developed a certain conception of modern capitalist society and modernity, which was essentially based on a critique of Hegel's idealism and Hegel's theory of the state in particular. Hegel rejects the Kantian view (discussed earlier) that human beings are free by nature. In his view, only the state, the objective manifestation of consciousness and the embodiment of "universal interests," can guarantee human liberty in society; without the state, human beings can never achieve actual freedom in society as an arena of conflict, characterized by antagonisms and contradictions. In contrast, Marx emphasizes the fact that modern capitalist society is based on a political abstraction, on a gap between civil society (Hegel's term for the socio-economic order) and the state (political society). Political life is detached from civil life, and public life from private life. In modern capitalist society, the individual leads a double life. As Marx puts it, "[The individual] lives in the *political community*, where he regards himself as a *communal being*, and in *civil society* where he acts simply as a *private individual*, treats other men as means, degrades himself to the role of a mere means, and becomes the plaything of alien powers" ("Bruno Bauer, *Die Judenferage*" 13). The state claims the individual as a member of a political community, but in reality, he/she is "an individual, separated from the community, withdrawn into himself, wholly preoccupied with his private interest and acting in accordance with his private caprice" (26). In its detachment from civil society, the state proves itself to be unreal, a mere "abstraction."

Marx distinguishes between two kinds of emancipation, political emancipation and human emancipation in modern bourgeois society. Political emancipation alone is incomplete, and, at best, is not enough, because the sphere of human life is greater than that of the political sphere. The state may be free, although the people themselves are not free. The state does not synthesize conflicts in society, as Hegel argues, but rather lies at their root, and unless the division of society into two separate spheres, the political and the private, which according to Marx is characteristic of bourgeois society alone, is abolished, "the modern state itself leaves *the real man* out of account or only satisfies the *whole* man in an illusory way" (51).

While Marx admits that "political emancipation certainly represents a great progress," it is not "the final form of human emancipation" (15). But what solution is capable of bridging the gap between human and political emancipation and regaining the lost unity and ensuring "real, practical" emancipation? For the young Marx, the resolution of the contradiction between the state and society is envisaged in political terms, in what Marx calls radical or "true" democracy. In his "Contribution to the Critique of Hegel's Philosophy of Right", he writes:

> Democracy is the solved *riddle* of all constitutions. Here, not merely *implicitly* and in essence but *existing* in reality, the constitution is constantly brought back to its actual basis, *the actual human being, the actual people*, and established as the people's *own* work. The constitution appears as what it is, a free product of man (*Marx-Engels* 20).

Marx further adds:

> All other *state forms* are definite, distinct, *particular forms of state*. In democracy the *formal* principle is at the same time the *material* principle. Only democracy, therefore, is the true unity of the general and the particular.
>
> In all states other than democratic ones the *state*, the *law*, the *constitution* is what rules, without really ruling—i.e., without materially permeating the content of the remaining, non-political spheres. In democracy the constitution, the law, the state itself, insofar as it is a political constitution, is only the self-determination of the people, and a particular content of the people (20-21).

Marx's critique, here, is directed against Hegel's defense of constitutional monarchy. As an alternative, Marx proposes a new vision of democracy. In his view, only some radical form of democracy, which guarantees the full participation of all citizens in the political and social processes, can put an end to the division and separation between society and the state, between civil society and political society. However, Marx does not define what such radical democracy entails, except that it is more than a mere political form.

Of course, there are limits to what can be achieved through radical democracy, and it would be naïve not to acknowledge these limits. But given the limits set on the Moroccan/Arab left at the current historical conjuncture, the inexistence of a large, well-organized working class capable of carrying out its historical mission, and the long history of totalitarian and oppressive regimes, working for some kind of radical democracy remains a very attractive and necessary political project. This does not mean that we give up the Marxist ideal: the creation of a socialist society must not be abandoned. In fact, radical democracy can pave the way, even facilitate and accelerate the coming of the socialist stage. Naturally, radical democracy, within the framework of a capitalist society, a society based on inherent injustice and inequality, cannot overcome all alienation, all social conflict, but it will be a major step forward, a major achievement for a society that has never enjoyed real democracy, not even real political democracy, throughout its colonial and post-colonial history. The kind of democracy envisioned here is different from the kind of liberal democracy advocated by Laroui; it is a radicalization of it. Instead of limiting democracy to the freedom to participate in the political sphere, leftist politics should work for the extension of that freedom into participation in decision-making processes in the economic sphere, as well. This would lead towards equal participation in all social processes, towards the abolition of private property and the establishment of a socialist society.

Currently, unceasing application of offensive revolutionary pressure (an echo of Trosky's notion of permanent revolution) would be an inappropriate policy in a country like Morocco, where, I believe, along with Al-Jabri, that a gradual building of tactical coalitions and alliances, or to use Gramsci's terminology, historical blocs, among oppressed groups is absolutely essential.

Throughout the Arab world, one is unlikely to see a radically and totally distinct socialist order fundamentally shaped by some form of collective consensus on economic decisions in the foreseeable future for reasons that are well-known. Systematic critiques and protests against the social ills endemic to capitalism—structural poverty and inequality and cyclical instability—should continue to play a central role in radical left politics. Other feasible possibilities and alternatives should be explored and encouraged. Some sort of semi-socialism under which laborers, in addition to receiving wages for their labor, participate through assemblies or councils in the decision-making of the producing organization and receive a share of its profits is an alternative which would at least help reduce the division between owners and non-owners while keeping economic decisions in a decentralized "private sector."

Under present conditions, radical politics should assume a radicalizing character, rather than a revolutionary one, and center on the demands of the new working class and poor peasants for better conditions, better wages, better lives, more chances...etc. Only by struggling for more immediate and practical concessions, by compelling the state to limit exploitation, by improving the conditions of life, however unevenly, can the working class become in the long run aware of its revolutionary potential and its historical mission as the true "gravedigger of the bourgeoisie."

The Socialist Project

Around 1845, Marx had developed his "materialist conception" of history, a conception which was to shape his later critique of modern capitalist society and modernity. There is no doubt that *The Communist Manifesto*, which according to its writers (Marx and Engels) "had as its object the proclamation of the inevitability impending dissolution of modern bourgeois property," contains the best summary of this later socialist project we are trying to sketch here (*Marx-Engels* 471). Marshall Berman was certainly right to base his classic reconstruction of the Marxian vision of modernity and modern life (as well as his title *All That Is Solid Melts Into Air*) almost exclusively on the *Manifesto*, despite the fact that he overlooks the vision Marx had developed prior to 1844 (before he had fully developed his materialist conception of history). Marx's greatest achievement in the *Manifesto* could be said to lie in his ability to identify, analyze, and critique the dialectical and self-destructive nature of the capitalist mode of production, as well as to highlight its precisely historical and transient nature. But he does more than that. He presents us with a theory of revolutionary praxis, a theory of socialist revolution.

According to Marx, modern capitalism has, on the one hand, weakened and replaced feudal relations and restrictions, traditional institutions and systems of thought. Thus, modern capitalism certainly represents great progress towards human emancipation. But, on the other hand, as Marx emphasized, modern capitalism does not represent the last form of human emancipation. To the process of capitalist development corresponds an increasingly alienated society, concealing, as it does, a much more fundamental antagonism: the exploitative nature of the relationship between those who own the means of production and those who have to labor to reproduce themselves, between the bourgeoisie and the proletariat. Radical democracy can minimize this antagonism, but is unable to put an end to it once and for all. Ultimately, only a total revolution, a revolution of the whole economic and social structure, is capable of ending social antagonism and ensuring "real, practical" emancipation within the framework of a socialist society.

What is socialism? In fact, Marx does not provide a systematic account of a future socialist society, but he does indicate some of its essential features.[3] Marx understands socialism in relation to capitalism, as the product of the latter's development, as a system of collective ownership and management of the means of production and distribution of goods, "an association in which the free development of each is the condition for the development of all" (491).

In arguing that socialism should be a long-term project for the Moroccan left and the Arab left in general, I do not mean to say that it is a mere dream. Socialism is an attainable reality. However, the current state of socio-economic development in Morocco (and all over the Arab world) is *not yet* ripe for the total abolishment of private property and capitalist production. While the social forces capable of making socialism a reality do exist, they are not ready to do so as of yet. In an 1870 letter to Dr. Kugelmann, Marx describes what he considered to be the conditions for the disintegration of capitalism:

> Although the revolutionary initiative will probably come from France, England alone can serve as the lever of a serious economic revolution. It is the only country where there are no more peasants and where property in land is concentrated in a few hands. It is the only country where the capitalist form—that is to say combined labor on a large scale under capitalist employers—has invaded practically the whole of production. It is the only country where the great majority of the population consists of wage laborers. It is the only country where the class struggle and the organization of the working class through the trade unions has acquired a certain degree of maturity and universality. As a result of its dominating position in the world market, it is the only country where every revolution in its economic conditions must react directly on the entire world (qtd. in Fisher 49-50).

Although Marx has been proven wrong, and the predicted revolution did not occur in England, that does not mean that the conditions that he set for a socialist revolution are irrelevant. Perhaps, the socialist revolution did not occur in England precisely because capitalism was not as developed as Marx thought it was. Now let us turn our attention to Morocco and the Arab world. Does Morocco, in fact the whole Arab world, meet the conditions described by Marx as being necessary for a *serious* socialist revolution? It is true that the capitalist form is invading more and more the whole sphere of economic production, but wage laborers are far from being the overwhelming majority; there are as many peasants as there are wage laborers. And as a result of Morocco's and the Arab world's peripheral position in the world market, it is far-fetched to envision that a revolution there would have an internationalist dimension.

Does this mean that we should abandon the Marxian project of socialism? Not at all. It simply means that we should first help bring about the conditions necessary for it by working for radicalizing democracy and preparing the social forces capable of making revolution a reality, because after all, socialist revolution is not the result of objective factors alone, it is also the result of intense class struggle. The *Manifesto* opens with the famous statement that, "The history of all hitherto existing society is the history of class struggles" (473). In a playful questionnaire prepared by one his daughters, Marx was asked "What is happiness?" His answer was "To fight!" Only by fighting and struggling can democracy be radicalized, and at a later stage, socialism fulfilled.

A New Understanding of Arab Culture

The concept of culture is highly complex, elusive, and problematic, and it is important to ask: what is culture? In 1939, the British-Polish anthropologist, Bronislaw Malinowski held that culture was "the most central problem of all social science" (588). The status of culture has not changed, and it comes as no surprise that Raymond Williams, early in his *Marxism and Literature*, makes a similar point about its centrality and complexity. As he puts it, "At the very center of a major area of modern thought and practice, which it is habitually used to describe, is a concept, "culture," which in itself, through variation and complication embodies not only the issues but the contradictions through which it has developed" (11). In *Culture: A Critical Review of Concepts and Definitions*, Kroeber and Kluckohn trace the development of the term culture and provide us with over one-hundred and sixty definitions and usages in the humanities and social sciences literature. These definitions, however, are closely related and could be said to fall under two general categories: the narrow elitist and the general anthropological meaning. The first can be traced back to the eighteenth century usage by such thinkers as Adelung, Kant, Hegel, Voltaire, etc, when culture was used fleetingly and most often interchangeably with the word "civilization." In this sense, culture is closely associated with its etymological derivation from the Latin word *cultura*, meaning tending or cultivation. The German word *Kultur*, which refers roughly to the distinctive "higher" values or enlightenment of a society, is closely related to this narrow meaning of the term. Kant, for example, used the German word *Kultur* in this sense to refer to the cultivation or the intrinsic improvement and development of the individual. Mathew Arnold understood culture in a similar way. In *Culture and Anarchy*, he defines culture as "the study and pursuit of perfection; and that of perfection as pursued by culture, beauty and intelligence, or, in other words, sweetness and light, are the main characters" (35). Here, culture is limited to so-called high art forms and practices, to the exclusion of popular cultural forms and practices.

How do Laroui, Al-Jabri, and Yassine understand culture? In his analysis of Moroccan folk culture, Laroui writes: "Folk cultural forms—musical, plastic, or literary—participate in the historical inferiority of the social structure that gives them birth and value. Expressive artistic forms, in contrast, seek to compensate for that inferiority through artistic expression itself, that is, by developing individual and collective consciousness of that inferiority" (*L'ideologie* 174). There are many reasons to be skeptical of such an elitist account where high artistic forms are juxtaposed against popular cultural forms, and where the latter are assumed to be intellectually and esthetically inferior. Al-Jabri's celebration of the progressive nature of medieval Islamic philosophy, while overlooking the important role of more popular cultural forms, and Yassine's distinction between authentic Islamic culture and inauthentic Islamic culture, both reveal their elitist, undialectical, and ahistorical understanding of culture. To claim that all high art forms are progressive and that all popular cultural forms are reactionary by definition is to have a static, fixed vision of culture, thus serving to reproduce and legitimize the domination of certain cultural forms and ideas and to preserve the *status quo*.

The second meaning of the word culture is a purely modern development and was established in English by Edward Tylor in 1871, although it did not come into common usage until more than half a century later. Tylor defines culture as "that complex whole which includes knowledge, belief, art, morals, law, custom, and any other capabilities and habits acquired by man as a member of society" (3). According to this conception, culture is an essentially descriptive term and is used to signify a whole way of life of a group of people.

There was, then, a contrast between the modern "anthropological" sense of culture and a narrower "humanistic" sense of it. For while the former included all the practices of everyday life, the latter emphasized the conscious self-cultivation of the individual and his attempt to raise himself out of the average mass to the level of the elite. This double meaning of culture and the accompanying tensions that come with it figure in the writings of Adorno and other critical theorists. In his *Adorno*, Martin Jay points out that for the Frankfurt School, and for Adorno in particular:

> To speak of culture means immediately to be confronted by the basic tension between its anthropological and elitist meanings. For the former, which in Germany can be traced back at least to Herder, culture signifies a whole way of life: practices, rituals, institutions, and material artifacts, as well as texts, ideas and images. For the latter, which developed in Germany as an adjunct of a personal inwardness contrasted with the superficiality of courtly manners, culture is identified with art, philosophy, literature, scholarship, theatre, etc., the allegedly "humanizing pursuits" of the "cultivated" man (112).

Marcuse addressed this problem in his undoubtedly important essay, "The Affirmative Character of Culture." Here, Marcuse makes a distinction between two main concepts of culture, the first of which I will call the dialectical and the second of which Marcuse calls the affirmative. According to the dialectical conception, culture "signifies the totality of social life in a given situation, insofar as both the areas of ideational reproduction (culture in the narrower sense, the "spiritual world") and of material reproduction ("civilization") form a historically distinguishable and comprehensible unity" (94). So while culture, in this narrower sense, refers to a transcendental realm of human fulfillment and autonomy, aiming as it does to end the struggle for existence, civilization refers to the realm of necessity and necessary social labor, reinforcing nothing other than human alienation.

According to the affirmative conception of culture, "the spiritual world is lifted out of its social context, making culture a (false) collective noun and attributing (false) universality to it...[C]ulture is distinguished from civilization and sociologically and valuationally removed from the social process" (95). For Marcuse, the project of affirmative culture, a peculiarly bourgeois phenomenon, is a fake project. Despite its abstract claims to universal human values, including freedom and equality, affirmative cultural manifestations serve only to stabilize the existing order without ever actually changing it. If the traditional goal of culture is to anticipate a better social order than the existing one, technological civilization and affirmative culture tend to destroy this revolutionary goal. One consequence of this is the assimilation of labor and relaxation, failure and enjoyment, art and household, psychology and management, as well as the disappearance of human autonomy and all forms of genuine critique and opposition.

To speak of Arab-Islamic culture is also to be confronted by the distinction between cultural practices as they are at present and cultural ideals as they should be, between the manipulative dimension of culture and its liberating potentials, between progressive and reactionary culture, between critical and conservative cultural forms. This distinction, however, does not necessarily correspond to the "high/low" culture dichotomy, for popular cultural forms can play, and have indeed played, a progressive role throughout Arab history. Cultural practices, regardless of whether they are high or low, can be critical or ideological, authentic or inauthentic; they can serve either to reproduce or to challenge dominant ideologies.

In liberal, nationalist, and Islamist accounts, Arab-Islamic culture is a static and fixed entity. This formulation denies the dynamics of history. Culture is nothing but a group's collective experience of reality at a certain place and time. It is continuously moving, developing, and changing, as new challenges and needs arise. Only a completely dead culture does not change. The whole notion of authenticity is based on the facile, essentialist assumption of the static, unchanging, and fixed nature of certain cultural practices and values.

The Historical Mission of Intellectuals

Central to the alternative emancipatory project of modernity that informs my understanding of culture is a reconsideration of the role of the intellectual. As I have already argued earlier, intellectuals can play a crucial role in the creation of a counter ideology and the development of mass consciousness. The whole notion that traditional intellectuals constitute a distinct social category independent of class is not tenable, and in reality, intellectuals either serve to conserve or resist the system, either consciously or unconsciously. The autonomy and independence of intellectuals is more apparent than real, and that is why, I would argue (in agreement with Gramsci) that intellectuals should be seen in specifically political terms.

In "The Need for Cultural Studies: Resisting Intellectuals and Oppositional Public Spheres," Henry Giroux, David Shumway, Paul Smith, and James Sosnoski provide a powerful critique of the fragmentation of the study of culture through disciplinary specialization. While the essay is a critique from within and in the context of North American academia, it raises important points that I think are relevant in the context of the Arab world, as well. Instead of regarding culture as a static canon of certain works and certain ideas, Arab leftist intellectuals should investigate culture as an "unfinished" process, in other words, "as a set of activities which is lived and developed within asymmetrical relations of power, or as irreducibly a process which cannot be immobilized in the image of a storehouse" (478).

The authors further note:

> We concur with Gramsci that it is important to view intellectuals in political terms. The intellectual is more than a person of letters, or a producer and transmitter of ideas and practices. Intellectuals are also mediators, legitimators, and producers of ideas and practices; they perform a function eminently political in nature (480).

As I mentioned earlier, Gramsci identifies two types of organic intellectuals—conservative and radical—both of whom are more directly related to the socio-economic structure of society. Conservative organic intellectuals, on the one hand, organically belong to the dominant social group, the ruling class, and are its thinking and directing element. It is through this group that the dominant class maintains its hegemony over the other classes in society. On the other hand, radical organic intellectuals are the thinking and directing element of the working class. Drawing on Gramsci's analysis, Giroux and others develop what they call "resisting intellectuals." These intellectuals differ from Gramsci's radical organic intellectuals, in the sense that they are not the thinking and directing element of the working class alone, but "can emerge from and work with any number of groups which resist the suffocating knowledge and practices that constitute their social formation" (480). These resisting intellectuals should be the thinking and directing element of all the oppressed groups in contemporary Moroccan (and Arab) society: workers, peasants, women, and minorities.

In a world where Orientalists depict the Arab-Islamic world as mired in unchanging tradition, and extremist Islamists wish to do something very similar to that, then the whole conversation cries out for just what cultural studies can offer: a view of culture that treats its object as historically contingent, socially constructed, and politically volatile; an emphasis on historicity and flux in the making of "traditions."

A Critique of Capitalist Globalization

One of the challenges facing the Arab world today is the globalization of capitalism. As I argued in my critique of Al-Jabri's analysis of globalization, globalization is not a new economic system, but rather a worldwide process of integration of national economies into the capitalist world market. It would be wrong to assume that globalization is a new phenomenon; as a set of processes, it has been an inherent feature of capitalism since its early development. The conventional understanding of globalization as a post-colonial, postmodern phenomenon is ahistorical and at best misleading. Marx was the first to identify and critique the globalizing tendencies and imperatives of capital.

Far from changing the nature of capital, globalization is the inevitable outcome of the advanced development of capitalist production. Contrary to conventional understandings, globalization is incapable of putting an end to the problem of exploitation in capitalist society. It would not be an exaggeration to say that the work of Marx provides the first critique of globalization as a process of capital accumulation (well before it became a buzz word). Marx highlights that part of the dialectic of capital is its inherent globalizing imperative, its inherent drive for self-expansion and its constant technological innovation on the one hand, and its tendency to deepen labor exploitation and social inequality, on the other. As Marx puts it, "The bourgeoisie cannot exist without constantly revolutionizing the instruments of production, and thereby the relations of production, and with them the whole relations of society" (*Marx-Engels* 476).

Marx makes it clear that the processes of self-expansion and technological innovation ultimately proceed without any consideration of national boundaries, and that the logical movement of capital is to create a world market, where national boundaries will become irrelevant as capital strives ceaselessly to secure new markets (and one might add cheap labor) for its increasing production. As he puts it:

> The need of a constantly expanding market for its products chases the bourgeoisie over the whole surface of the globe. It must nestle everywhere, settle everywhere, and establish connections everywhere.... In place of the old local and national seclusion and self-sufficiency, we have intercourse in every direction, universal inter-dependence of nations (476).

But if Marx's account of the globalization of capital helps us understand the nature and logic of capital, it also raises a number of problems. During Marx's lifetime, the globalization of capital assumed the form of colonialism. There is textual evidence that Marx supported colonization, arguing that it would bring "civilization" to less developed countries in Asia, Latin America, the Middle East, and elsewhere (477). He held that colonialism, especially British colonialism, was a catalyst for industrialization and capitalization processes. This has not been the case. Colonialism introduced capitalism to many countries, but it also blocked their natural development, thus leading to an immediate crisis that continues up to this day. The same is true of globalization today. While large transnational corporations may have introduced manufactures to several underdeveloped regions, global forces have also served to reinforce pre-capitalist economic forms, given their interest in rent and interest, rather than in industrial development.

I would concur with Al-Jabri that globalization (which I understand as a mere stage of capitalist development—and an advanced one of course—while he understands it as a new economic system), is unable to bring about true, stable, deep-rooted development and modernity into the Arab world, nor is it capable of decreasing the growing gaps between nations and classes. In fact, it exists and continues to exist thanks to those injustices and inequalities which are inherent in the system.

Tasks for the Moroccan/Arab Left

At present, the Moroccan and with it the whole Arab left finds itself impaired in its political struggle against capitalism. Left politics and the critique of culture and capital informed by them are everywhere under attack.

Marxism has never been popular among the masses. The common sense (in Gramsci's sense) construction in Morocco, of course, as well as in many parts of the Arab and Muslim world, is that the political concepts, theoretical ideas, and historical methodologies of Marxism are not useful because they are based on an atheistic, immoral philosophy. Many people have taken the collapse of socialism in the Soviet Union and Eastern Europe (and their third world replicas) to be a further proof of its immorality and futility. Everyday, they are being proved wrong; for the questions that Marxism has addressed are very much with us as long as capitalism continues to survive.

The kind of radical-socialist modernity that I propose here would enrich democratic political liberties and human rights, the historic achievements of centuries of struggles and revolutions. Obviously, that is not enough. This new modernity would also give to these liberties and rights a new economic and social dimension.

There is no doubt that the state apparatuses, ideological and repressive, as a whole are (directly or indirectly) instruments of the ruling classes, of capitalism. The state is not above classes, nor is it an arbiter between them, as Laroui claims. However, at this point in history, the capitalist state is a reality, and it would be naïve to just ignore it.

The left should act as left in the Third World countries in which it is operating in the twenty-first century. My propositions are not valid for everyone and every country; they are valid for the Moroccan society and for other countries at similar stages of development. Socialism and socialist modernity will mean different things and take different forms in different countries at different historical stages. To set up a model of general laws for revolution and socialism goes against one of the basic tenets of Marxism itself. Marxism is based on the concrete analysis of concrete reality. Otherwise, it turns into mere ideology. The realities of present-day Morocco and other Arab and Third-World countries have very concrete peculiarities which we cannot avoid. The conservative forces in Morocco (and elsewhere) would be much happier if all they had to face is dogmatic Left politics, adhering rigidly to outdated positions, with no consideration of history and material realities. As the current marginalization of the Left demonstrates, politics along those lines would be necessarily vulnerable and weak, incapable of emerging from isolation and of being taken seriously. The left would never be able to make its mark on the political process and become a great revolutionary force. It would never be able to contribute to establishing the hegemony of the working class in the life of the country.

As far as the Moroccan left is concerned, no new version of a socialist, or at least a non-capitalist society that might amount to a genuine "alternative society" to capitalism has been developed or considered with any degree of seriousness. The Marxist critique of the undeniable inequalities and injustices that continue to exist (and in a sense more dramatically than ever) under the capitalist mode of production is still relevant and has much to say about capitalism. Though we are not yet looking at the signs of a socialist alternative, as a collectivist mode of production involving the abolition of private ownership and control of the means of production, the Marxist tradition provides the left with another project, that of radicalizing democracy, a possible path to freedom and socialism.

Conclusion

The Marxian project remains the most acceptable, persuasive, and useful project not only because it goes beyond other projects, but also because it provides the theoretical approach and framework within which the merits and weaknesses of other projects, and itself, can be judged. Marx's work, as well as its development by Lukacs and by the theorists of the Frankfurt School, provides some insight into a different vision of modernity, into *another* modernity. There are at least two projects of modernity in Marx, two complementary projects, one paving the way for the other.

As I have shown, some aspects of the projects of Laroui, Al-Jabri, and Yassine are complementary to the Marxist vision of modernity. It is my contention that a useful critical theory of modernity, while fundamentally Marxist, should also incorporate the insights of many other theories, including those analyzed earlier. However, I would argue that although these non-Marxist analyses —analyses which have enjoyed more currency than Marxism in current debates and studies of modernity throughout the Arab world—have achieved only partial understandings of modernity and modernization processes, they each fail to give us a complete and scientific understanding. Marxism is the only critique able to incorporate the various strong points of non-Marxist theories, avoid their weaknesses, and successfully provide us with a much more convincing and useful critique of life under modern capitalist conditions.

However, it would be wrong to assume that Marx alone offers us a complete understanding of modernity. The work of Marx is part of the modern world, an important, original, fruitful, indispensable, and irreplaceable element in capitalist development. The work of Marx demonstrates and at the same time calls for the necessity of ongoing critique and self-critique. As David Harvey rightly points out, the work of Marx "teems with ideas on how to explain our current state" (*Limits to Capital* xiv). In many ways, the work of Marx is much more pertinent today than it was during Marx's lifetime. But while the work of Marx provides us with the "theoretical base" for a theory and practice for a radical and socialist modernity and is indispensable for understanding late capitalist society, it is only the starting point. While the theoretical concepts and categories developed by Marx and others are not alone sufficient and have to be elaborated, refined, and even complemented by other concepts and categories whenever necessary, they remain an important part of any emancipatory political project of modernity in Morocco and the Arab world.

NOTES

1. Marx's critique would have never been complete even if Marx had lived to finish it.
2. These two projects are incomplete in two ways. First, they have never been fulfilled in practice; second, they still need to be developed at the theoretical level as well.
3. Marx rightly thought that even the attempt to describe what a socialist society that did not exist would be like was a foolish endeavor.

Conclusion

The colonial interventions of the nineteenth and twentieth centuries throughout the Arab world have inaugurated the entry of the region into the world of capitalism and capitalist modernity. These interventions have had many significant implications and critical consequences for all—social, political, and cultural—aspects of life and society in the post-colonial Arab world. The dualities, contradictions, paradoxes, ironies, and even achievements of Arab societies today often hide the dualities, contradictions, paradoxes, ironies, and achievements of old imperialisms and colonialisms, which have stretched into the present and continue to haunt the life and dreams of the Arab subject.

One of the ironies of colonialism has been the realization on the part of those colonized of the superiority of the colonizing West and of the necessity of modernization and national *nahda* [renaissance]. But, alas, the realization of the need for Arab national renaissance and modernity has not led to their actual implementation. Throughout the modern history of the Arab world, a number of projects and ideologies have developed: liberalism, nationalism, and Islamism. The stated aim of all these has been to bring about national independence; to bring about a political project of unity of all Arabs and/or all Muslims; to achieve true modernity; and to preserve Arab cultural authenticity and identity.

By relating Arab ideologies and discourses of modernity and modernization to the particular historical situation within which they have developed and to which they have responded, my critique has aimed at demonstrating why these ideologies were (and still are) unable to fulfill the objectives they have prescribed for themselves. The liberal, nationalist, and Islamist projects and ideologies—each of which has been politically and culturally dominant at one conjuncture or another in modern Arab history—have carried with them the seeds of their own defeat. They have not failed because of purely cultural, religious, or ideological factors, as orientalists, liberals, nationalists, and Islamists seem to suggest. They have not failed either because the Arab mind is inherently irrational, nor because Islam is naturally backward, nor because Arab culture is unable to change, nor because Islam lost its authenticity. Rather, they have failed because they have all remained within the sphere of capitalism and the capitalist world system; they have been unable to truly break away from capitalism. They have failed because they did not represent the whole of society and have chosen instead to speak on behalf of the bourgeois and petty bourgeois classes, without any consideration of the needs and wishes of the masses of poor workers and poor peasants. Just as liberalism remained unable to transcend its bourgeois origins, state capitalism was unable to transcend its petty bourgeois origins. Many contradictions set limits on their functioning, contradictions which were very apparent in the deepening of the social crisis at all levels of society—social, cultural, and political. The failure of modernist ideologies of economic development in the Arab world—as well as in other areas of Muslim majorities and elsewhere; the international reorganization of capitalist production under a "flexible accumulation" system; increasing proletarianization; deepening impoverishment of the masses; all these factors have contributed to the rise of Islamic fundamentalism and Islamist ideologies and movements and the decline of liberalism and state capitalism in the Arab world.

I have chosen to concentrate on the work of three Moroccan intellectuals, politicians, and activists, Abdallah Laroui, Mohammed Abed Al-Jabri, and Abdessalam Yassine, as representatives of three different ideologies and projects: liberalism, nationalism, and Islamism respectively. My aim has been to reveal and to problematize the methodological and ideological assumptions informing the work of these men, to locate them in their proper historical context, and to reveal their hidden contradictions. I have also tried to go beyond this work to propose an alternative project of radical modernity and change.

Laroui's work was a defense of liberalism and liberal capitalism. In his early work, when Marx and Marxism were dominant ideologies throughout the South, Laroui employed a Marxist phraseology to justify and naturalize liberalism. In his later work, at a time when actually existing socialism was in decline, however, Laroui dissociated himself from Marx and Marxism. The absence of a consistent program in Laroui is best understood as a reflection of the ideological incoherence and vacuity of the Arab petty bourgeoisie (a class to which he belongs) and of state capitalism in general.

The work of Al-Jabri, another petty bourgeois intellectual, also reflects the failure of Arab state capitalism and its nationalist project of Arab unity. But it was more than that; it was also a critique, an attempt to make sense of that defeat. Al-Jabri's work took shape in the wake of the Arab defeat in 1967 war against Israel, and from here its concern with Islamic tradition and *turath* [heritage]. In the aftermath of the war, intellectual discussion shifted; many intellectuals attributed defeat to the dismissal of tradition and adoption of foreign ideologies, liberalism, nationalism, and socialism. This was a period of revival of medieval Islamic heritage.

At around the same time, new social forces were emerging and Islamist movements were becoming more and more powerful. Unlike Al-Jabri, who still had "faith" in the nationalist project of state capitalism, Yassine—like other fundamentalist Islamists—called for the end of all ideologies and the return to Islam not as mere heritage, but as a comprehensive political system capable of guiding all aspects of Arab society—social, political, cultural, and personal life. As we have argued, Islamism revealed itself as a modern phenomenon implicated in world capitalism and incapable of breaking with it without destroying some of its central claims and assumptions about humanity and society. The experiences of Islamist revolutions in Iran and Sudan, for example, further support my claims about the political and ideological vacuity and stagnation of Islamism.

My whole effort throughout this book has been an argument for the continued relevance of Marx and Marxism. As I believe I have shown, the work of Marx and other Marxists is indispensable for understanding the complicity of capitalism and colonialism and for the development of any serious emancipatory project of true modernity in the post-colonial Arab world. Like orientalist ideologies, liberal, nationalist, and Islamist ideologies often—whether consciously or unconsciously—overlook the historical nature of social and cultural phenomena, and end up naturalizing and eternalizing them. In the context of this book, we have seen how Laroui's blind celebration of liberal capitalism as the highest stage of social and economic development, how Al-Jabri's emphasis on the irrational nature of the Arab mind and the role of religious tradition in underdevelopment, and how Yassine's project to regain some kind of unchanging, eternal, fixed Islam, all tended to reveal the idealistic, ahistorical, undialectical nature and logic of their own work and projects. The vision emerging from their work was that of a society and culture that either hardly changes or does not change at all.

Marx provides us with a set of theoretical categories and analytical tools that are indispensable for understanding the implication of the postcolonial Arab world in the history of capitalist/Western imperialism and also for developing an emancipatory project of modernity there. However, it would be wrong to conclude from this that these theoretical categories and analytical tools, Marxian though they are, are sufficient or complete. To do so would be to go counter to one of the central claims of Marx's method: the transitory and fluid nature of categories and tools themselves. That is why, these categories and tools have to be consistently elaborated, refined, and complemented by other concepts and categories.

The Marxian project provides an alternative to conventional, ahistorical (orientalist, liberal, nationalist, and Islamist) analyses of society, as well as a guide for emancipatory political practice. Marxian dialectical historicism does not examine social phenomena as static entities but rather looks at them in the processes of their production, development, movement, existence, and transformation.

In a world where orientalists and auto-orientalists (Arab liberals, nationalists, and Islamists) regard Arab-Islamic society as mired in an unchanging tradition, Marx and Marxism have much to offer: a view of culture that treats its object as historically contingent, socially constructed, and politically volatile; an emphasis on historicity and flux in the making of traditions. By showing how Arab liberalism, nationalism, and Islamism are themselves artifacts of ongoing social and cultural contestations, a dialectical understanding of Arab culture represents a substantial intervention in Arab societies and cultures; it can serve as a check on auto-orientalizing ideologies, discourses, and movements, and are essential in the West (especially after 9/11), where depictions of a timeless "Arab mind" have always been popular.

The Marxian analysis of the nature and logic of the capitalist mode of production is still relevant and has much to say about capitalism. At different stages of his life, in his attempt to account for and overcome the contradictions of modern capitalism, Marx develops two *complementary, interconnected* projects of modernity, one of radical democracy and the other of socialist revolution.

These two projects, I argue, provide the Arab left with two critical strategies of political practice, one short-term and the other long-term. At the current historical juncture, it is very unlikely that the establishment of a socialist society, of a collectivist mode of production involving the abolition of private ownership and control of the means of production, will be fulfilled in the foreseeable future. That is why, the Marxist tradition calls on the left to work toward another project, that of radicalizing democracy, thereby paving the way for a socialist society characterized by freedom, equality, and justice.

At a time when leftist politics are everywhere in crisis and under attack, capitalism, without of course being "eternal," remains a highly probable mode of production under conditions of economic surplus, extensive division of labor, urbanism, and the increasing globalization of capital. The inequalities of capitalism inevitably exist and will certainly continue to exist, and as long as they do, complaints about them inevitably persist and will certainly continue to do so. And, inevitably, some degree of variation, no matter how wide, in capitalism—which is one of its characteristic features—will in no way amount to its decline and subsequent replacement by a socialist mode of production. In the Arab world, and in Morocco in particular, it is not unlikely that a radically and totally distinct socialist order fundamentally shaped by some form of collective consensus on economic decisions may be fulfilled in the foreseeable future for reasons that have been discussed throughout the book. The development of systematic critiques and protests against the social contradictions that are endemic to capitalism—structural poverty and inequality and cyclical instability—should continue to play a central role in radical leftist politics. As I have suggested, some sort of semi-socialism under which laborers, in addition to receiving wages for their labor, participate through assemblies or councils in the decision-making of the producing organization, would at least eliminate the division between owners and non-owners while keeping economic decisions in a decentralized "private sector."

At present, radical politics should assume both a reformist and revolutionary character and should center on the demands of the new working class and poor peasants for better conditions, better wages, better lives, and better opportunities. Only struggling for more immediate and practical concessions, by compelling the state to limit exploitation, by improving the conditions of its life, however unevenly, can the working class become in the long run aware of its revolutionary potential, and of its mission as the true "gravedigger" of the bourgeoisie. As a matter of fact, in Morocco and the Arab world, capitalism as a mode of production under which commodities and services are produced for sale, with a few people and groups owning the means of production and employing the labor of the vast majority is unlikely to be completely replaced by a non-capitalist mode of production because of the structurally dependent nature of capitalism in this part of the world. It is my contention that the best hope for the new left lies in the emergence of an international third-world movement against global capitalism. Those who want to see real change should be challenging the logic of the market rather than, like our mid-left politicians, extending its dominion.

Under present conditions, what is likely to follow from a conservative, fundamentalist revolution other than barbarism, historical reactionarism and regression? The march to a serious socialist revolution is long and hard, and yet falls in the realm of the possible.

Select Bibliography

A'arab, Ibrahim. *Al-Islam al-Siyyasi wa al-Hadata* [Political Islam and Modernity]. Casablanca: Afrique Orient, 2000.

Abduh, Mohammed. *Al-A'amal Al-Kamila [Complete Works]*. 5 vols. Cairo: Dar Al-Shuruq, 1993.

Abdullatif, Kamal. *Al-Fikr Al-Falsafi fi Al-Maghrib* [Philosophical Thought in Morocco]. Casablanca: Afrique Orient, 2003.

Abdunnaser, Walid. *Al-Yasar wa Al-Aawlama* [The Left and Globalization]. Cairo: Nahdet Misr, 2003.

Abdurrahman, Taha. *Al-Amal al-Dini wa Tajdid al-Aaq'l* [The Religious Act and Renewal of Reason]. Casablanca: Arab Cultural Center, 2000.

Abu Jaber, Kamel. *The Arab Ba'th Socialist Party*. Syracuse: Syracuse University Press, 1966.

Adorno, Theodor. *Can One Live After Auschwitz?: A Philosophical Reader*. Ed. Rolf Tiedemann. Stanford: Stanford University Press, 2003.

———. *Critical Models: Interventions and Catchwords*. Trans. Henry W. Pickford. New York: Columbia University Press, 1998.

———. *The Culture Industry: Selected Essays on Mass Culture*. Ed. J.M. Bernstein. London: Routledge, 1991.

———. *Minima Moralia: Reflections from Damaged Life*. Trans. E.F.N. Jephcott. London: Verso, 1974.

———. *Negative Dialectics*. Trans. E.B. Ashton. New York: Continuum, 1973.

———. *Notes to Literature*. Ed. Rolf Tiedmann. Trans. Shierry W. Nicholsen. Vol. 1. New York: Columbia University Press, 1991.

———. *Notes to Literature*. Ed. Rolf Tiedmann. Trans. Shierry W. Nicholsen. Vol. 2. New York: Columbia University Press, 1992.

———. *Prisms*. Trans. Samuel and Shierry Weber. Cambridge: MIT Press, 1983.

———. *The Stars Down to Earth and Other Essays on the Irrational in Culture*. Ed. Stephen Crook. London: Routledge, 1994.

Afaq Al-Tahawul Al-Dimoukrati fi Al-Maghrib [Prospects of Democratic Transition in Morocco]. Nawafid. 6-7 (2000).

Aksikas, Jaafar. *The Sirah of Antar: An Islamic Interpretation of Some Aspects of Arab and Islamic History*. Casablanca: Impremerie Najah El Jadida, 2002.

Al-Afghani, Jamal Eddine. *Al-A'amal Al-Kamila [Complete Works]*. Cairo: Dar Al-Katib Al-Arabi, 1971.

Alam Al-Tarbiyya [The World of Education]. Al-Tarbiyya wa Al-Hadata [Education and Modernity]. 13 (2003).

Alami, E. Ahmed. *Al-Masar Al-Dimokrati fi Al-Maghrib [Democracy in Morocco].* Mohammedia: Impression Fedala, 2002.

Al-Asbi, Lahcen and Safi Ennasiri. *Aqsa al-Yasar fi al-Maghrib [The Extereme Left in Morocco].* Casablanca: Arab Cultural Center, 2002.

Al-Awni, Abdelhamid. *Harb al-Bintagoun ala Al-Maghrib [The War of the Pentagon on Morocco].* Fez: Arabic Publishing, 2003.

Al-Azmeh, Aziz. *Islams and Modernities.* London: Verso, 1993.

Al-Buti, Mohammed Said Ramadan. *Al-Jihad fi Al-Islam [Holy War in Islam].* Beirut: Dar Al-Fikr, 1997.

Al-Ghazali, Abu Hamid. *Tahafut Al-Falisifa [The Incoherence of Philosophers].* <http://www.ghazali.org/books/tahfut-bejou.pdf>.

Al-Ghiyyat, Mohammed. *Al-Siyyasa wa al-Shabab al-Maghribi [Politics and Moroccan Youth].* Rabat: Top Press, 2004.

———. *Al-Haq Al-Arabi fi Al-Ikhtilaf Al-Falsafi [The Arabic Right to Philosophical Difference].* Casablanca: Arab Cultural Center, 2002.

Al-Hajwi, A. Hassan. *Al-Fikr al-Dimoukrati wa Ishkaliyat al-Dimoukratiya fi al-Moujtamaat al-Mouaasira [Democratic Thought and the Problematic of Democracy in Contemporary Societies].* Rabat: El Maarif El Jadida, 1995.

Al-Harwi, Al-Hadi. *Al-Maghrib al-Mouaasir wa Rihanat al-Moustaqbal [Contemporary Morocco and the Challenges of the Future].* Editions Imperial, 2004.

Al-Haymer, Abdessalam. *Al-Nukhba al-Maghribiyya wa Ishkaliyat al-Tahdith [The Moroccan Elite and the Problematic of Modernization].* Casablanca: Ennajah Al-Jadida, 2001.

Ali, Nabil. *Aalam Al-Maarifa. Al-Arab wa Asr Al-Maaloumat [Arabs in the Information Era].* 184 (1994).

Al-Irhabi [The Terrorist]. Dir. Nader Jalal. Perf. Adil Imam, Ahmed Rateb, Sherine, and Madiha Youssri. POK, 1994.

Al-Irhab wal Kabab [Terrorism and Bar.b.que]. Dir. Sherif Arafa. Perf. Adil Imam, Ahmed Rateb, Youssra, and Kamal El-Shennawi. 1993.

Al-Ittihad Al-Ishtiraki. *Al-Taghyir Al-Dimoukrati Wa Moutatallabat Al-Tanmiyya Al-Shamila [Democratic Transition and the Demands of Total Development].* Casablanca: Dar Ennashr Al-Maghribiyya, 1994.

Al-Jabri, Mohammed Abed. *Al Masala Al-Taqafiyya [The Cultural Question].* Beirut: Arab Unity Studies Center, 1994.

———. *Al-Dimoukratiyya wa Huquq Al-Insan [Democracy and Human Rights].* Beirut: Arab Unity Studies Center, 1994.

———. *Al-Maghrib Al-Muasir [Modern Morocco].* Casablanca: Muasasat Binahsra, 1988.

———. *Al-Turath wa al-Hadatha [Tradition and Modernity].* Casablanca: Arab Cultural Center, 1991.

———. *Arab-Islamic Philosophy: A Contemporary Critique.* Trans. Aziz Abbassi. Austin: The Center for Middle Eastern Studies, the University of Texas at Austin, 1999.

———. *Masaalat Al-Houwiyya [The Question of Identity: Arabism and Islam...and the West]*. Beirut: Arab Unity Studies Center, 1995.

———. *Mawaqif [Attitudes]*. 11 (2003).

———. *Mawaqif [Attitudes]*. 24 (2004).

———. *Nahnu wa al-Turath [We and Tradition]*. Casablanca: Arab Cultural Center, 1993.

———. *Naqd Al-Aql Alarabi (1): Takwin Al-Aql Al-Arabi [Critique of Arab Reason: The Genesis of Arab Reason]*. Beirut: Center for Arab Unity Studies, 1984.

———. *Naqd Al-Aql Alarabi (2): Binyat Al-Aql Al-Arabi [Critique of Arab Reason: The Structure of Arab Reason]*. Beirut: Center for Arab Unity Studies, 1986.

———. *Naqd Al-Aql Alarabi (3): Al-Aql Al-Siyasi Al-Arabi [Critique of Arab Reason: Arab Political Reason]*. Beirut: Center for Arab Unity Studies, 1990.

———. *Naqd Al-Aql Alarabi (4): Al-Aql Al-Akhlaqi Al-Arabi [Critique of Arab Reason: Ethical Arab Reason]*. Beirut: Center for Arab Unity Studies, 2001.

———. *Wijhat Nadar [Viewpoint]*. Beirut: Center for Arab Unity Studies, 1994.

Al-Karawi, Idriss. *Al-Nisaa Al-Muwadafat fi Al-Maghrib [Working Women in Morocco]*. Casablanca: Toubqal Editions, 2002.

Al-Khawli, Ousama. *Alam Al-Maarifa: Al-Biaa wa Qadaya Al-Tanmiyya wa Al-Tasniaa [World of Knowledge Journal: Environment and Issues of Development and Industrialization]*. 285 (2002).

Al-Mansouri, Abdullah. *Mouqaddimat likuli Dimoukratiyya Muqbila [Introductions to Any Future Democracy]*. Casablanca: Dar Al-Nashr Al-Maghribiyya, 2002.

Al-Masbahi, Hamid. *I'idamu Mayyit [Executing a Dead Man]*. Casablanca: Afrique Orient, 2003.

Al-Muthaqafun al-Maghariba wa Tafjirat 16 May [Moroccan Intellectuals and the Terroirst Attacks of 16 May]. Casablanca: El Najah Al Jadida, 2003.

Al-Mutaqafun al-Maghariba wa Al-Haraka Al-Ousouliyya [Moroccan Intellectuals and the Fundamentalist Movement]. Editions Al Ahadath Al-Maghribiyya, 2004.

Al-Rummani, Abdelaziz. *Limada Aajazna an Islah al-Idara [Why Are we Unable to Correct the Administration]*. Rabat: Imperial, 1998.

Al-Sahmarani, Asaad. *Al-Tatarruf wa al-Mutatarrifun [Extremism and Extremists]*. Beirut: Dar An-Nafaes, 1999.

Al-Sahraa: Al-Hal Al-Watani Al-Dimokrati [The Sahara: The Nationalist Democratic Solution]. Nawafid. 10-11 (2001).

Al-Sahrawi, Faqihi. *Rihan al-Tajdid fi al-Riwaya al-Magharibiyya al-Maktouba bi-Logha al-Faransiyya [The Challenge of Innovation in the Maghrebi Novel Written in French]*. Casablanca: Al-Najah al-Jadida, 2001.

Al-Slawi, A. Mohammed. *Al-Irhab Wuridu Hallan [Terrorism Needs A Solution]*. Kenitra: Impression Boukili, 2004.

Althusser, Louis. *For Marx*. London, Verso, 2005.

Al-Wakili, A. Mohammed. *Ahdat Maghrib Li Ahdat Maghrib [A Modern Era, A Modern Morocco]*. Rabat: Rabat Net, 2003.

Al-Zawi, Mustapha. *Al-Islam wa al-Hadatha, wa al-Dimoqratiyya [Islam,

Modernity, and Democracy]. Rabat: Axions, 2003.

Akhyat, Ibrahim. *Silsilat Al-Dirassat Al-Amazighiyya: Limada Al-Amazighiyya? [Berber Studies Series: Why the Berber Language?]*. Kenitra: Boukili Impressions, 1994.

Amin, Qasim. *The Liberation of Women*. Cairo: The American University in Cairo Press, 2000.

———. *The New Woman*. Cairo: The American University in Cairo Press, 2000.

Amin, Samir. *The Arab Nation: Nationalism and Class Struggle*. Trans. Michael Pallis. London: Zed Press Ltd., 1978.

———. *Re-Reading the Postwar Period: An Intellectual Itinerary*. Trans. Michael Wolfers. New York: Monthly Review Press, 1994.

———. *Specters of Capitalism: A Critique of Current Intellectual Fashions*. Trans. Shane Henry Mage. New York: Monthly Review Press, 1998.

Annales marocaines d'économie. Rabat: El Maarif Al Jadida, 1998.

Anderson, Benedict. *Imagined Communities: Reflections on the Origin and Spread of Nationalism*. New York: Verso, 1991.

Arnold, Mathew. *"Culture and Anarchy" and Other Writings*. Cambridge: Cambridge University Press, 1993.

Arroub, Hind. *Al-Makhzen fi Al-Taqafa Al-Siyyasiyya Al-Maghribiyya [Al-Makhzen in Moroccan Political Culture]*. Casablanca: Ennajah Al Jadida, 2003.

Asheqrq, Othmane. *Al-Atab Al-Maghribi: Baht fi Ousoul Al-Tahdit wa Iaqatuhu Bil-Maghrib [The Moroccan Breakdown: A Study on the Origins of Modernity and Its Failure in Morocco]*. Casablanca: Ennajah Al Jadida, 2003.

Ayache, Albert. *Etudes d'histoire sociale marocaine*. Rabat: Editions Okad, 1997.

Barnett, N. Michael. *Dialogues in Arab Politics*. New York: Columbia University Press, 1998.

Baudrillard, Jean. *The Spirit of Terrorism*. Trans. Chris Turner. London: Verso, 2003.

Bauman, Zygmunt. "Postmodernity, or Living with Ambivalence." Natoli and Hutcheon. 9-24.

Bell, Daniel. *The Cultural Contradictions of Capitalism*. New York: Basic Books, Inc., 1976.

Bendourou, Omar, Abdelmoughit Benmessaoud, and Mohammed Hammoudi, ed. *Alternance et transition démocratique*. Casablanca: Ennajah Al Jadida, 2001.

Benedict, Ruth. *Patterns of Culture*. Boston: Houghton Mifflin, 1934.

Benjamin, Andrew, ed. *The Problems of Modernity: Adorno and Benjamin*. London: Routledge, 1989.

Benjamin, Walter. *The Arcades Project*. Trans. Howard Eiland and Kevin McLaughlin. Cambridge: Harvard University Press, 1999.

———. *Illuminations*. Ed. Hanna Arendt. Trans. Harry Zohn. New York: Schocken Books, 1969.

———. *Selected Writings: 1913–1926*. Ed. Marcus Bullock and Michael W. Jennings. Vol. 1. Cambridge: Harvard University Press, 1996.

———. *Selected Writings: 1927–1934*. Eds. Michael W. Jennings, Howard Eiland, and Gary Smith. Vol. 2. Cambridge: Harvard University Press, 1999.

———. *Reflections: Essays, Aphorisms, Autobiographical Writings*. Trans. Edmund Jephcott. Ed. Peter Demetz. New York: Schoken, 1986.

Benjelloun, Taher. *L'Enfant des sables*. Trans. Mohammed Al-Sherghi. Casablanca: Toubkal Publishing, 2001.

———. *L'Auberge des pauvres*. Trans. Mohammed Al-Hilali. Casablanca: Toubkal Publishing, 2001.

———. *La Nuit sacrée*. Trans. Mohammed Al-Sherghi. Casablanca: Toubkal Publishing, 2001.

"Berber Manifesto." <http://www.amazighworld.org/human_rights/morocco/manifesto2000.php>.

Berman, Marshall. *All That is Solid Melts into Air*. London: Penguin Books, 1982.

Berman, Paul. *Terror and Liberalism*. New York: W.W. Norton and Company, 2003.

Berrada, Mohammed. *Lu'abat Al-Nisyan [The Game of Forgetting]*. Rabat: Dar Al Aman, 2002.

Berrada, Mohammed Abderrahaman. *La Presse écrite au maroc: distribution and diffusion*. Rabat: Editions Stouky, 2003.

Best, Steven, and Douglas Kellner. *Postmodern Theory: Critical Interrogations*. New York: Guilford, 1991.

Bhabha, Homi, ed. *Nation and Narration*. London: Routledge, 1990.

Blumenberg, Hans. *The Legitimacy of the Modern Age*. Trans. Robert M. Wallace. Cambridge: The MIT Press, 1983.

Bronner, Stephen and Douglas Kellner, ed. *Critical Theory and Society*. New York: Routledge, 1989.

Brouksy, Lahcen. *Makhzénité et modernité*. Rabat: El Maarif Al Jadida, 2002.

Brown, J. David and Robert Merril, ed. *Violent Persuasions: The Politics and Imagery of Terrorism*. Seattle: Bay Press, 1993.

Bottomore, Tom. *The Frankfurt School*. London: Routledge, 1989.

Boutaleb, Abdelhadi. *Nahwa Awlama Oukhra, Aktaru Adlan wa Insaniyya [Towards Another Globalization, More Just and Human]*. Casablanca: Dar Ennashr Al-Maghribiyya, 2004

Cailleux, Yves. *Le Royaume des défis*. Lille: Edition Hayak, 2002.

Cassier, Ernest. *The Philosophy of the Enlightenment*. Trans. Fritz C.A. Koelln and James P. Pettegrove. Boston: Beacon Press, 1955.

Centre D'études et de recherches en sciences sociales (CERSS). *Rapport Stratègique du Maroc: 2001-2002*. Casablanca: Ennajah Al Jadida, 2004.

Cesaire, Aime. *Discourse on Colonialism*. New York: Monthly Press Reviews, 1972.

Charters, David, ed. *The Deadly Sin of Terrorism*. Westport: Greenwood Press, 1994.

Cherkaoui, Abdessaid. *Mondialisation ou Christianisation!?* Rabat: Impremerie Librairie Omnia, 2000.

Choukri, Mohammed. *Al Khoubz Al-Hafi [For Bread Alone]*. London: Dar Al Saqi, 2002.

Cleveland, William. *The Making of an Arab Nationalist: Ottomanism and

Arabism in the Life and Thought of Sati al-Husri. Princeton: Princeton University Press, 1971.

Dalle, Ignace. *Maroc: 1961–1999, L'espérance brisée*. Paris: Maisonneuve et Larose, 2001.

Deleuze, Gilles, and Felix Guattari. *A Thousand Plateaus: Capitalism and Schizophrenia*. Trans. Brian Massumi. Minneapolis: University of Minnesota Press, 1987.

Duara, Prasenjit, ed. *Decolonization: Perspectives from Now and Then*. London: Routledge, 2004.

Durkheim, Emile. *The Division of Labor and Society*. Trans. W. D. Halls. New York: Free Press, 1997.

———. *The Elementary of Forms of Religious Life*. Trans. Karen Fields. New York: The Free Press, 1995.

El Abdaimi, Mohammed. *Maroc: Pays Emergent?* Marrakech: Berepie, 1994.

El Aouni, Abdelhamid. *Siyyasat Al-Giniralat [Policy of Generals after the Bloody Attacks of May 16th]*.

El Hanafi, Mohammed. *Haqaiq Jihawiyya: Al-Islam/Al-Marxiyya [Regional Facts: Islam/Marxism, a Comparative Study]*. 1 (2003).

El Kurdi, Bassam. *Debating Laroui's Theory*. Casablanca: Arab Cultural Center, 2000.

El Malki, Habib. *Al-Maghrib al-Mutahawil [Morocco in Transformation]*. Morocco: Dar Al-Manahil Publishing, 2003.

El Masaoudi, Amina. *Al Wuzaraa fi Al-Nidam Al-Siyyasi Al-Maghribi: 1955-1992 [Ministers in the Moroccan Political System]*. Casablanca: Ennajah Al Jadida, 2001.

———. *Humiliation à L'Ere du Méga-Impérialisme*. Casablanca: Ennajah Al Jadida, 2004.

———. *La décolonisation culturelle, défi majeur du 21e Siécle*. Marrakech: Editions Walili, 1996.

El Mossadeq, Rkia. *Les labyrinthes de la transition démocratique*. Casablanca: Najah El Jadida, 2001.

El Qabbaj, M. Mohammed. *Al Oumiyya fi Al-Maghrib: Hal Min Ilaj [Illiteracy in Morocco: Any Solution?]*. Rabat: Ramssis Publications, 1998.

El Qasmi, Ali. *Al-Jamiaa wa Al-Tanmiyya [The University and Modernization]*. Rabat: Ramssis Publications, 2002.

El Wasini, Zouhair. *Shiraa: Qat'l Al-Arabi [Shiraa Series: Murdering the Arab, the Image of the Arab in Western Media]*. 38 (1998).

Fanon, Franz. *Black Skin, While Masks*. Trans. Charles Lam Markmann. New York: Grove Press, 1967.

———. *A Dying Colonialism*. Trans. Haakon Chevalier. New York: Grove Press, 1956.

———. *Toward the African Revolution*. Trans. Haakon Chevalier. New York: Grove Press, 1967.

———. *The Wretched of the Earth*. Trans. Constance Farrington. New York: Grove Press, 1963.

Ferguson, Russell et al, ed. *Out There: Marginalization and Contemporary*

Cultures. Cambridge: The MIT Press, 1999.

Fiqr wa Naqd [Thought and Critique]. Casablanca: Dar Al-Nashr Al-Maghribiyya, 1997.

Fi Maarakat Al-Islah Al-Dimoukrati. Casablanca: Dar Qourtuba, 1999.

Fisher, J. Marguerite. *Communist Doctrine and the Free World*. Syracuse: Syracuse University Press, 1952.

Friedman, Jonathan. *Cultural Identity and Global Process*. London: SAGE Publications, 1994.

Friedman, Milton. *Capitalism and Freedom*. Chicago: University of Chicago Press, 2002.

Foucault, Michel. *The Birth of the Clinic: An Archaeology of Medical Perception*. Trans. Sheridan Smith. New York: Vintage Books, 1975.

———. *Discipline and Punish: The Birth of the Prison*. New York: Vintage Books, 1995.

———. *The History of Sexuality: An Introduction*. Vol. 1. New York: Vintage Books, 1990.

———. *The History of Sexuality: The Use of Pleasure*. Vol. 2. New York: Vintage Books, 1990.

———. *The Order of Things*. New York: Vintage Books, 1994.

———. "What Is Enlightenment?" In *The Essential Foucault*. Ed. Paul Rabinow and Nikolas Rose. New York: The New Press, 2003.

Freud, Sigmund. *Civilization and Its Discontents*. New York: Norton, 1961.

Fromm, Erich. *On Being Human*. New York: Continuum, 1999.

Gallaire, Fatima. *Theatre et nouvelles*. Mohammedia: Faculté des Lettres et Sciences Humaines, 1993–4.

Geertz, Clifford. *Islam Observed: Religious Development in Indonesia and Morocco*. New Haven: Yale University Press, 1968.

Gerth, H. and Wright Mills, trans. *From Max Weber: Essays in Sociology*. New York: Oxford University Press, 1958.

Giddens, Anthony. *The Consequences of Modernity*. Cambridge: Polity Press, 1990.

———. *The Constitution of Society*. Berkeley: University of California Press, 1984

———. *Modernity and Self-Identity: Self and Society in the Late Modern Age*. Stanford: Stanford University Press, 1991.

Gholiane, Charle André. *Tarikh Shamal Ifriqya [History of North Africa]*. 2 vols. Tunis: Eddar Tounisiyya, 1978.

Gramsci, Antonio. *The Antonio Gramsci Reader: Selected Writings, 1916–1935*. Ed. David Forgacs. New York: New York University Press, 2000.

———. *Selections from the Prison Notebooks*. Trans. Quintin Hoare and Geoffrey Smith. New York: International Publishers, 1999.

Habermas, Jurgen. "Modernity versus Postmodernity." Natoli and Hutcheon. 91-104.

———. *The Philosophical Discourse of Modernity*. Trans. Frederick Lawrence. Cambridge: MIT Press, 1987.

———. "The Public Sphere: An Encyclopedia Article." Bronner and Kellner. 136–

142.

———. *The Structural Transformation of the Public Sphere*. Trans. Thomas Burger and Frederick Lawrence. Cambridge: MIT Press, 2001.

———. "The Tasks of Critical Theory of Society." Bronner and Kellner. 292-312.

Haddour, Azzedine. *Colonial Myths: History and Narrative*. Manchester: Manchester University Press, 2000.

Hall, Stuart, D. Held, and T. McGrew. *Modernity and Its Futures*. Cambridge: Polity Press and Open University, 1992.

Hallward, Peter. *Absolutely Postcolonial: Writing between the Singular and the Specific*. Manchester: Manchester University Press, 2001.

Harzani, Ahmed. *Al-Intiqal Al-Dimoukrati fi Al-Maghrib [Democratic Transition in Morocco]*. Rabat: Awdad Lilittisal, 2004.

Harvey, David. *The Condition of Postmodernity: An Enquiry into the Origins of Cultural Change*. Cambridge, MA: Blackwell, 1989.

Hayek, Friederich. *The Fatal Conceit: The Errors of Socialism*. Ed. W.W. Bartley. Chicago: The University of Chicago Press, 1991.

Held, David. *Introduction to Critical Theory: Horkheimer to Habermas*. Berkeley: University of California Press, 1980.

Hegel, Georg. *Phenomenology of Spirit*. Trans. A.V. Miller. Oxford: Oxford University Press, 1977.

———. *The Philosophy of History*. Trans. J. Sibree. New York: Dover Publications, Inc., 1956.

———. *Philosophy of Right*. Trans. S.W. Dyde. New York: Prometheus Books, 1996.

Heggoy, A. Alf. *The French Conquest of Algiers, 1830: An Algerian Oral Tradition*. Athens: Ohio University, 1986.

Himmich, Ben Salem. *Au Pays de nos crises : essai sur le mal marocain*. Casablanca: Afrique Orient, 1997.

———. *Naqd Taqafat al-Hajr wa Badawat al-Fikr [Critique of Affirmative Culture and Primitive Thought]*. Casablanca: Arab Cultural Center, 2004.

———. *Zahrat Al-Jahiliyya [The Rose of Ignorance]*. Beirut: Dar Al Adab, 2003.

Hof, I. Ulrich. *The Enlightenment*. Oxford: Blackwell, 1994.

Hoffman, G. Bernard. *The Structure of Traditional Moroccan Rural Society*. Paris: Mouton & Co., Publishers, 1967.

Hoogvelt, Ankie. *Globalization and the Postcolonial World*. Baltimore: The John Hopkins University Press, 2001.

Horkheimer, Max. *Critique of Instrumental Reason*. Trans. Mathew J. O'Connell et al. New York: Continuum, 1994.

———. *Eclipse of Reason*. New York: Continuum, 1996.

——— and T. Adorno. *Dialectic of Enlightenment: Philosophical Fragments*. Trans. Edmund Jephcott. Ed. Gunzelin S. Noerr. Stanford: Stanford University Press, 2002.

Hourani, Albert. *A History of the Arab Peoples*. Harvard: Harvard University Press, 2003.

Hudson, C. Michael, ed. *Middle East Dilemma: The Politics and Economics of Integration*. New York: Columbia University Press, 1999.

Hume, David. *Essays: Moral, Political, and Literary.* London: Longmans, Green, 1875.

———. *An Inquiry Concerning Human Understanding.* Ed. Eric Steinberg. Indianapolis: Hackett Publishing Company, 1977.

Hutcheon, Linda. *The Politics of Postmodernism.* London: Routledge, 1989.

Huyssen, Andreas. *After the Great Divide: Modernism, Mass Culture, Postmodernism.* Bloomington: Indiana University Press, 1986.

Hyland, Paul, Olga Gomez and Francesca Greensides, Eds. *The Enlightenment: A Sourcebook and Reader.* London: Routledge, 2003.

Ibn Khaldun, Abderrahman. *The Muqaddimah: An Introduction to History.* Trans. Franz Rosenthal. Princeton: Prinseton University Press, 2005.

Imarah, Mohammed. *Al-Islamu wa Al-Siyyasa [Islam and Politics].* Cairo: Dar Al-Tawzi'a wa Nashr Al-Islamiyya, 1993.

Jameson, Fredric. *Late Marxism: Adorno, or the Persistence of the Dialectic.* London: Verso, 1990.

———. *Marxism and Form: Twentieth Century Dialectical Theories of Literature.* Princeton: Princeton University Press, 1971.

———. *The Political Unconscious: Narrative as a Socially Symbolic Act.* Ithaca: Cornell University Press, 1981.

———. *Postmodernism or, the Cultural Logic of Late Capitalism.* Durham: Duke University Press, 2001.

———. *A Singular Modernity: Essay on the Ontology of the Present.* London: Verso, 2002.

——— and Masao Miyoshi, eds. *The Cultures of Globalization.* Durham: DUP, 1998.

Josephson, Eric and Mary Josephson, ed. *Man Alone: Alienation in Modern Society.* New York: Dell Publishing, Inc., 1962.

Jay, Martin. *Dialectical Imagination: A History of the Frankfurt School and The Institute of Social Research, 1923–1950.* Boston: Little Brown, and Co., 1973.

———. *Adorno.* Cambridge: Harvard University Press, 1984.

Kant, Immanuel. "An Answer to the Question: What Is Enlightenment?" *Perpetual Peace.* 41-46.

———. *Perpetual Peace and Other Essays on Politics, History, and Morals.* Trans. Ted Humphrey. Indianapolis: Hackett Publishing Co, Inc., 1983.

Karam, Souhail. "Moroccan Berbers Reject Arab Identity." *Middle East Times.* Rabat, 2001.

King, A., ed. *Culture, Globalization and the World-System.* London: Macmillan, 1991.

Khatibi, Abdelkebir. *Al-Ismu Al-Arabi Al-Jarih [The Broken Arab Name].* Rabat: Oukad Publications, 2000.

———. *Al-Tanawub wa Al-Ahzab Al-Siyyasiyya [Alternating and Political Parties].* Trans. Aaz Eddine K. El-Idrissi. Rabat: Oukad Publications, 1999.

———. *Al-Siyyassa wa Al-Tasamouh [Politics and Tolerance].* Trans. Aaz Eddine K. El-Idrissi. Rabat: Oukad Publications, 1999.

———. *Maghreb pluriel.* Paris: Editions Denoel, 1983.

———. *Penser le maghreb.* Rabat: Société Marocaine des Editeurs Réunis,

1993.

Koran. Meddina: Mujammaa Al-Malik Fahd Littiba'a, 2003.

Korsch, Karl. *Marxism and Philosophy*. New York: Monthly Review Press, 1971.

Kroeber, A. L., & Kluckhohn, C. "Culture: A Critical Review of Concepts and Definitions." Harvard University Peabody Museum of American Archeology and Ethnology Papers, 1952.

Koselleck, Reinhart. *Futures Past: On the Semantics of Historical Time*. Trans. Keith Tribe. Cambridge: The MIT Press, 1985.

Kumar, Ashok, ed. *Terrorism and New World Order*. New Delhi: Anmol, 2002.

Laclau, Ernesto and Chantal Mouffe. *Hegemony and Socialist Strategy: Towards a Radical Democratic Politics*. London: Verso, 2001.

Laroui, Abdallah. *Al-Ghourba [Alienation]*. Casablanca: Arab Cultural Center, 2000.

———. "Hiwar: Al-Tahdith wa Dimuqratiyya [Interview: Modernization and Democracy]." Afaq. March-April 1992.

———. "Hiwar [Interview]." *Al-Siyyasa Al-Jadida*. 23 October 1998: 5

———. *Awraq [Papers]*. Casablanca: Arab Cultural Center, 2002.

———. *Al Yatim [The Orphan]*. Casablanca: Arab Cultural Center, 2002.

———. *Ghila*. Casablanca: Arab Cultural Center, 1998.

———. *Islam et modernité*. Casablanca: Arab Cultural Center, 2001.

———. *Islamisme, modernisme, libéralisme*. Casablanca: Arab Cultural Center, 1997.

———. *L'idéologie arabe contemporaine*. Paris: François Maspero, 1967.

———. *La crise des intellectuelles arbes: traditionalisme ou historicisme*. Paris: François Maspero, 1974.

———. *Mafhum Al-Aql [The Concept of Reason]*. Casablanca: Arab Cultural Center, 2001.

———. *Mafhum al-Dawla [The Concept of the State]*. Casablanca: Arab Cultural Center, 2001.

———. *Mafhum al-Houriyya [The Concept of Freedom]*. Casablanca: Arab Cultural Center, 2002.

———. *Mafhum al-Idyulujiyya*. Casablanca: Arab Cultural Center, 1984.

———. *Muhawarat Fikr Abdallah Laroui [Debating Laroui's Theory]*. Ed. Bassam El Kurdi. Casablanca: Arab Cultural Center, 2000.

———. *Mujmal Tarikh al-Maghrib [History of the Maghrib]*. 3 vols. Casablanca: Arab Cultural Center, 2000.

———. *Taqafatuna fi Dawii al-Tarikh [Our Culture in the Light of History]*. Casablanca: Arab Cultural Center, 2002.

Lanfry, Jacques. "Les berbers, leur langue, leur culture." *Etudes et Documents Berbers*. Paris: La Boîte à Documents, 1986. 41-67.

Larrain, Jorge. *Identity and Modernity in Latin America*. Cambridge: Polity Press, 200.

———. *Ideology and Identity: Modernity and the Third World Presence*. Cambridge: Polity Press, 1994.

Lash, Scott. *Another Modernity: A Different Rationality*. Malden: Blackwell,

1999.

Lash, S. and J. Friedman, eds. *Modernity and Identity.* Oxford: Blackwell, 1992.

Laurent, Michel. *Le Maroc de L'Espoir.* Rabat: Editions la Porte, 1996.

Leymarie, Serge and Jean Tripier. *Maroc: Le Prochain Dragon.* Casablanca: Editions Eddif, 1992.

L'khal, Said. *Sheikh Abdessalam Yassine: Mina Al-Qawma Nahwa Dawalat Al-Khilifa [Sheikh Yassine: From Rebirth to the Caliphate State].* Dar Ennashr Al-Maghribiyya, 2003.

Lukacs, Georg. *History and Class Consciousness: Studies in Marxist Dialectics.* Cambridge: The MIT Press, 2000.

Lyotard, Jean-François. *The Postmodern Condition: A Report on Knowledge.* Minneapolis: University of Minnesota Press, 1984.

Maher, Vanessa. *Women and Property in Morocco.* Cambridge: Cambridge University Press, 1974.

———. *Reflections on Fieldwork in Morocco.* Berkeley: University of California Press, 1977.

Mandel, Ernest. *Late Capitalism.* Trans. Joris De Bres. London: New Left Books, 1975.

Marcuse, Herbert. *The Aesthetic Dimension: Towards a Critique of Marxist Aesthetics.* Boston: Beacon Press, 1978.

———. *Counter-Revolution and Revolt.* Boston, Beacon Press, 1972.

———. *Eros and Civilization: A Philosophical Inquiry into Freud.* Boston: Beacon Press, 1966.

———. *An Essay on Liberation.* Boston: Beacon Press, 1969.

———. "The Affirmative Character of Culture." *Negations: Essays in Critical Theory.* Boston: Beacon Press, 1969.

———. *One-Dimensional Man: Studies in the Ideology of Advanced Industrial Society.* Boston: Beacon, 1964.

Martin, Hans-Peter and Harald Schumann. Fakh Al-Awlama. 295 (2003).

Marx, Karl. *Capital: A Critique of Political Economy.* Trans. Ben Fowkes. Vol. 1. London: Penguin Books, 1976.

———. *Capital: A Critique of Political Economy.* Trans. David Fernbach. Vol. 2. London: Penguin Books, 1978.

———. *Capital: A Critique of Political Economy.* Trans. David Fernbach. Vol. 3. London: Penguin Books, 1981.

———. *Grundrisse: Foundations of the Critique of Political Economy.* Trans. Martin Nocolaus. London: Penguin Books, 1973.

———. *Later Political Writings.* Trans and Ed. Terrell Carver. Cambridge: Cambridge University Press, 1996.

———. *Manifesto of the Communist Party.* Tucker. 469-500.

———. *The German Ideology.* Amherst: Prometheus Books, 1998.

——— and Frederick Engels. *Collected Works.* Vol. 11. New York: International Publishers, 1979.

Mashruh, Ibrahim. *Nahwa Siyyasa Jihawiyya Linnidam al-Taalimi bil-Maghreb*

[Towards a Regional Policy for the Educational System in Morocco]. Mohammedia: Fdala Publishing, 2000.

M'didsh, Jawad. *Derb [Neighborhood] Moulay Sherif.* Trans. Abderrahim Huzal. Casablanca: Afriqya al-Sharq, 2002.

Memmi, Albert. *La poésie algérienne de 1830 à nos jours.* Paris : Mouton, 1963.

Mernissi, Fatima. *Le harem Européen.* Trans. Fatima al-Zahra Azerwil. Casablanca: Arab Cultural Center, 2003.

———. *Hal Antum Mouhassanoun Didda al-Harim? [Are you Protected against Women?]* Trans. Nahla Baydoun. Casablanca: Arab Cultural Center, 2000.

———. *Shahrazad Laysat Maghribiyya [Shehrazad Is Not Moroccan].* Trans. Marie Touk. Casablanca: Arab Cultural Center, 2003.

Mohammed, Yahya. *Naqd Al-Aql Al-Arabi fi Al-Mizan [Critique of the Arab Mind Reconsidered].* Beirut: El Intishar Al-Arabi, 1997.

Moudawanat Al-Ahwal Al-Shakhsiyya [Moroccan Family Code]. 1957.

Moudawanat Al-Ahwal Al-Shakhsiyya Maaa Akhir Al-Taadilat [Moroccan Family Code with Latest Changes]. Casablanca: Maktabat Al-Wahada Al-Arabiyya, 1993.

Mourad, E. Farida. *Ma femme, ce démon angélique.* Casablanca: Imprimerie Eddar El Beida, 1987.

Muck, Thomas. *The Enlightenment: A Comparative Social History, 1721-1794.* London: Arnold, 2000.

Munson, Henry. *Religion and Power in Morocco.* New Haven: Yale University Press, 1993.

Nef, U. John. *Cultural Foundations of Industrial Civilization.* Hamden: Archon Books, 1974.

Nietzsche, Friedrich. *The Anti-Christ: Fragments from a Shattering Mind.* Trans. Domino Falls. Creation Books, 2002.

———. *Basic Writings of Nietzsche.* Trans. Walter Kaufmann. New York: The Modern Library: 1992.

———. *Thus Spake Zarathustra.* Trans. Thomas Common. New York: Prometheus Books, 1993.

Q'runful, Hassan. *Al-Mujtamaa Al-Madani wa al-Nukhba al-Siyyasiya [Civil Society and the Political Elite].* Casablanca: Afrique Orient, 2000.

Prakash, Gyan, ed. *After Colonialism: Imperial Histories and Postcolonial Displacements.* Princeton: PUP, 1995.

Rabinow, Paul. *Symbolic Domination.* Chicago: Chicago University Press, 1975.

Rao, Deepak and Seema Rao. *Terrorism: A Comprehensive Analysis of World Terrorism.* New Delhi: APH, 2004.

Rousseau, Jean-Jacques. *Of the Social Contract and Discourses on Political Economy.* Trans. Charles M. Sherover. New York: Harper and Row, Publishers, 1984.

Roy, Oliver. *The Failure of Political Islam.* Cambridge: Harvard University Press, 1994.

Rutherford, J., ed. *Identity, Community, Culture, Difference.* London: Lawrence and Wishart, 1990.

Saaef, Abdullah. *Rihanat Al-Tahawul Al-Siyyassi fi Al-Maghrib [Challenges of*

Political Transition in Morocco]. Casablanca: Ennajah Al Jadida, 2004.

Sabila, Mohammed. *Al-Idyoloujya [On Ideology]*. Beirut: Arab Cultural Center, 1992.

——— and Abdessalam Ben Abdelali, eds. *Dafatir Falisafiyya: Al-Hadata [Philosophical Portfolios: Modernity]*. 6 (2004).

Said, Edward. *Culture and Imperialism*. New York: Vintage Books, 1994.

———. *Orientalism*. New York: Vintage Books, 1979.

Saintouchi, Jean-Claude. *Al-Ahzab Al-Siyyasiyya Al-Maghribiyya Tahata Al-Majhar [Moroccan Political Parties under Examination]*. Trans. Mohammed Hammadi. Casablanca: Ennajah Al Jadida, 2003.

Saqi, Rachida. *Marocaines en mâle-vie*. Casablanca: Eddif, 1998.

Sebbar, Khadija. *Al-Maraa bayna al-Mitulujya wa al-Hadatha [Woman between Mythology and Modernity]*. Casablanca: Afriqya al-Sharq, 1999.

———. *Al-Islam wa Al-Maraa [Islam and Woman]*. Casablanca: Afrique Orient, 1999.

Schmidt, James. *What Is Enlightenment?* Berkeley: University of California Press, 1996.

Seligson, Mitchell and John Passe-Smith, ed. *Development and Underdevelopment: The Political Economy of Global Inequality*. London: Lynne Reinner Publishers, 2003.

Simmel, Georg. *The Philosophy of Money*. Trans. Tom Bottomore and David Frisby. Ed. D. Frisby. London: Routledge, 1990.

Shafiq, Mounir. *Fi al-Hadata wa al-Khitab al-Hadati [On Modernity and the Discourse of Modernity]*. Casablanca: Arab Cultural Center, 1999.

Shaghmoun, El Miloudi. *Aryana*. Casablanca: Arab Cultural Center, 2003.

Shaqir, Mohammed. *Tatawwur Al-Dawla fi Al-Maghrib [State Evolution in Morocco]*. Casablanca: Afrique Orient, 2002.

Sheikh, Mohammed. *Shurfat: Masalat Al-Hadata fi Al-Fikr Al-Maghribi Al-Hadith [Views Magazine: The Question of Modernity in Contemporary Moroccan Thought]*. 13 (2004).

Smith, Adam. *Wealth of Nations*. New York: Prometheus Books, 1991.

Smith, Paul. *Millennial Dreams: Contemporary Culture and Capital in the North*. London: Verso, 1997.

Smith, Tony. *The Pattern of Imperialism*. Cambridge: Cambrdige University Press, 1981.

Sondhi, M. L., ed. *Terrorism and Political Violence: A Sourcebook*. New Delhi: Har-Anand, 2000.

Spivak, Gayatri. "Can the Subaltern Speak?" *Marxism and the Interpretation of Culture*. Ed. Cary Nelson and Lawrence Grossberg. Chicago: University of Illinois Press, 1988. 271–313.

———. *A Critique of Postcolonial Reason: Toward a History of the Vanishing Present*. Cambridge: Harvard University Press, 1999.

———. *In Other Worlds: Essays in Cultural Politics*. New York: Routledge, 1988.

Steel, Ronald, ed. *North Africa*. Vol. 38. 5. New York: The H.W. Wilson Company, 1968.

Talal, Mohammed. *Al-Maraa Al-Arabiyya fi Al-Din wa Al-Siyyassa [The Arab

Woman in Religion and Politics]. Rabat: Dar Al-Nashr Al-Maghribiyya, 1998.

Tanit- Equipe Pluridisciplinaire de Recherche sur la Femme. *La femme marocaine et la moudawana: tutelle et divorce.* Meknes: Moulay Ismail University, 1993.

Tankoul, Abderrahman. *Al Adab Al Maghribi Al Hadith [Contemporary Moroccan Literature: A Bibliography].* Casablanca: Al-Jamiaa, 1984.

Tebaa, Jamal. "Le maroc à la fin du XIX° siècle." *Al-Asas.* 1982: 14–24.

Therborn, G. *European Modernity and Beyond.* London: Sage, 1995.

Thompson, B. John. *The Media and Modernity: A Social Theory of the Media.* Cambridge: Polity Press, 1995.

Tourabi, Hassan. *Mustalahat Siyyasiya in Islam [Political Terms in Islam].* Beirut: Dar Al-Saqi, 2000.

———. *Ideology and Modern Culture.* Cambridge: Polity Press, 1990.

Tucker, C. Robert, ed. *The Marx-Engels Reader.* New York: W.W. Norton & Company, Inc., 1978.

Université Conviviale D'Essaouira. *Art, environment, et dialogue des cultures.* Essaouira: Editions Sefrioui, 1996.

Vermeren, Pierre. *Histoire du maroc depuis l'indépendance.* Paris: La Découverte, 2002.

———. *Maghrib Al-Marhala Al-Intiqaliyya [Morocco in the Stage of Transition].* Casablanca: Traik Editions, 2002.

Waarab, Mustapha. *Al Mu'ataqadat Al-Sihriyya fi Al-Maghrib [Magic Beliefs in Morocco].* Dar Ennashr Al-Maghribiyya, 2003.

Waazi, El Houssein. *Nashaat al-Haraka al-Taqafiyya al-Amazighiyya bil-Maghreb [The Development of the Amazegh (Berber) Cultural Movement in Morocco].* Rabat: El Maarif Al Jadida, 2000.

Wagner, P. *A Sociology of Modernity, Liberty, and Discipline.* London: Routledge, 1994.

Waqidi, Mohammed. *Juraat Al-Mawqif Al-Falsafi [The Daring Philosophical Attitude].* Casablanca: Afrique Orient, 1999.

Weber, Max. *Basic Concepts in Sociology.* Trans. H. P. Secher. New York: Carol Publishing Group, 1993.

———. *Economy and Society: An Outline of Interpretive Sociology.* Ed. Guenther Roth. California: University of California Press, 1986.

———. *The Protestant Ethic and the Spirit of Capitalism.* Trans. Talcott Parsons. London: Routledge, 2002.

Wellmer, Albrecht. *The Persistence of Modernity: Essays on Aesthetics, Ethics, and Postmodernism.* Cambridge: MIT, 1993.

Westermarck, Edward. *Wit and Wisdom in Morocco.* London: George Routledge & Sons, Ltd., 1930.

Williams, Raymond. *The Country and the City.* Oxford: Oxford University Press, 1982.

———. *The Long Revolution.* Ontario: Broadview Press, 2001.

———. *Marxism and Literature.* Oxford: Oxford University Press, 1977.

Women and Writing. Meknes: Moualy Ismail University, 1996.

World Bank Reprot: 2003.

Yacoubi, Rachida. *Ma vie, mon cri.* Rabat: Editions Eddif, 1995.

Yassine, Abdessalam. *Al-Adl: Al-Islamiyyun wa Al-Hukm [Justice: Islamists and Power].* Morocco: Al-Safaa Impressions, 2000. <http://www.yassine.net/Main.aspx?article=ADL00Fatiha&m=2&sm=24>.

———. *Al-Ihssan [Spirituality].* 2vols. Casablanca: Al-Ofok Impressions, 1989. <http://www.yassine.net/Main.aspx?article=Books_Ihssan_intro&m=2&sm=10>.

———. *Al-Islam wa Al-Qawmiyya Al-Ilmaniyya [Islam and Secular Nationalism].* Mohammedia: Fdala Impressions, 1989.

———. *Al-Islamu bayna Al-Daawa wa al-Dawla [Islam between the Appeal and the State].* 1971. <http://www.yassine.net>.

———. *Al-Islamu Ghadan [Islam Tomorrow!].* 1972. <http://yassine.net>.

———. *Al-Islamu wa Tahdid Al-Marxiyya-Lininiyya [Islam and the Challenge of Marxism-Leninism].* 1987. <http://www.yassine.net>.

———. *Al-Islamu wa Tufan [Islam or the Deluge].* 1974. <http://www.yassine.net/letters/arab-toufane.htm>.

———. *Al-Khiliafa wa Al-Mulk [Caliphate and Monarchy].* Casablanca: Dar Al-Afaq, 2001. <http://www.yassine.net/khilafa/intro.htm>.

———. *Al-Minjah Al-Nabawi [The Prophetic Method].* Publisher Unknown. 1989.

———. *Al-Shura wa Al-Dimuqratiyya [Shura and Democracy].* Casablanca: Al-Ofok Impressions, 1996.

———. *Fi Al-Iqtisad [On the Economy].* Casablanca: Al-Ofok, 1995.

———. *Hiwar maa Al-Fudalaa Al-Dimuqratiyyin [A Dialogue with Honorable Democrats].* Casablanca: Al-Ofok Impressions, 1994.

———. *Hiwar maa Sadiqi Al-Amazighi [Dialogue with my Tamazight [Berber] Friend].* Casablanca: Al-Ofok Impressions, 1997.

———. *Islamiser la modernité.* Casablanca: Al-Ofok Impressions, 1998.

———. "Jamaat Al-Adl wa Al-Ihssan: Taarikh [Al-Adl wa Al-Ihssan: A History]" http://www.yassine.net.

———. *Mihnat Al-Aql Al-Muslim [The Muslim Mind on Trial: Divine Revelation versus Secular Rationalism].* Trans. Muhtar Holland. Iowa City: Justice and Spirituality Publishing, 2003.

———. *Mudakkira: Ila man Yahummuhu Al-Amr [Memorandum: To Whom It May Concern]* 2000. <http://www.yassine.net/letters/arab-memo.htm>.

———. *Muqaddimat fi Al-Minhaj [Introductions to Method].* 1989. <http://www.yassine.net/Main.aspx?book=muqaddimat&m=1&sm=8>.

———. "Pour un dialogue avec l'élite occidentalisée." 1980. <http://www.yassine.net/letters/frensh-dialog.htm>.

———. *La revolution a l'heure de l'islam.* Casablanca: 1980. <http://www.yassine.net>.

———. *Rijal Al-Qawma wa Al-Islah [Exemplary Men in Islam].* Casablanca: Afrique Orient, 2001.

———. *Tanwir Al-Mouaminat [Enlightening Believeing Women].* Tanta: Dar Al Bashir, 1995.

Znayber, Mohammed. *Arouss Aghmat [Aghmat Bride].* Casablanca: Dar Ennashr Al Maghribiyya, 1991.

Index

A

Abderrahman, Taha, 65
Abduh, Mohammed, 19–20, 66
Activism, 97, 112
Adorno, Theodor, 132, 143
Afghanistan, 29
Aksikas, Jaafar, 66
Al-Adl wa Al-Ihssan, 8, 29, 95–98
Al-Afghani, Jamal ud-Din, 19–20, 66
Al-Alawi, Mohammed Ben al-Arbi, 19
Al-Fassi, Allal, 16
Al-Ghannushi, Rashid, 65
Algeria, 15–16, 23–24, 29, 32, 65, 94
Al-Ghazali, Abu Hamid, 70–71, 80
Al-Husri, Sati, 20
Ali, Mohammed, 17, 18
Al-Jabri,Mohammed, 5, 7–10, 13, 29, 31, 58, 61–95, 100, 105, 133–134, 138, 142, 146–147, 149, 152–153
Al-Jihad, 105
Al-Kindi,Ibn Ishaq, 71
Amazigh. See Berber
Amin, Qasim, 19
Amin, Samir, 17, 21–22, 25, 27
Anti-Colonialism, 5, 16, 18–19
Anti-Colonial Struggle. See Anti-Colonialism
Arab East. See *Mashreq*
Arab-Israeli Conflict, 8
Arab Left, 68, 88, 129, 135, 137, 140, 145, 147, 155
Arab Nationalism, 1, 20, 30, 33
Arab West. See *Maghreb*

Arabic, 20, 37–38, 49, 57, 60, 62, 66, 78–79, 102, 120–121
Arabism, 8, 27, 30, 43, 46, 153
Arab Unity. See Arabism
Arkoun, Mohammed, 65, 94
Arnold, Mathew, 142

B

Bacon, Francis, 4
Berber, 95, 119–123
Bourgeoisie, 89
  Petty Bourgeoisie, 22, 24–29, 41–42, 45, 52–53, 58–59, 64, 73, 152–153
Britain, 14, 22, 47, 55, 140

C

Caliphate, 96, 107–109, 112–119, 122
Capitalism, 2, 4–5, 24, 26
  Late Capitalism, 3, 150
  State Capitalism, 5, 7–8, 14, 24–29, 43, 58–59, 64, 84, 152–153
Christ, Jesus, 2
Colonialism, 2, 5, 9, 14–18, 20, 23, 31, 43, 46, 58, 82–83, 86, 102, 104, 130, 147, 151, 153,
Colonization. See Colonialism
Communism, 25, 27, 81
Cultural Studies, 6, 10, 145–146
Culture, 6, 9–10, 15, 19, 36, 45–46, 52, 67, 69, 77–78, 83, 96, 103, 110–111, 114, 121, 125, 127, 132–133, 141–147, 152, 154,

D

Democracy, 3, 9–11, 24, 43, 49–50, 61, 63, 66, 87–92, 94, 105, 116–117–119, 128, 134–139, 141, 149, 154–155
Descartes, René, 4, 76
Dialectics, 10, 41, 46, 134,
Diderot, Denis, 3
Discursive Formation, 3
Domination, 27, 40, 53, 59, 75, 79, 85, 91, 142,
Doukkali, Chouaib, 19

E

Education, 17, 23–24, 26, 34, 38, 61 63, 74, 82–85, 94, 96–97, 100, 107, 109, 111, 113, 120
  Policies, 63
  Reforms, 17
  Religious, 107
Egypt, 13, 16–30, 34, 38, 64–65, 88, 100, 105, 125
Elite, 16, 20, 31, 36, 38–39, 46, 51, 83, 88–90, 97, 100–101, 107, 143
Enlightenment, 3–4, 49, 56, 92
England. *See* Britain
Essentialism, 9, 49, 110–111, 119, 130, 144
Ethnicity, 14, 78, 87, 101, 121
  Politics, 119–120

F

Family Law. *See Moudawana*
Fitna, 106–107, 116
Fitra, 110
France, 14, 22–23, 33–38, 47, 65, 94, 102, 140
Freedom, 3, 11, 24, 35, 49–53, 90–92, 111, 117, 122, 127, 136, 138, 143, 149, 155,
French Occupation, 16–17, 62
Fundamentalism. 1, 19, 52, 65–79, 84, 91, 99–100, 105, 119, 125–126, 153, 156, *See also* Islamism

G

Gender, 108, 121, 123–124,

Globalization, 5, 61, 63, 81, 85–87, 146–147, 155,
Gramsci, Antonio, 40, 41, 44, 138, 145, 148

H

Hanafi, Hassan, 65
Hassan I, 16–17
Hassan II, 23, 96, 98, 122
Hegel, 51–52, 56, 136–137, 141
Hegemony, 16, 24, 29, 30, 41, 44, 50, 53, 69, 81, 90–91, 101, 145, 149
Historicism, 35, 56, 154,
Holy War. *See Al-Jihad*
Horkheimer, Max, 132
Hourani, Albert, 71
Human Nature, 48, 57, 110
Hume, 3
Hussein, Mahmoud, 27

I

Ibn Abdurrahman, Mohammed, 16
Ibn Rushd, 61, 75, 79, 80
Ibn Sina, 62, 79, 80
Ibrahim Pasha, 18
Identity Politics, 119
Ideology, 2–9, 13, 18, 22, 27–29, 35–38, 44–49, 51, 53–55, 58, 64, 67, 73, 80–81, 99, 103, 104, 116, 124–131, 135, 144, 148
  Political Ideologies, 35, 44–45, 47–48
IMF, 92
Imperialism, 14
Independence, 62
Industrialization, 2, 25, 31, 40, 89, 124, 147
Intellectuals, 18, 144, 145
  Organic Intellectuals, 41, 145
  Traditional Intellectuals, 40–41, 100, 144
Iran, 29, 153
  Iranian Revolution, 8, 29, 64
Iraq, 18, 25, 29, 30, 32, 94, 98
  First Gulf War, 32, 95
  Second Gulf War, 30, 98

Islam, 1, 6, 8, 9, 19, 20, 28, 35, 37, 43, 52, 64–65, 70, 93, 96–97, 103–108, 112–124, 127, 133, 152–153

Islamic *Caliphate*. *See Caliphate*
Islamic Fundamentalism. *See* Fundamentalism
Islamic Philosophy, 61, 63–66, 70, 74, 76–77, 80, 84, 93, 142
Islamic Community. *See Umma*
Islamic Spain, 79–80
Islamic Tradition. *See Turath*
Islamism, 1, 5–8, 14, 28–29, 44, 46, 54, 58, 95, 99–100, 116, 124–125, 127, 151–154
Israel, 22, 27–28, 30, 64, 153

J

Jameson, Frederic, 2, 6, 14
Jihad. *See Jihad*

K

Koran, 43, 65, 71, 96, 102, 107, 109–110, 113–115, 117–119, 121, 127
Kuwait, 30

L

Laroui, Abdallah, 5–13, 27, 31–60, 65, 78, 92, 95, 105, 133–134, 138, 142, 148–149, 152–153
Lebanon, 20, 22, 24, 88
Lefebvre, Henri, 129, 134–135
Left, 10–11, 24, 29, 31, 51, 60, 62–65, 68, 88, 92–93, 99–100, 104, 108, 127, 129, 135, 137–138, 140, 145, 147–149, 155–156
Lenin, 27, 98
Liberalism, 1, 5–9, 14, 20, 23, 25–26, 28–30, 33, 38, 42–50, 52, 55, 57–60, 80, 82, 84, 87, 92, 124, 127, 133, 151, 154
Liberty. *See* Freedom

M

Machiavelli, Niccolò, 4
Maghreb, 14, 26, 34–35, 60, 63, 79, 93
Marcuse, Herbert, 143
Marx, Karl, 1, 7, 9–10, 28, 39, 44, 50, 53–54, 59, 108, 129–141, 146–147, 149–154

Marxism, 9–10, 25–28, 36, 44–47, 57–60, 68, 86, 88–89, 97, 108, 129–134, 137, 141, 148–149, 152–154
Mashreq, 14, 19, 20
Middle East, 1, 5, 14, 51, 100, 147
Midhat Pasha, 18
Mill, John Stuart, 47–48
Modernism, 38, 47, 95, 103, 165
Modernity, 1–10, 13, 16, 25, 27, 35–36, 38–39, 43, 45–49, 51–55, 57, 59, 61, 65–67, 69–70, 75, 77–78, 80, 87, 89, 91–93, 95, 99, 101–106, 112, 116, 119, 121, 124, 126–131, 133–136, 139, 144, 147, 154
  Discourses, 1, 5–6, 77
  Problematic, 1, 7, 13–14, 35, 37, 40, 65, 70, 72–76, 80, 88–90, 93–94, 123, 141
Modernization, 1–2, 4–6, 8, 13, 16–19, 23, 29, 31, 43, 45, 51, 55, 61, 65, 83, 91, 99–100, 121, 149, 151, 158, 162, 166
Montesquieu, 3, 47, 48
Morocco, 8–9, 13–19, 21, 23–24, 26, 33–37, 40–42, 46–47, 49, 58, 60, 62–63, 65, 71, 77, 79, 91–100, 108, 120–125, 131, 133–134, 138, 140–141, 148, 150, 155–156
Moudawana 23, 122
Musa, Salamah, 20

N

Nahda, 5, 7, 13, 74, 151
Napoleon, 16
Nasser. *See* Nasserism
Nasserism, 7–8, 14, 24, 27–28, 64
Nation, 17, 19–21, 27, 30–31, 75, 86–87, 147
  Nation-State, 4, 56, 82, 85–86, 89
Nationalism, 5–8, 14, 16–17, 20, 27–28, 30, 33, 35, 42, 44, 58–59, 61, 98, 151–154
Neo-Liberalism, 29
North, 2, 8, 14, 34, 38, 78, 81, 86, 95, 100, 112, 119–120, 145

O

Orientalism, 67, 110, 130
Other, 37, 45, 56, 84, 103

Ottoman Empire, 14, 20

P

Palestine, 24
   Partition of Palestine, 22
Periodization, 6, 13–14
Political Economy, 2, 131
Political Movements, 1, 6, 17, 19, 99, 124–125
Post-Colonial Studies, 58
Post-Modernism, 14,
Postmodernity, 2
Privatization, 49, 80–82, 84–85
Proletarianization, 21, 26, 152
Progress, 3, 16,43, 46, 50, 60, 65, 78, 81, 91–93, 101, 103–105, 124, 136, 139

Q

Qawma, 98, 106–108

R

Radical Democracy, 10, 134, 136–139, 154
Radical Politics, 138, 155
Rationality, 61, 69–70, 72, 75, 78–80, 84, 93, 103
Rationalization, 3, 52, 92–93, 105
Reforms, 16–19, 22–25, 84, 122, 125
Renaissance. *See Nahda*
Revolution, 4, 8, 10, 20, 24, 26, 29, 48, 64, 68, 97, 100, 107–108, 125, 131, 135, 138–141, 148, 153–154, 156
Russia, 25, 69

S

Sayyid, Lotfy, 47
Second Gulf War. *See* US Attack on Iraq
Second World War, 22, 88
Secularism, 3, 15, 20, 43, 80, 98, 103–106, 115–119, 122–125, 127
Self, 4, 37, 45, 56, 67, 84
Shari'a, 65, 113–115, 119, 123
Shura, 43, 116–119
Smith, Paul, 6, 86, 145

Social Change, 5, 28, 38–40, 46, 53, 63, 77, 106, 116, 123, 131,
Social Justice, 65, 87, 89, 116, 125
Social Totality, 6, 10, 132–134, 39, 75, 78, 93, 131–135, 143
Socialism, 23, 25–28, 30, 80–81, 84–85, 88, 90, 92, 125, 127, 138, 140–141, 148–149, 153–155
South, 2, 9, 104, 130, 152
State, 20, 26, 30, 31, 35, 42–45, 51–53, 56–58, 79, 82, 84, 89, 91, 93, 96–97, 99, 111–115, 119, 127, 135–138, 148, 150, 155
Syria, 18, 20, 22, 24, 25, 30, 34, 62, 65, 88

T

Taqlid, 19
Terrorism, 29, 98–99, 113, 126
Third World, 26, 41, 54, 59, 86–87, 130, 148, 156
Totalitarianism, 74, 114, 137
Tourabi, Hassan, 65
Tradition, 7, 19, 27–29, 39, 43, 46, 55, 61, 63–85, 92–93, 110, 112, 124, 126, 133–134, 146, 153
Tunisia, 23, 65, 116
Turath, 8, 63–65, 70, 74, 77, 153

U

Umma, 19–20, 112–114
Underdevelopment, 9, 27, 51, 87, 102–103, 133–134, 153
United States, 27, 32, 87, 94
United Kingdom. *See* Britain
Urbanization, 3, 21, 155
US Attack on Iraq, 30, 98

V

Voltaire, Francois-Marie Arouet, 3, 141

W

World Bank, 82
World War II. *See* Second World War

West, 3, 5, 14–15, 20, 25, 33, 37, 43, 45–47, 51–54, 57, 61, 67, 80, 82, 84–85, 88–89, 100, 103, 108, 112, 122–127, 151, 154
Women, 19, 121–124

Y

Yassine, Abdessalam, 5, 7–10, 13, 27, 29, 31, 58, 60, 65, 95–128, 133–134, 142, 149, 152–153

POSTCOLONIAL STUDIES
Maria C. Zamora, *General Editor*

The recent global reality of both forced and voluntary migrations, massive transfers of population, and traveling and transplanted cultures is seen as part and parcel of the postindustrial, postmodern, postcolonial experience. The Postcolonial Studies series will explore the enormous variety and richness in postcolonial culture and transnational literatures.

The series aims to publish work which explores various facets of the legacy of colonialism including: imperialism, nationalism, representation and resistance, neocolonialism, diaspora, displacement and migratory identities, cultural hybridity, transculturation, translation, exile, geographical and metaphorical borderlands, transnational writing. This series does not define its attentions to any single place, region, or disciplinary approach, and we are interested in books informed by a variety of theoretical perspectives. While seeking the highest standards of scholarship, the Postcolonial Studies series is thus a broad forum for the interrogation of textual, cultural and political postcolonialisms.

The Postcolonial Studies series is committed to interdisciplinary and cross cultural scholarship. The series' scope is primarily in the Humanities and Social Sciences. For example, topics in history, literature, culture, philosophy, religion, visual arts, performing arts, language & linguistics, gender studies, ethnic studies, etc. would be suitable. The series welcomes both individually authored and collaboratively authored books and monographs as well as edited collections of essays. The series will publish manuscripts primarily in English (although secondary references in other languages are certainly acceptable). Page count should be one hundred and twenty pages minimum to two hundred and fifty pages maximum. Proposals from both emerging and established scholars are welcome.

For additional information about this series or for the submission of manuscripts, please contact:

>Maria C. Zamora
>c/o Acquisitions Department
>Peter Lang Publishing
>29 Broadway, 18th floor
>New York, New York 10006

To order other books in this series, please contact our Customer Service Department:
>(800) 770-LANG (within the U.S.)
>(212) 647-7706 (outside the U.S.)
>(212) 647-7707 FAX

Or browse online by series:
>www.peterlang.com